Pioneer Children on the Journey West

"Thought There Was Nothing But Fun in a Journey"

PIONEER
CHILDREN
on the
JOURNEY
WEST

EMMY E. WERNER

Westview Press
Boulder • San Francisco • Oxford

Frontispiece: "Thought There Was Nothing But Fun in a Journey," *Harper's New Monthly Magazine,* October 1874; courtesy *Harper's Magazine* and The Denver Public Library, Western History Department, #F19906

Published in 1995 in the United States of America by Westview Press, Inc., 5500 Central Avenue, Boulder, Colorado 80301-2877, and in the United Kingdom by Westview Press, 12 Hid's Copse Road, Cumnor Hill, Oxford OX2 9JJ

Library of Congress Cataloging-in-Publication Data
Werner, Emmy E.
  Pioneer children on the journey west / Emmy E. Werner.
    p.   cm.
  Includes bibliographical references and index.
  ISBN 0-8133-2026-7
  1. Pioneer children—West (U.S.)—History.   2.Frontier and
pioneer life—West (U.S.)   3. Overland journeys to the Pacific.
I. Title.
F596.W467   1995
917.804'1'083—dc20   94-38427
                                                                          CIP

Printed and bound in the United States of America

The paper used in this publication meets the requirements
of the American National Standard for Permanence of Paper
for Printed Library Materials Z39.48-1984.

10   9   8   7   6   5   4   3   2

For Dale Harris and Louise Bachtold—loyal friends;
for Stanley Jacobsen—cherished husband;
and in memory of Michael David Jacobsen

Contents

Illustrations

Acknowledgments and Credits

MANY THANKS TO Dorothy Suhr for patiently typing several versions of the manuscript for this book and to the following people at Westview Press: Nancy Carlston, Allison Sole, Cheryl Carnahan, Connie Oehring, and Polly Christensen.

Grateful acknowledgment is made to the following for permission to reprint from manuscripts and previously published material.

The Bancroft Library for permission to quote from John Breen's "Pioneer Memories," 1877, and "Letters to C. F. McGlashan," 1879; Patrick Breen's "Diary," 1846–1847; John B. Chiles's "A Visit to California in Early Times," 1898; Nicholas Dawson's "Notebook Kept on a Journey to California," 1841; Eliza, Frances, Georgia, and Leanna Donner's "Letters to C. F. McGlashan," 1879; Maria J. (Norton) Elliot's "Diary," microfilm typescript, 1859; Henry Ferguson's "Recollections of a 1849 Journey," 1918; William Graves's "Letters to C. F. McGlashan," 1879; Maggie Hall's "Recollections," 1853; Sarah Ide's "Recollections," in Simeon Ide, *The Conquest of California: The Biography of William B. Ide*, 1888; Ada Millington's "Journal Kept While Crossing the Plains," 1862; Rebecca Hildreth Woodson Nutting's "Recollections," 1850–1858; Martha and Virginia Reed's "Letters to C. F. McGlashan," 1878; Virginia Reed's "Letter Written to her Cousin, Mary C. Keyes," May 16, 1847; Warren Saddler's "Journal of a Gold Prospector," 1849; and Mary Eliza Warner's "Diary," 1864.

California Historical Society Library for permission to quote from Sally Fox Allen's "Diary," 1859, MS 42.

California State Library, Sacramento, California, for permission to quote from Kate Furniss McDaniel, "From Prairie to Pacific. A Narrative of a Trip Across the Plains of a Family from Illinois with a Covered Wagon and Oxen in 1853." Edited by Mai Luman Hill. Typescript. qCBF98; and from Mary Fetter Sanford Hite, "A Biographical Sketch of Abraham Hite and Family. A Trip Across the Plains March 28–October 27," 1853. Typescript. qcBH67s.

Arthur H. Clark Co. for permission to quote from Tamsen Donner's "Letter of May 11," 1846, and Louisiana Strentzel's "Letter from San Diego," 1849, both in *Covered Wagon Women,* vol. 1, 1983; and Eliza McAuley's "Diary," 1852, in *Covered Wagon Women,* vol. 4, 1983; and to reprint Sallie Hester's "Diary of a Pioneer Girl" (March 20, 1849–June 3, 1850), and parts of Elizabeth Keegan's "A Teenager's Letter from Sacramento," December 12, 1852.

Columbia University Press for permission to quote from J. Goldsborough Bruff, *Gold Rush: The Journals, Drawings and Other Papers of J. Goldsborough Bruff,* edited by Georgia Willis Reed and Ruth Gains, 1949. Copyright © 1949 by Columbia University Press, New York.

Holt-Atherton Center for Western Studies, Department of Special Collections, University of the Pacific Libraries, for permission to quote from Florence Blacow Weeks's "Notes to Diary of Lorina Walker Weeks," 1859.

Nevada State Historical Society for permission to quote from Edith A. Lockhart's "Diary," 1861.

State Historical Society of Iowa for permission to quote from Henry W. Haight, "We Walked to California in 1850."

Yale University Press for permission to quote from Sarah Royce, *A Frontier Lady: Recollections of the Gold Rush and Early California,* 1932. Copyright © 1932 by Yale University Press.

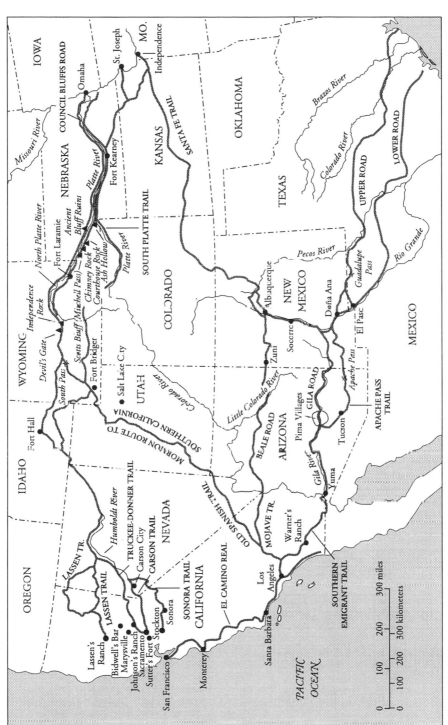

Trails to California

Introduction

N OT FAR FROM THE WHITE HOUSE, in the Corcoran Gallery of Art in Washington, D.C., hangs a painting of an emigrant train bedding down for the night. Among the weary travellers is a group of children, ranging in age from an infant in her mother's arms to a teenage boy driving the oxen within the enclosure of the covered wagons.

Other youngsters are busily engaged in chores: A boy is drawing water in a bucket from a nearby stream; a small girl is comforting the baby. A teenage girl is putting a large kettle over the open campfire to start the evening meal; another girl kneels beside her on the ground, unpacking plates and pitchers wrapped in cloth to shield them from the dust of the prairie.

Around forty thousand children, like the youngsters depicted on Benjamin Franklin Reinhart's canvas, participated in the great overland journeys between 1841 and 1865 from the banks of the Missouri to the Pacific shores. Others joined them on the Gila Trail, travelling north from Texas and Arizona to southern California. Except for the Gold Rush years, one of every five emigrants on the way West was a child.[1] Their young voices are seldom heard among the tales of the trail.[2]

The familiar accounts of the overland journeys that have captured the nation's imagination came from adults.[3] However, children's diaries, letters to relatives "back in the States," and reminiscences of the young emigrants *have* survived, and so have the narratives of adults who accompanied them on the journey or met them on the trail.[4] Only a few have been published and are still in print; most can be found in the manuscript collections of the Bancroft Library at the University of California at Berkeley, at the California Historical Society in San Francisco, at the California State Library in Sacramento, and at the Huntington Library in San Marino.

The Emigrant Train Bedding Down for the Night by Benjamin Franklin Reinhart (courtesy The Corcoran Gallery of Art, Washington, D.C.)

The stories of the youngsters on the emigrant trails are a remarkable testimony to the resiliency of the human spirit, for the hardships they encountered were unusual. They parted from their homes, friends, relatives, and familiar surroundings, never to return. For six months or more, they travelled around two thousand miles across uncharted prairies, deserts, and mountain ranges. Unless they were infants or toddlers, they walked most of the way.

They endured desolation and detours, excessive heat, floods, and cold. They suffered from cholera, dysentery, fever, and scurvy. When water and provisions ran out—as they often did—they faced thirst and starvation. They met with accidents and death along the way—the deaths of strangers and of friends and family members. Occasionally, children on the trail got lost, were abandoned, or were kidnapped. Some survived massacres and were held as hostages; others witnessed scenes of cannibalism among the famished members of their own party.

As one reads their narratives, one cannot help but be deeply impressed by the children's hardiness. Their eyewitness accounts tell of enduring qualities that helped them overcome the odds: competence and self-reliance, curiosity and determination, enthusiasm and cheerfulness, concern for the needs of others, and a sense of responsibility far beyond their years. Above all, they shared a faith that things would work out well for them in the end—a faith that sustained them and gave meaning to their lives.

There were familiar and sometimes unexpected sources of support for the children on the trail: older brothers and sisters; cousins, aunts, and uncles; a beloved grandparent; friends and neighbors; cherished family pets; books and dolls. When all else failed, there was the kindness of strangers they met along the trail or at the end of their journey: preachers and prospectors, soldiers and Indians.

Most of the child emigrants on the overland trail were sons and daughters of farmers and of businessmen and professionals from small towns in the Midwest who headed for California to find economic prosperity. Around fifteen hundred children were part of the great Gold Rush that attracted fortune seekers from all walks of life—from the East, the Midwest, and even from abroad.[5] Other children came West with parents who were in search of better health for themselves or their offspring.

Some of the young diarists, letter writers, and journal keepers had kinfolk who were school teachers, preachers, printers, or lawyers. When goods had to be abandoned toward the end of the journey, when the draft animals wore out and the covered wagons or oxcarts broke down, they threw out the bacon rather than the books they carried with them. Some, like Sarah Royce, who was to become the mother of a professor of philosophy at Harvard University, picked up books left in the trail dust by other emigrants so that her children might learn to read from them.

On the whole, the children and young people who wrote accounts of their journey were an intelligent and a perceptive lot. Like their parents, they valued books and education. This was true for the girl emigrants as well as for the boys. By the time their families were heading West, school attendance had become compulsory in the eastern and midwestern states, and the literacy gap between males and females in the North was closing. By 1850 the United States could claim one of the highest female literacy rates in the world.[6] Hence, it is not surprising that among the diarists and letter writers on the trail were many young girls.

My focus throughout this book is on the children's perspective of the overland journey—their subjective experiences of hardships along the way and how they managed to cope with them. My primary sources are eyewitness accounts of the experiences of approximately 120 children and young people on the California trail in the period between 1841 and 1865—from the time the first emigrant party with a child reached California to the end of the Civil War.

Among the primary materials are diaries, letters, and journals written on the journey or shortly after arrival at the destination—mostly by youngsters in their early and middle teens—supplemented by reminiscences of child emigrants. The youngest in this group was four years old at the time of the crossing. Psychologists consider this the age at which autobiographical memory has developed that enables children to recall an image of an important event in their lives.[7]

We need to keep in mind that the term *children* had a broader connotation in midnineteenth-century America than it has today. It was often applied to anyone under age eighteen. Teachers, preachers, diarists, and newspaper editors spoke and wrote interchangeably of "children," "youth," and "young persons." In the farm communities from which most young emigrants came, physical size, and hence capacity for work, was more important than chronological age. Many children performed important household chores by the time they were five to seven years old. Most became full participants in the workforce by the time they were fifteen or sixteen. The term *adolescence,* indicating a separate stage of life between childhood and adulthood, had not yet been developed.[8]

The stories of the child emigrants are, of course, affected by the passage of time, filtered as they were through the screen of subsequent events.[9] When both a child's diary or letter and his or her adult reminiscences are available, I contrast the difference, if any, in their perspectives over time. As complementary or corroborating evidence, I also draw on the eyewitness accounts of others (siblings, cousins, friends, and travelling companions) who were present and who recorded their impressions of the children's experiences in *their* diaries, letters, or memoirs.

On the whole, the younger children reacted differently to the overland journey than those who had passed puberty. Their narratives reflect their excitement about leave-taking, meeting new people in unfamiliar surroundings, and anticipating the high adventure that seemed the promise of each new day. Their age and lack of experience limited their ability to envision the enormity of the undertaking and its inherent uncertainties and dangers. Secure within the circle of their extended family, they had a sense of trust and safety they could hold on to, even when the journey brought hardships to themselves and to the people they loved. Only the loss of a parent, especially the mother, could unravel this basic sense of security.

The older children, especially those in their midteens, revealed a growing sense of competence and confidence, as the adults relied heavily on their active contributions to the welfare of the wagon train. Parents asked them to assume responsibilities rarely expected of a teenager today. Often wagon trains allowed boys as young as fourteen to vote on company decisions because they carried burdens equal to those of the male adults. Among their major responsibilities were ensuring the health and safety of the livestock, on which the success of the overland journey depended. Many teenage girls, in turn, cared for sick relatives, including parents, and took on full responsibility for the welfare of younger brothers and sisters.

I first present the tales of young people whose spirit of survival was severely tried. Among them was Nancy Kelsey, a teenage mother who walked barefoot across the Sierras in the snow of 1841, carrying in her arms her infant daughter, Ann, the first emigrant child to enter California (Chapter 1). The children of the Donner party tell of their ordeals in the winter of 1846–1847 and describe how they managed to survive in Chapter 2.

Chapter 3 relates the fate of emigrant children caught in the snowstorms of 1849 on the Lassen Trail, recorded by the men who rescued and took care of them. The Gold Rush brought many "unaccompanied minors" to California—youngsters who were abandoned, kidnapped, or orphaned; their stories are told in Chapter 4. Chapter 5 presents eyewitness accounts of the travel of children who struggled through the waterless desolation of Death Valley in the winter of 1849–1850.

Chapter 6 tells of "ordinary" overland journeys along the Platte River route, recorded by young diarists in the late 1840s and 1850s. When seen through the eyes of children and teenagers, even a relatively uneventful journey west was filled with adventure and provided extraordinary experiences that tested the young people's mettle.

Chapter 7 is based on narratives of youngsters who came along the Gila Trail from Texas and Arizona to southern California in the 1850s and encountered mayhem and massacres along the way. Chapter 8 contains accounts of children and teenagers travelling to California's mining towns and accounts of overland journeys during the Civil War, when young emigrants were settling on wheat and cattle ranches in a state that, in time, was to become the largest and most prosperous in the Union.

Chapter 9 sums up the general theme that runs through the stories of the emigrant children heading west—the theme of human resilience in the face of great odds. The analysis of the narratives of these midnineteenth-century travellers poses the same interpretative challenges as the life histories of contemporary children who were exposed to unusually stressful life events and yet managed to grow into competent, confident, and caring individuals.

Such children were able to attract affection and encouragement from members of their extended family, from friends and neighbors, and from strangers. They usually had a special skill or talent that was valued by their elders. At some point in childhood or adolescence, they assumed responsibilities that were essential to the well-being of their family or community. This experience bolstered their self-confidence and strengthened their belief that they *could* surmount the hardships in their lives. They never lost hope—even though the odds were against them.[10]

Most young emigrants who wrote about their experiences on the overland trails drew on similar sources of strength in the face of adversity. Their eyewitness accounts are thus like a "distant mirror" that reflects the timelessness of human resilience. Three of these accounts are reprinted in Chapter 10: a letter from a thirteen-year-old survivor of the Donner tragedy in 1846–1847, the diary of a fourteen year old who participated in the 1849 Gold Rush, and a letter from a twelve year old who rode horseback all the way from Kansas to California in 1852, the year with the most travel on the overland trails. Their stories speak for themselves.

1

Ho for California

Weadquarters of the San Joaquin River ... [and] camped on the summit. It was my eighteenth birthday."

The year is 1841. The voice is that of Nancy Kelsey, a young mother who was the first white woman to reach California in an overland emigrant party. She crossed the snow-covered mountains barefoot, carrying her infant daughter, Ann, in her arms and leading her packhorse behind her. "It was a sight I will never forget," wrote one of her companions, Nicholas Dawson, in a diary he kept on their journey.

Married at age fifteen, Nancy had joined her husband, Benjamin Kelsey, in the first band of emigrants to set out for California from Missouri in May 1841. Those who completed the seven-month trip, after the fainthearted had dropped away or chosen the easier course to Oregon, consisted of thirty-one men and the young woman with her one-year-old child. John Bidwell, a twenty-one-year-old schoolteacher who had organized the group, noted in his journal, "Our ignorance of the road was complete. We knew that California lay west, and that was the extent of our knowledge. I doubt whether there was one hundred dollars in the whole party, but all were enthusiastic and anxious to go."

They had only learned through word of mouth about what lay ahead—from letters written by John Marsh, a fellow Missourian who had lived in California since 1836. He and a Swiss immigrant, Captain John A. Sutter, had been given large land grants by the Mexican government, and both were eager to entice Americans to settle on the property they owned. But to get to this promised land, they would have to cover a greater distance in one season than their ancestors had traversed in a century.

It was considered almost rash for a woman to venture on so perilous a journey, but when questioned about going to California, Nancy Kelsey replied

Approaching Chimney Rock by William Henry Jackson (courtesy Scotts Bluff National Monument, Gering, Nebraska)

without hesitation, "Where my husband goes, I go." She added, "I can better endure the hardships of the journey than the anxieties for an absent husband."

"So she was received in the company," wrote John Chiles, one of her travel companions, "and her cheerful nature and kind heart brought many a ray of sunshine through the clouds that gathered around ... so many weary travellers. She bore the fatigue of the journey with so much heroism, patience, and kindness that there still exists a warmth in every heart for the mother and her child."

The emigrants travelled 2,000 miles, with the goal of reaching Sutter's Fort, on the site of present-day Sacramento. Starting near Independence, Missouri, on May 12, they crossed the Kansas and Platte Rivers, passed Chimney Rock, and reached Fort Laramie—the end of the first leg of their journey—on June 22. They had covered 635 miles; their daily average was 15 miles. Nancy Kelsey, with baby Ann, rode horseback or travelled in one of the nine wagons.

On August 8 they reached Soda Springs, after crossing the South Pass and the Green River, from where henceforth all water would flow toward the Pacific. They had finished the second leg of their journey, travelling about 560 miles from Fort Laramie, averaging less than 12 miles a day. As they pushed out over the desert north of Salt Lake, their team animals began to fail. They were tired and half starved. Nancy Kelsey reported matter-of-factly, "We left our wagons this side of Salt Lake and finished our journey on horseback and drove our cattle. I carried my baby in front of me on the horse."

Their journey gradually became a starvation march. They killed their oxen one by one for food. In mid-October they approached the Sierra Nevada and crossed the summit at Sonora Pass. West of the pass they were ensnared in the canyon country of the Stanislaus River. Nancy Kelsey remembered:

We had a difficult time to find a way down the mountains. At one time I was left alone for nearly half a day, and as I was afraid of Indians I sat all the while with my baby in my lap on the back of my horse. ... It seemed to me while I was there alone that the moaning of the winds through the pines was the loneliest sound I had ever heard.

We were then out of provisions, having killed and eaten all our cattle. I walked barefeeted until my feet were blistered and lived on roasted acorns for two days. ... My husband came very near dying with cramps, and it was suggested to leave him, but I said I would never do that, and we ate a horse and remained over till the next day, when he was able to travel.

Finally, on October 30, they reached the wooded banks of the Stanislaus River. A few days later they arrived at John Marsh's ranch at the foot of Mount Diablo. Some horses and mules were still alive, and so was Nancy Kelsey's resilient spirit. She and her baby rested for some weeks and then set forth to the final destination of her overland journey.

In December we went up with Sutter in a leaky rowboat to his fort at what is now Sacramento. We were fifteen days making the trip. The boat was manned by Indians, and Sutter instructed them to swim to the shore with me and the child if the boat should capsize. We arrived at the fort on Christmas Day.

There they met Joel Walker, his wife, and their children who had crossed into California from Oregon three weeks earlier. At Sutter's Fort Nancy gave birth to a son, who died about a week later. She had been pregnant during the entire journey from Missouri to California. In spring 1842, John Marsh wrote a letter to his parents "back in the states" in which he paid tribute to the indomitable young mother and her infant.

A company of thirty of my old neighbors in Missouri arrived here the first of November last. ... A young woman with a little child in her arms came

with the company ... and was about a month in my house. After this, the
men ought to be ashamed to think of the difficulties [of the journey].

In 1843 Nancy and her young daughter were on the trail again, this time heading for Oregon. En route, Indians stole twenty-five of their horses, but one of the natives swam across the Sacramento River and towed the canoe in which the mother and child were sitting to safety. In 1844 her restless husband returned to California with Nancy, Ann, and a newborn daughter, to settle in Napa Valley. Near Mount Shasta Native Americans stampeded their stock of horses and cattle. "While the arrows were flying into our camp," said Nancy, "I took one babe and rolled it in a blanket and hid it in the brush and returned and took my other child and hid it also."

In 1846 Nancy and her children joined her husband in Sonoma, where American settlers staged the Bear Flag Rebellion. She sewed the first flag of the short-lived "California Republic"—a piece of muslin, crudely painted with a grizzly bear and a red star. It was raised on June 14 as a symbol of the settlers' defiance against the Mexican government, only to be replaced three and a half weeks later by the Stars and Stripes of the United States.

The Kelseys kept on the move, turning up in Mexico, Texas, and southern California. In 1861 Nancy's twelve-year-old daughter was scalped by Comanche Indians in a raid and later died from her injuries.

After her husband's death, Nancy Kelsey lived her final years alone in a remote cabin in the mountains of Santa Barbara County, supporting herself by raising chickens and practicing herbal medicine. She died in 1896 at age seventy-three. "Up to within a few weeks of her death," wrote a friend, "she would mount her pinto pony and ride across the mountains to help bring a baby into the world, bind splints on a broken leg or minister to a fever-ridden child."

In 1843 John Chiles, a companion of the Kelseys on the first overland journey, headed back to Missouri to prepare for another expedition. This one consisted of sixteen men, three women, and five small children. They left toward the end of May from the vicinity of Independence—"with high spirits, but much anxiety."

They followed the trail of the first emigrant party, crossing the Kansas and Platte Rivers but travelling more slowly because rainy weather had created a muddy trail and necessitated frequent halts at swollen streams. At the crossing of the South Fork of the Platte River, the Chiles party overtook the last of the more than one hundred wagons that composed the "Great Emigration to Oregon." Among the occupants of one of the wagons was seven-year-old Jesse A.

Applegate, who narrowly survived an accident that befell him as his family was fording the river.

> *Mother, myself, and the other children were in the little red wagon; it . . .*
> *was attached to the last end of the train. As we were just getting up the bank*
> *from the ford, our team broke loose and wagon and team backed into the*
> *river. Being swept below the ford, the team swam and the wagon sank down,*
> *and was drifting on the sand; and I remember the water came rushing into*
> *the wagon box to my waist, compelling me to scramble up on the top of a*
> *trunk. . . . But several men came swimming, held up the wagon, and soon*
> *assisted us to the shore.*

The boy recovered quickly and soon delighted in a chase between his dog, Fleet, and an antelope that had been separated from the herd and ran through the train.

> *The black dog as he sped on with all his might looked like a crane flying*
> *along the plain. We were all excited, for the dog was gaining on the antelope*
> *and would soon overtake him. The dog gave a yelp, but that antelope, in a*
> *few seconds after the bark, was flying over the plain as if it had been shot out*
> *of a gun. . . . The dog was so astounded that he stopped short, turned about*
> *and trotted back to the train.*

At one of the emigrant camps, an ox was slaughtered. The gutted stomach, left lying on the ground in the warmth of the afternoon sun, swelled up to the size of a large barrel. This was a splendid opportunity for young Jesse and some other boys in his train to invent a rather "original and uncanny" game.

> *The sport consisted in running and butting the head against the swollen*
> *paunch and being bounced back, the recoil being in proportion of the con-*
> *tact. The sport was found to be very exciting and there grew up a rivalry be-*
> *tween the boys . . . as to who could butt the hardest. There was a boy by the*
> *name of Andy Baker . . . who was ambitious to excel all the others, and he*
> *backed off as to have a long run for it. He . . . charged the paunch at the top*
> *of his speed, and when within a couple of yards of the target, leaped up from*
> *the ground . . . and came down like a pile driver against the paunch, but he*
> *did not bounce back. We gathered around to see what the matter was, and*
> *discovered that Andy had thrust his head into the stomach, which had closed*
> *so tightly around his neck that he could not withdraw his head. We took*
> *hold of his legs and pulled him out.*

At Fort Laramie eighteen of Jesse's travel companions joined the Chiles party, induced by the "very handsome young ladies" in the California company. They pushed on to Soda Springs, which they reached on August 28. By the time they arrived at Fort Hall two weeks later, provisions were short. Chiles split the company in two—most of the food was left in the wagons, and the women and children went with the wagons. The men went by horseback, living off the land.

The horsemen reached Sutter's Fort on November 10, 1843, but the wagons with the women and children were late arriving. The mules that pulled them were exhausted by the time they reached the eastern boundaries of the Sierra Nevada. The emigrants abandoned the wagons near Owens Lake and packed the little food that was left. The four women rode; the five small children were carried or stowed in saddlebags.

The snow was six inches deep in some places when the party crossed the Sierra Nevada in the first week of December. Then, descending to the San Joaquin valley, they encountered desert conditions and went without food for three days and nights. At last they reached the Coastal Range. Camped in Peach Tree Valley, they celebrated Christmas, feasting on the "finest haunches of venison." Shortly after New Year's Day, they reached the California settlements on the Salinas River.

That year, 1844, another train of emigrants was bound for California, numbering twenty-three men, eight women, and fifteen children. Two of the women were pregnant. The company started in mid-May from Council Bluffs, at the western border of the Iowa territory. Their route followed the North Bank of the Platte River in present-day Nebraska. Seven weeks later they halted near Independence Rock to celebrate the Fourth of July and the arrival of the newest member of the party, baby Ellen Independence Miller.

They reached Fort Hall on about August 10 and then swung south, following the Humboldt River until they reached Truckee Meadows (where Reno now stands). By then it was mid-October. Confronted by the seemingly impenetrable range of the snow-covered Sierra Nevada, six wagon owners decided to abandon their vehicles with their valuable cargo at a winter camp near Truckee Lake. The other five wagons managed to find an opening in the vertical ledge ahead. On November 25 they crossed the summit of the Sierra at what today is Donner Pass.

On the west slope they welcomed another baby to their party: Elizabeth Yuba Murphy, her middle name taken from the mountain stream by which she was born. In five feet of snow they established a mountain camp for the women and children and the five wagons that had come across the Sierra.

Most of the cattle were butchered for food. Two men were left as guards. The others rode on to Sutter's Fort, where they arrived in early December. They had hoped to organize a relief party and return for the women and children, but they found California in the throes of a revolution. Mexican rebels were threatening to overthrow Governor Micheltorena. The men were drafted by Captain Sutter to fight the rebels.

It was more than three months before they could rescue their snowbound families in the mountains near Big Bend. By then, some of the women and children were living on hides; miraculously, no lives had been lost, and no harm had come to the two babies born on the trail.

Another survivor was left alone that winter at Truckee Lake. A lanky, seventeen-year-old boy named Moses Schallenberger had volunteered to guard the abandoned wagons and their cargo. Here is his account of how he faced his solitary winter ordeal.

There seemed little danger to me in undertaking this. Game seemed to be abundant. We had seen a number of deer, and one of our party had killed a bear, so I had no fears of starvation. The Indians in that vicinity were poorly clad, and I therefore felt no anxiety in regard to them, as they probably would stay further south as long as cold weather lasted. Knowing that we were not far from California, and being unacquainted with the climate, I did not suppose that the snow would at any time be more than two feet deep, nor that it would be on the ground continually. After I had decided to stay, Mr. Joseph Foster and Mr. Allen Montgomery said they would stay with me, and so it was settled, and the rest of the party started across the mountains. They left us two cows, so worn out and poor that they could go no further. The morning after the separation of our party, which we felt was only for a short time ... we set about making a cabin, for we determined to make ourselves as comfortable as possible, even if it was a short time. We cut saplings and yoked up our poor cows and hauled them together. These we formed into a rude house, and we covered it with rawhides and pine brush. A hole was cut for a door. ... On the evening of the day we finished our little house it began to snow, and that night it fell to a depth of three feet. ... It did not worry us much, however, for the weather was not at all cold, and we thought the snow would soon melt. But we were doomed to disappointment. A week passed, and instead of any snow going off more came. At last we were compelled to kill our cows, for the snow was so deep that they could not get around to eat. ... It kept on snowing continually, and our little cabin was almost covered. It was now about the last of November ... and we began to fear that we should all perish in the snow. … We now began to feel very blue, for there seemed no possible hope for us. We had already eaten about half our meat, and with the snow on the ground getting deeper and deeper each day, there was no chance for game. … Death by starvation stared us in the face. At last, after due consideration, we determined to start for California on foot. Accordingly we dried some of our beef, and each of us carrying ten pounds of meat, a pair of blankets, a rifle and ammunition, we set out on our perilous journey.

Foster and Montgomery were mature men and could stand a greater amount of hardship than the teenage boy Moses. When they reached the summit of the mountain at about sunset, he could scarcely drag one foot after another and was seized with violent cramps. He was so stiff he could barely move. His companions were beginning to have grave doubts as to whether he could stand the journey. Moses volunteered to return to the cabin, and live as long as possible on the quarter of beef that was still there, while awaiting assistance from California. His companions reluctantly agreed.

We did not say much at the parting. The feeling of loneliness that came over me as the … men turned away I cannot express, though it will never be forgotten. … My companions had not been long out of sight before my spirits began to revive, and I began to think like Micawber that something might "turn up." So I strapped on my blankets and dried beef, shouldered my gun, and began to retrace my steps to the cabin. … As soon [as] I was able to crawl around the next morning, I put on my snow-shoes, and, taking my rifle, scoured the country thoroughly for foxes. The result was … plenty of tracks, but no fox.

Discouraged and sick at heart, I came in from my fruitless search and prepared to pass another night in agony. As I put my gun in the corner, my eyes fell upon some steel traps that Captain Stevens [the leader of the party] had left behind in his wagon. In an instant the thought flashed across my mind, "If I can't shoot a coyote or fox, why not trap one?" … My spirits began to rise immediately. … I set my traps. That night I went to bed with a lighter heart, and was able to get some sleep.

As soon as daylight came I was out to inspect the traps. … To my great delight I found in one of them a starved coyote. I soon had his hide off and his flesh roasted in a Dutch oven. I ate his meat, but it was horrible. I next tried boiling him, but it did not improve the flavor … for three days that was all

I had to eat. On the third night I caught two foxes. I roasted one of them, and the meat ... was delicious.

I now gave my whole attention to trapping. ... I caught, on average, a fox in two days, and every now and then a coyote. I never really suffered for something to eat, but was in almost continual anxiety for fear the supply would give out. ... As soon as one meal was finished I began to be distressed for fear I could not get another one. My only hope was that the supply of foxes would not become exhausted. ... For bread and vegetables I had no desire. Salt I had plenty, but never used. I had just coffee enough for one cup, and that I saved for Christmas.

The daily struggle and the uncertainty under which I labored were very wearing. I was always worried and anxious, not about myself alone, but in regard to the fate of those who had gone forward. I would lie awake nights and think of these things. ... Fortunately, I had plenty of books, Dr. Townsend [the company's surgeon] having brought out quite a library. I used often to read aloud, for I longed for some sound to break the oppressive stillness. For the same reason, I would talk aloud to myself. At night I built large fires and read by the light of the pine knots as late as possible, in order that I might sleep late the next morning, and thus cause the days to seem shorter. What I wanted most was enough to eat, and the next thing I tried hardest to do was to kill time. I thought the snow would never leave the ground, and the few months I had been living here seemed like years.

One evening, a little before sunset, about the last of February, as I was standing a short distance from my cabin, I could distinguish the figure of a man moving toward me. I first thought it was an Indian, but very soon I recognized the familiar face of Dennis Martin. My feelings can be better imagined than described.

Moses and his rescuer started their return the next morning. His companion was familiar with snowshoes and fixed them for the boy in such a way that he could travel with little labor, but a scanty diet and limited exercise made this a trying journey for him. They arrived safely at the emigrants' camp, just as the women and children were being moved into Sacramento valley by the relief party. It was now March 1, 1845, exactly a year from the day Moses's travelling companions had left their homes in Missouri.

In spring 1845 the journey west had become a family affair. The muster roll of one party alone showed sixty-one children, thirty-one men, and thirty-two

women. Among the emigrants headed for California in April 1845 was fifty-
year-old William B. Ide, a prosperous Illinois farmer who was to become governor of the short-lived "California Republic." He set out with thirteen people, including his wife, four children, and five young men who drove the ox
teams for their board and passage. His seventeen-year-old daughter, Sarah,
had vivid memories of their departure from Springfield, Illinois.

> *On April 1st we bid our good friends farewell. It was a sad day for us. All
> our old neighbors came to help us pack our things into our three wagons,
> and see us off. ... We packed our cooking utensils, tin cups, tin plates—with
> provisions to last six months. Mother, my little brothers—Daniel, aged ten,
> and Lemuel, aged eight, and Thomas Crafton, (a little boy that had been
> given to my Mother), all rode in a wagon. Our drove of cattle numbered 165,
> including 28 working oxen.*

The Ide family camped the first night about ten miles from their old home
and cooked their first supper by campfire. Sarah and the other children slept
with their mother in the wagon—as they were to do all the way to California.
The others pitched tents. It took them four weeks to reach Independence,
where they laid in ammunition, guns, and pistols, as well as clothing for the
men, "and many little things needful on so long a journey."

On May 10 they left Independence and travelled to the "Big Camp," where
they joined a large train consisting of one hundred wagons. "The cattle of this
large emigrant company was so numerous," wrote Sarah, "that it was difficult
to find grass for them, and it was a great deal of work to control them—also
dangerous." A cattle guard was organized, and Sarah's father became the captain of the guard and chief herdsman. Sarah rode horseback sidesaddle and
helped him drive the cattle.

Her family travelled in one of three companies along the Platte River, then
to the South Pass and Fort Hall. At the fort they camped for several days and
traded horses with the Native Americans. "One offered a very pretty pony for
two calico dresses," remembered the young girl. A company of mountain
trappers told them of a good road to California, with plenty of good grass for
cattle.

> *After we started for California, the Pilot said there was no longer any danger
> from the Indians, and our company began to scatter. I remember one night
> in particular, my Father, with one other family, camped alone, with no
> other guard than a faithful watch-dog we were so fortunate as to bring with*

*us from our old home in Sangumon county, Illinois. This dog would not al-
low an Indian to come near the camp. None of our company were killed.*

They wound their way along the Humboldt River and traversed the forty-
mile desert. Wrote Sarah:

*Some of our best oxen became poor and unfit for work, and were left on the
sandy desert, some 40 miles this way of it, to shirk for themselves; and they
probably died, or were "cared for" by the Indians. An ox would lie down in
his yoke, and could not be got up; so we would unyoke and leave him.*

*After passing the 40-miles desert, and crossing the Truckee River thirty-
two times, we came to Truckee Lake: ... some of the way being obliged to
drive our wagon on the edge of the Lake; some of the time the water coming
almost up to our feet—keeping the women in constant dread of being
drowned. It was a fearful time for the timid female passengers, both young
and old. At night we camped at the foot of the Sierra Nevada; and were told
by the Pilot that we would have to take our wagons to pieces, and haul them
up with ropes.*

Instead, Sarah's father and his men built a "road bridge." By rolling stones
and piling dirt, they built up steep, narrow lanes from one level spot to the
next, taking the oxen and empty wagons slowly up the slope of the mountain.
Sarah remembered:

*It took us a long time to go about two miles over our rough, new-made road
up the mountain, over the rough rocks, in some places, and so smooth in
others, that the oxen would slip and fall on their knees; the blood from their
feet and knees staining the rocks they passed over. Mother and I walked, (we
were so sorry for the poor, faithful oxen), all those two miles—all our clothing being packed on the horses' backs. It was a trying time—the men swear-
ing at their teams, and beating them most cruelly, all along the rugged way.*

Eventually, they reached the summit of the Sierra Nevada and found there
some of the remnants left by the emigrant party that had crossed in 1844.
Sarah observed:

*Somewhere near the summit we came to a place where a company of ten or
twelve wagons had camped the year before, and emptied their feather beds.
They left their wagons and "packed" their oxen into the valleys. We could see*

the tracks of these wagons very plainly—there having been no rain since the melting of the snow last spring.

As they descended into the canyons on the western slopes of the Sierra, Sarah experienced several mishaps with two of her favorite animals:

In driving down into "Steep Hollow," the men cut down small trees to tie to the hind of each wagon, to keep it from turning over ... and also to hold it back. In attempting to ride my pony down, the saddle came off her head. She was so gentle as to stop for me to alight, and I lead her the rest of the way down. We camped that night in "Steep Hollow." Our best milch cow died the next morning. We did all we could to doctor her. We supposed she was poisoned by eating laurel leaves—grass being so scarce.

The rest of the journey into Sacramento was uneventful but very slow, since the surviving sixty-five cattle—a small remnant of the herd they had started with in Illinois—were nearly worn out. They reached Sutter's Fort on October 25. In spite of her weariness, Sarah had not lost her youthful enthusiasm. "To me the journey was a pleasure trip," she remembered, "so many beautiful wild flowers, such wild scenery, mountains, rocks and streams—something new at every turn, or at least every day!"

Seven-year-old Benjamin Franklin Bonney was heading west that same year. His parents and their seven children, four girls and three boys, left Illinois on April 12, 1845. In Independence they joined the Barlow wagon train. They were well equipped for the journey. Young Benjamin remembered:

Father ... built a large box in the home-made wagon and put in a lot of dried buffalo meat and pickled pork. He had made over a hundred pounds of maple sugar which we took along instead of loaf sugar. He also took along plenty of corn meal. ... He laid in a plentiful supply of home twist tobacco. Father chewed it and mother smoked it ... in an old corn cob pipe.

As they crossed the Nebraska prairies, they witnessed a severe thunderstorm that came upon them in the middle of the night. Benjamin never forgot it.

The thunder seemed almost incessant, and the lightning was so brilliant, you could read by its flashes. ... Our tents were blown down as were the covers of our prairie schooners and in less than five minutes we were wet as drowned rats. Unless you have been through it, you have no idea of the confusion re-sulting from a storm on the plains, with the oxen bellowing, the children crying and the men shouting ... with everything as light as day and the next second as black as the depth of a pit.

Benjamin's father had originally wanted to settle in the Willamette valley, but he changed his mind in Fort Hall when he met Caleb Greenwood, a mountain man who had been employed by Captain Sutter to divert Oregon-bound emigrants to California. He promised that Sutter would supply them with plenty of potatoes, coffee, and dried beef and would give every head of a family six sections of his Mexican land grant if they chose to settle near his fort.

After an all-night powwow, the Bonneys were among the first of eight wagons to pull out of the Oregon-bound train to head southwest for California. Young Benjamin recalled:

After two weeks of traveling we struck a desert of sand and sage brush. On this sage brush plain we found lots of prickly pears. We children were bare-footed and I can remember yet how we limped across the desert, for we cut the soles of our feet on the prickly pears. ... They also made the oxen lame, for the spines would work in between the oxen's hoofs.

He also remembered an ugly incident between one of the California-bound emigrants in his party and a Native American they met along the way.

While we were crossing the sage brush desert, one of the men in our party, named Jim Kinney, who hailed from Texas, came upon an Indian. When he saw this Indian in the sage brush, he called his driver to stop. His wagon was in the lead, so the whole train stopped. Going to the wagon, he got a pair of handcuffs and started back to where the Indians was. He jumped off his mule, and struck the Indian over the head. The Indian tried to escape. He put up a fight, but was no match for Kinney. In a moment or two, Kinney had knocked him down, gotten his handcuffs on him and ... fastened a rope around his neck. ... For several days he rode back of the Indian, slashing him across the back with his black-snake whip to "break his spirit."

After the Indian had been with Kinney for over three weeks, one dark windy night he disappeared. In the morning when Kinney got up he found the Indian had taken a blanket as well as Kinney's favorite Kentucky rifle. ... He had also taken his powder horn, some lead, and three hams. Kinney was furious but everyone in the train rejoiced that the Indian had escaped.

At the foot of the Sierra Nevada, Bonney's party was met by ten Mexicans with a pack train loaded with flour, potatoes, and dried beef. They then began their laborious ascent. At each rimrock ledge along the Sierra, their wagons were disassembled and hoisted to the top of the rim, then reassembled and reloaded. It took them four days to reach the summit. Benjamin remembered:

At the foot of the Sierras we camped by a beautiful, ice-cold, crystal-clear mountain stream. We camped there for three days to rest the teams and let the women wash the clothing and get things fixed up. My sister Harriet was fourteen, and with my cousin Lydia Bonney, Truman Bonney, myself and other boys of the party, we put in three delightful days wading in the stream. It was October and the water was low. In many places there were sand and gravel bars. On one of these gravel bars I saw what I thought was wheat, when I picked it up I found it was heavy. ... I took one of the pieces about the size of a small pea into camp with me. [One of our companions] Dr. Gildea asked me for it. That evening he came to my father and, showing him the dull yellow metal I had given him, said "What your boy found today is pure gold. Keep the matter to yourself; we will come back here next spring and get rich."

When the Bonneys reached Fort Sutter, they were made welcome. Captain Sutter gave them furnished quarters, plenty of food, and work for the men. The families who joined his colony received regular allowances in accordance with the number of children they had. Young Benjamin was intrigued by the people at the fort.

There was a large cookhouse at the fort, where we children liked to watch them doing the cooking. They cooked here for a large number of Indian laborers. In addition to the Indian workers, there were a lot of Indian boys who were trained to do the work. The Indian boys were fed in a peculiar way. They ground barley for them, made it into a gruel, and emptied it in a long trough. When the big dinner bell rang, the Indian boys would go to the trough and with their fingers pick up the porridge and eat it.

So many emigrants were crowded into the fort that winter that as a result there was a good deal of sickness. ... A large number of the natives died as well as some of the emigrants, mainly children.

Among those who succumbed to typhoid, or "mountain fever," were Benjamin's oldest brother, his sister Ann, and his old friend Dr. Gildea. With the latter died the dream of returning to the camping place in the foothills and getting rich by picking up gold nuggets in the mountain stream. Two years later gold was discovered at Sutter's Mill, but by then young Benjamin and his family had moved on.

In spring 1846 the Bonneys went to Oregon after all because the Mexican government in California insisted that if they stayed there they must renounce their U.S. citizenship. On the way north, around three hundred miles out of Sacramento, the family came to a beautiful lake surrounded by green meadows. They camped there for the night. Young Benjamin remembered:

The young man who took the horses out for pasture found near the lake an Indian girl about eight years old. The little girl was perfectly naked, her long black hair was matted, and she was covered with scars from head to feet. She could only make a pitiful moaning noise. Dr. Truman Bonney, my uncle, examined her and said she was suffering from hunger and that the flies had almost eaten her up. Near by we could see where two tribes of Indians had fought. She had apparently crept to one side, out of danger, and had been left. ... A council among the men was held to see what should be done with her. My father wanted to take her along; others wanted to kill her and put her out of her misery. ... A vote was taken and it was decided to do nothing about it, but to leave her where we found her. My mother and my aunt were unwilling to leave the little girl. They stayed behind to do all they could do for her. When they finally joined us their eyes were red and swollen from crying. ... Mother said she had knelt down by the little girl and had asked God to take care of her. One of the young men in charge of the horses felt so badly about leaving her, he went back and put a bullet through her head and put her out of her misery.

A few days later, the Bonney party came to an encampment beside the trail. The Indians appeared peaceful, and the Bonneys decided to spend the night nearby. That evening the children in the party visited the Native Americans, who gave them some blackish bread that looked like fruitcake. Some of the youngsters ate it, but many were rather squeamish about it because they had discovered what it was made of: dried acorns and crickets, pounded together in a stone mortar and shaped into loaves.

Later that night an Indian came to the camp and brought a boy about twelve years old. Benjamin related what happened next.

Alan Sanders traded a Pinto pony for the boy. He cut the Indian boy's long hair, bought him clothing from one of the other members of the party, and named the boy Columbus. The first night Columbus was very unhappy, but after Sanders had given him a sound thrashing, he seemed more contented.

The early emigrant parties owed much to the assistance provided by the chief of the Piute Indians, who showed them the location of a river that flowed east from the Sierra Nevada. Along its banks were large trees and good grass. His granddaughter, Sarah Winnemucca, was born around 1844, at the time when the first wagon trains crossed her native land. In *Life Among the Piutes* she describes the swift deterioration that took place in the relationship between members of her tribe and the people her grandfather called "my white brothers."

I was a small child when the first white people came into our country. My people were scattered at that time over nearly all the territory now known as Nevada. My grandfather was chief of the Piute nation, and was camped near Humboldt Lake, with his tribe, when a party travelling eastward from California was seen coming. When the news was brought to my grandfather, he asked what they looked like? When told that they had hair on their faces, and were white, he jumped up and clasped his hands together, and cried aloud: "My white brothers—my long-looked-for white brothers have come at last!"

The next year came a great emigration, and camped near Humboldt Lake. … During their stay my grandfather and some of his people called upon them, and they all shook hands, and when our white brothers were going away they gave my grandfather a white tin plate. … My grandfather called for all his people to come together, and he showed them the beautiful gift he had received from his white brothers. … My grandfather thought so much of it that he bored holes in it and fastened it on his head, and wore it as a hat.

The third year more emigrants came, and gave my grandfather the name of Captain Truckee, and also called the river after him. Truckee is an Indian word; it means "all right," or "very well."

The following spring there was a great excitement among my people on account of fearful news coming from different tribes. Our mothers told us that the whites were killing everybody.

What a fright we all got one morning to hear some white people were coming. Everyone ran as best they could. ... My aunt said to my mother: "Let us bury our girls, or we shall all be killed and eaten up." ... So our mothers buried me and my cousin, planted sage bushes over our faces to keep the sun from burning them, and there we were left.

With my heart throbbing and not daring to breathe, we lay there all day. It seemed that the night would never come. ... At last we heard some whispering. Then I heard my mother say, "T'is right here!" Oh, can anyone in this world imagine what were my feelings when I was dug up by my poor mother and father? ... Those were the last white men that came along that fall. This whole band of white people perished in the mountains, for it was too late to cross them. We could have saved them, only my people were afraid of them. We never knew who they were, or where they came from. So, poor things, they must have suffered fearfully, for they all starved there. The snow was too deep.

Those who perished in the Sierra Nevada that winter were members of the Donner party, who had set out in the spring with high hopes and great expectations.

The Children
of the Donner Party

TWO EMIGRANT TRAINS pulled out of Springfield, Illinois, in mid-April 1846. Three wagons belonged to James Frazier Reed, a wealthy contractor and furniture maker. The Reeds travelled in style. They owned a two-story Pioneer Palace car, probably the largest prairie schooner ever to be seen on the overland trails.

Reed's thirteen-year-old stepdaughter, Virginia, the main chronicler of the journey, described the vehicle's splendor.

> *The entrance was on the side, like that of an old-fashioned stage coach, and one stepped into a small room, as it were, in the center of the wagon. At the right and left were spring seats with comfortable high backs, where one could sit and ride with as much ease as on the seats of a Concord coach. In this little room was placed a tiny sheet-iron stove, whose pipe, running through the top of the wagon, was prevented by a circle of tin from setting fire to the canvas cover. A board about a foot wide extended over the wheels on either side the full length of the wagon, thus forming the foundation for a large and roomy second story in which were placed our beds. Under the spring seats were compartments in which were stored many articles useful for the journey, such as a well filled work basket and a full assortment of medicines, with lint and bandages for dressing wounds. Our clothing was packed ... in strong canvas bags.*

Two other wagons were loaded with provisions—enough for the anticipated six-month journey—and supplies to last through the first winter in

California. Among them was a good library of standard books. Virginia remembered:

> *The family wagon was drawn by four yoke of oxen, large Durham steers at*
> *the wheel. The other wagons were drawn by three yoke each. We had saddle*
> *horses and cows, and last but not least my pony. He was a beauty and his*
> *name was Billy. I can scarcely remember when I was taught to sit on a horse.*
> *I only know that when a child of seven I was the proud owner of a pony and*
> *used to go riding with papa. That was the chief pleasure to which I looked*
> *forward in crossing the plains.*

The Reed party numbered nine, not counting the three teamsters: the parents, James Frazier Reed (age forty-six) and his wife, Margaret (thirty-two); Virginia Reed (thirteen), a daughter from Mrs. Reed's first marriage; Virginia's half sister, Martha, called "Patty" (eight); and her two little half brothers, James (five) and Thomas (three). Also on board were Virginia's grandmother, Mrs. Sarah Keyes (seventy), and two servants. Virginia described their departure.

> *Never can I forget the morning when we bade farewell. … We were sur-*
> *rounded by loved ones, and there stood all my little schoolmates, who had*
> *come to kiss me good-bye. My father with tears in his eyes tried to smile as*
> *one friend after another grasped his hands in last farewell. Mama was over-*
> *come with grief.*

The other six wagons in the emigrant train that left Springfield that morning belonged to the Donner brothers, George and Jacob. Both were prosperous farmers heading west in search of better land.

George Donner (age sixty-two) travelled with his wife, Tamsen (forty-five), their three children—Frances (6), Georgia (four), and Eliza (three)—and George's daughters from a previous marriage, Elitha (fourteen) and Leanna (twelve). His older brother Jacob (sixty-five) was accompanied by his wife, Elizabeth (forty-five), and their five children—George Jr. (nine), Mary (seven), Isaac (five), Samuel (four), and Lewis (three)—as well as two of Elizabeth's children from an earlier marriage, Solomon Hook (fourteen) and William Hook (twelve).

Among the supplies carried in the Donner wagons were seeds and implements for their prospective farms in the new country, bolts of cotton prints and flannels, handkerchiefs, glass beads, necklaces, chains, brass finger rings, earrings, pocket looking glasses, and other knicknacks intended as "peace of-

No 6 from the Starved Camp as it is Called,
and som would not come thare was 3 diead and the rest eat them thay was 10 days without anny
thing to eat but the Dead Pa braught Thomas and puddy on to where we was none of the men
Pa had with him ware able to go back fer Some people stell at the Cabins,
thare feet was froze very bad so thare was a nother Compana went and
braught them all in thay are all in from the mountains now but four men
went out after them and was caught in a storm and had to come back thare was
nother compana sent to thair relief
sumise that all of them got we ware one Mary I have not wrote you half of the
truble but I hav wrote you anuf to let you know that you dont know what truble is
but thank god we have all got throw and the onely family that did not eat
human flesh we have left every thing but i dont cair for that we have got through with our lives
but Dont let this letter dishaten anybody never take no cutofs and hury along as fast as you can

My Dear Cousin

we are all very well pleasd with the Callifornia particulary with the climate let
it be ever so hot a day thare is allwais cool nights it is a beautiful Country it is
mostley in vallies it aut to be a beautiful Country to pay us for our trubel getting
the greatest place for cattel and horses you ever saw it would Just suit Charley
for he could ride down 300 horses a day and he could lern to be Bocarro that one who
lases cattel the spanards and Indians are the best riders i ever saw thay have a span
sadel and wodon sturups and great big spurs 5 inches in
diameter they could not manage the Callifornia horses without the spurs thay
wont go a tol if thay cant hear the spurs rattle thay have littel bells to them to make
them rattle thay blindfold the horses till thay the wild sadel them and git on them and
take the blindfole of and let run and if thay cant set on thay tie themselves on and
let them run as fast as they can and go out to a band of bulllock and throw the
reatter on a wild bullluck and but it around the horn of his sadel and he can
hold it as long as he wants a nother Indedn thr0wes his reatter on its feet and throw
them and when thay take the reatter of of them thay are very dangerous

No 7

thay will run after you them hook there horses and run after any — person
thay see thay ride from 50 to 100 miles a day ——— some of the spanard have from 50 to ——
head of horse and from 15 to 16000 head cattel we are all verry ——— Ma wares 100 & 40 pons
and i tell again I weigh 80 tel Henriet if she wants to get married to come to
Callifornia she can get a spanyard any time that Eliza is a going to marry a
a spanyard by the name of Armeho and Eliza weighs 10072 We have not saw
uncle Cadon yet but we have had 2 letters from him he is well and is a coming
here as soon as he can Mary take this letter to uncle Gursham and to all that
and tell daughter Maneel.
I know to all of our neighbors and every girl i know and let them read it
Mary kiss little Sue and Maryann for me and give my best love to all i
know to uncle James aunt Lida and all the rest of the family and to uncle
Gursham aunt Percilla and all the children and to all of our neighbors and
to all the girls i know ——————————————— and to uncle James aunt
Lida and all the rest of the family and to uncle Gursham and all of the children
and to all of our neighbors and to all she knows so no more at presand

My Dear cousins

Virginia Elizabeth B Reed

Letter of Virginia Reed to Her Cousin Mary C. Keyes, May 17, 1847 (courtesy Bancroft Library, University of California–Berkeley) ferings for the Indians." There were also rich stores of laces, silks, satins, and velvets, "destined to be used in exchange for Mexican land-grants." Last but not least, there was material for women's handiwork, an apparatus for preserving botanical specimens, watercolors and oil paints, and books and school supplies that were the special province of Tamsen Donner, a former teacher who hoped to establish a "young ladies' seminary" in faraway California.

On the day of their departure, all the Donner children were dressed in new travelling suits, and, as the final packing progressed, they would peep out of the window at the covered wagons in the yard. Eliza, the youngest of Tamsen Donner's daughters, described the scene.

> *In the first wagon we stored the merchandise and articles not to be handled until they should reach their destination; in the second, provisions, clothing, camp tools, and other necessaries of camp life. The third was our family home on wheels, with feed boxes attached to the back of the wagon-bed for Fanny and Margaret, our favorite saddle-horses.*

Early in the day, the first two wagons started off, each drawn by three yoke of powerful oxen. The beef cattle and milk cows quickly followed, with a faithful watchdog at their heels. Finally, by noon the family wagon was ready. Eliza remembered:

> *I sat beside my mother with my hand clasped in hers, as we slowly moved away from that quaint old house on its grassy knoll, from the orchard, the corn land, and the meadow; as we passed through the last pair of bars, her clasp tightened, and I, glancing up, saw tears in her eyes.*

THE JOURNEY

After travelling for four weeks, the Reeds and Donners reached Independence, Missouri. There they found busy crowds of men, women, and children ready to join the pioneer trains. An agent from the American Tract Society came to their wagons and gave each child a copy of the Bible.

On May 11, 1846, one day before they left Independence, Tamsen Donner, Eliza's mother, wrote a letter to her sister.

> *My Dear Sister*
>
> *… Now in the midst of preparation for starting across the mountains I am seated on the grass in the midst of the tent to say a few words to my dearest & only sister. … My three daughters are round me, one at my side*

trying to sew, Georgeanna fixing herself up in old india rubber cap & Eliza Poor knocking on my paper & asking me ever so many questions. … I can give you no idea of the hurry of the place at this time. It is supposed there will be 7000 waggons will start from this place this season. We go to California, to the bay of San Francisco. It is a four months trip. I am willing to go & have no doubt it will be an advantage to our children & to us. I came here last evening & start to-morrow on the long journey.

Farewell, my sister, you shall hear from me as soon as I have an opportunity …
Farewell
T(amsen) E. Donner

After leaving Independence, the first part of the journey was relatively easy. The Donners and the Reeds travelled for two weeks across the northeast corner of Kansas. The older children did their daily chores, milking the cows, churning the butter, and cleaning the cooking utensils with sand. The younger ones gathered buffalo "chips" for fire. But there was also time for carefree play. Eliza Donner remembered:

We little folk sat in the wagons with our dolls, watching the huge white-covered "prairie schooners". … During a rest break, we children, who had been confined to the wagon so many hours each day, stretched our limbs, and scampered off on Mayday frolics. We waded the creek, made mud pies, and gathered posies in the narrow glades between the cottonwood, beech, and alder trees. … The staid and elderly matrons spent most of their time in their wagons, knitting, or patching designs for quilts. The younger ones and the girls passed theirs in the saddle. The wild, free spirit of the plain often prompted them to invite us little ones to seats behind them, and away we would canter with the breeze playing through our hair.

Virginia Reed was perfectly happy. "How I enjoyed riding my pony, galloping over the plain, gathering wild flowers! At night the young folks would gather about the camp fire chatting merrily, and often a song would be heard, or some clever dancer would give us a barn-door jig on the hind gate of a wagon."

Virginia's mood turned from happiness to sadness within a fortnight. On May 29, 1846, her seventy-year-old grandmother, Sarah Keyes, died from consumption and was buried near the Big Blue River. Virginia reported in her first letter to her cousin Mary in Illinois that "she became spechless the day before she died. We buried her verry decent. … We miss her verry much every time we come in the wagon we look up at the bed for her."

Crossing the Nebraska plains, the girl's exuberance returned. She joined her father in buffalo hunts on the prairies and was especially intrigued by a party of Sioux who were on the warpath against the Crow and Blackfeet Indians.

> *They are fine-looking Indians and I was not the least afraid of them. …*
> *They never showed any inclination to disturb us … but our wagon with its*
> *conspicuous stove pipe and looking glass attracted their attention. They were*
> *continuously swarming about trying to get a look at themselves in the mir-*
> *ror. … I picked up a large field glass which hung on a rack, and as I pulled*
> *it out with a click, the warriors jumped back, wheeled their ponies and scat-*
> *tered. … When ever they came near trying to get a peep at their war-paint*
> *and feathers I would raise the glass and laugh.*

By the middle of June, travel had become more difficult. The emigrant train was constantly enveloped by clouds of dust. Wood became scarce, and water had to be saved in casks. The children saw many dead oxen and crippled cattle that had been abandoned by their owners.

They reached Independence Rock in time for a Fourth of July celebration. "Paw treted the company with a botel of licker," wrote Virginia to her cousin, "and we all had some leminade."

Around the second week of July, the Donner and Reed families were joined by the Breens, an Irish family with seven children, ranging from fourteen-year-old John to Isabella, a nursing infant of six months. They had left their farm in Iowa territory in early April with three wagons, drawn by seven yoke of oxen, and some cows and horses. John traced the journey.

> *We crossed the Missouri river after a very tedious journey. … In due time we*
> *arrived at a camp called Lone Elm. … This place was thought to be the*
> *limit of civilization. At this camp were some hunters returning with furs &*
> *they gave us some dried bufalow meat and told us that we had no idea what*
> *we would suffer before we reached California—at this camp was a Elm tree,*
> *the only tree of any kind in sight. I shall never forget the loneliness of the*
> *scene. … Still we were fairly on our way across the plains, and were after-*
> *wards joined by other parties.*

By July 20 the emigrant train had reached the Sandy River. "There," wrote Eliza Donner, "my father and others deliberated over a new route to California. They were led to do so by a letter written by Lansford W. Hastings … stating that the better route by way of the south end of Salt Lake was nearly two hundred miles shorter than the old one by way of Fort Hall."

The proposition seemed feasible, and a party was formed to take the new route. Eliza's father was elected captain of this company, which from that time on was known as the Donner party.

Nine families with a total of forty-one children joined the party: the Reeds, the two Donner families, the Eddys, and the Graves, all from Illinois; the Breens from Iowa; the McCutchens and the children and grandchildren of widow Murphy from Tennessee and Missouri; and the Kesebergs from Germany. There were also eighteen single men, including the teenager John Baptiste Trudeau, son of a French trapper and a Mexican mother, who joined the Donners as a teamster at Fort Bridger. He became a loyal friend and helpmate to their children.

On July 31 the Donner party left Fort Bridger. "Without a suspicion of impending disaster," wrote Virginia Reed, "we set out with high spirits on the Hastings Cut-off." In the first days the emigrant party, now consisting of about twenty-two wagons, travelled a respectable twelve miles a day. Patty Reed, Virginia's eight-year-old half sister, had found a new friend, thirteen-year-old Edward Breen. Later his son would tell of an incident that befell the boy not far west of Fort Bridger.

He says that Patty Reed and he were galloping along on their saddle ponies, when his horse put one or both front feet into a badger or prairie dog burrow and took a hard fall. He was knocked out and when some of the others came to pick him up they found he had a break of his left leg between the knee and ankle. Someone was sent back to the Fort for aid in repairing the damage, and after what seemed to him a long time, a rough-looking man with long whiskers rode up on a mule. He examined the boy's leg and proceeded to unroll a small bundle he had wrapped in canvas and tied behind his saddle. Out of this came a short meat saw and a long bladed knife. The boy set up a loud cry when he sensed what was to be done and finally after a long discussion convinced his parents that he should keep his leg. The old mountain man was given five dollars and sent back to the Fort, muttering to himself for not being given a chance to display his skill as a surgeon.

Splints for Edward's leg were fashioned from wood strips, and by the time the party reached Humboldt River, about eight weeks later, he was able to ride his horse again.

By the end of the first week of August, the Donner party knew the "cutoff" was not as it had been represented in Hastings's letter. There was no road, not even a trail. Heavy underbrush had to be cut away and used for making a road bed. It took the men in the company six days to chop their way through eight miles of wooded canyon. The party was now travelling two miles a day. Wrote Virginia Reed, "Finally we reached the end of the canyon. ... Worn with travel and greatly discouraged we reached the shore of the Great Lake. It had taken an entire month, instead of a week, and our cattle were not fit to cross the desert." John Breen remembered:

> *When we got out on the valley ... there was fine grass and water, and no one to molest us as the Indians were not troublesome. We should have wintered here, as the season was late [it was the end of August], but there was no one in the company that had ever been to California and it was not supposed that we would be stopped by snow.*

Instead, men, women, and children began to cross the salty desert. After two days and nights, "suffering from thirst and heat by day and piercing cold by night," Virginia Reed's father went ahead in search of water. While he was gone, his oxen bolted and disappeared in the desert. The other wagons moved out of sight. Virginia Reed:

> *Towards night the situation became desperate and we had only a few drops of water left; another night there meant death. We must set out on foot and try to reach some of the wagons. ... Dragging our selves along about ten miles, we reached the wagon of Jacob Donner. The family were all asleep, so we children lay down on the ground. A bitter wind swept over the desert, chilling us through and through. We crept closer together, and, when we complained of the cold, papa placed all five of our dogs around us.*

Patty Reed:

> *As soon as day light appeared, we went to their wagon. ... We had crackers and some lump of suger (the sugar was to quench thirst) with us to eat, as we moved on this salt desert, but Mrs. Donner said ... "Mr. Reed, let Mrs. Reed and the children stay with us and ride in our wagon." ... We little ones were glad with the thought of riding with Aunt Betsy.*

A week was spent in a fruitless search for the cattle. The Reeds had lost thirty-six oxen and had to abandon their heavy palace wagon. The company lent them two yoke of oxen, so they could load one wagon with necessities. The rest of their possessions were cached in the desert. They resumed the journey across the waterless wasteland. Eliza Donner described the crossing.

All who could walk did so, mothers carrying their babes in their arms, and fathers with weaklings across their shoulders moved slowly as they urged the famishing cattle forward. Disappointment intensified our burning thirst, and my good mother gave her own and other suffering children wee lumps of sugar, moistened with a drop of peppermint, and later put a flattened bullet in each child's mouth to engage its attention.

On September 26 the Donner party reached the Humboldt River at the point at which it met the old trail coming down from Fort Hall, near present-day Elko. They were now the last emigrant train of 1846 that was still on the trail. All the others had arrived in California.

Food supplies were low. Two men—William McCutchen, the father of an infant girl, and Charles Stanton, a bachelor—volunteered to go ahead to Sutter's Fort on horseback to obtain provisions for the party. The cattle were weary, and tempers were fraying. On October 7 Virginia Reed's stepfather killed a man in self-defense and was banished from the train, leaving behind his wife and four children. Virginia had vivid memories of the event.

My father was sent out into an unknown country without provisions or arms—even his horse was at first denied him. When we learned of this decision, I followed him through the darkness, taking Elliott [the head teamster] with me, and carried him his rifle, pistols, ammunition and some food. I had determined to stay with him, and begged him to let me stay ... but he placed me in charge of Elliott, who started back to camp with me—and papa was left alone. I had cried until I had hardly strength to walk, but when we reached camp and I saw the distress of my mother, with the little ones clinging around her and no arm to lean upon, it seemed suddenly to make a woman of me. I realized that I must be strong and help mama bear her sorrows.

The one wagon that now carried the Reeds' possessions was found to be too heavy and was abandoned, along with everything they could spare. What was left was packed in another family's wagon. They still had two horses, which carried the two youngest Reed children, five-year-old Jimmy and three-year-old Tommy. Virginia, Patty, and their mother walked beside the horses and held on to the boys.

Every day, Mrs. Reed and her children would look for some sign from James Reed. Even young Tommy fretted and worried every time the family had a meal lest his father should find nothing to eat. When Stanton came back on October 19, with two Native Americans from Fort Sutter and seven mules loaded with provisions, they heard the good news that he had seen James Reed alive in California. Virginia Reed continued her tale of their journey.

We now packed what little we had left on one mule and started with Stanton. My mother rode on a mule, carrying Tommy in her lap; Patty and Jim rode behind the two Indians, and I behind Mr. Stanton, and in this way we journeyed on through the rain, looking up with fear towards the mountains, where snow was already falling although it was only the last week in October.

After crossing the Humboldt sink, the Donner party reached the Truckee River the third week in October. The Breen family, fearful of the snows and anxious to get going, took the lead in the drive up the Truckee. By the time they reached the area west of Truckee Meadows (today's Reno), they had forded the river forty-nine times. John Breen remembered:

After leaving the sink of the Humboldt the company as if by mutual consent dissolved, or gradually separated, some wanted to stop and rest their cattle; others in fear of the snow were in favor of pushing ahead as fast as possible, as provisions were getting short which fact greatly increased the danger of delay—My father and some others after getting on the Truckey river concluded to travel as fast as they could, as there began to be heavy clouds on the high range of mountains to the West.

The wagons stretched out for miles. The Donners, in the rear, fell further behind when an axle on their wagon broke. Fourteen-year-old Elitha Donner told her half sister, Eliza, about the mishap.

Our five Donner wagons ... were a day or more behind the train ... when an accident happened which nearly cost us your life. ... Your mother and Frances were walking on ahead; you and Georgia were asleep in the wagon; and father was walking beside it, down a steep hill. It had almost reached the base of the incline when the axle to the fore wheels broke, and the wagon tipped over on the side, tumbling its contents upon you two children. Father and uncle, in great alarm, rushed to your rescue. Georgia was soon hauled out safely through the opening in the back of the wagon sheets, but you were nowhere in sight, and father was sure you were smothering because you did not answer his call. … Finally uncle came to your limp form. You could not have lasted much longer, they said.

On October 31 the Breen family approached Truckee Lake, located at an altitude of six thousand feet—twelve hundred feet below the pass. They drove their team toward the main ridge. Snow was falling fast, but they made a last-ditch effort to cross the mountains. They failed. The Reed family was behind the Breens. Virginia remembered:

When it was seen that the wagons could not be dragged through the snow, their goods and provisions were packed on oxen and another start was made, men and women walking in the snow up to their waists, carrying their children in their arms and trying to drive their cattle, camped within three miles of the summit. That night came the dreaded snow. We children slept soundly on our cold bed of snow. … Every few moments my mother would have to shake the shawl—our only covering—to keep us from being buried alive. In the morning the snow lay deep on mountain and valley. With heavy hearts we turned back.

THE ENTRAPMENT

The Breens settled into the cabin at the eastern end of Truckee Lake in which young Moses Schallenberger had spent the winter of 1844. It was about sixteen by twenty feet long, built of rough logs, with a fireplace and chimney at one end and sleeping space at the other. All of the others had to construct their own shelters. There were three camp sites near the lake.

1. The Breen and Keseberg cabin—with Patrick and Margaret Breen, their seven children, ranging in age from one to fourteen, and bachelor Patrick Dolan; and the Keseberg extension to the Breen cabin, with Lewis and Philippine Keseberg and their two children, ages one and three.

2. The Murphy and Eddy camp—a double cabin about two hundred yards from the Breens. In one cabin were widow Murphy; five of her unmarried children, ranging in age from ten to fifteen; her daughter Sarah Murphy Foster, Sarah's husband, William Foster, and their four-year-old son; and another daughter, Harriet Murphy Pike, and her two children, ages one and three. In the other cabin were William and Eleanor Eddy and their two small children, ages one and three.

3. The Graves and Reed Camp—three cabins on Donner Creek, more than half a mile from the Breen cabin. In the cabin of the Graves family were seven children, ranging in age from one to eighteen; in the Reed cabin were Mrs. Reed and her four children, ranging in age from three to thirteen. The third cabin was for the hired help.

The Donner brothers, caught in the heavy snows, never reached the lake camps and built shelters for themselves, their children, and their hired men about six miles away at Alder Creek. Eliza Donner wrote:

> *All plans for log cabins had to be abandoned. There was no sheltered nook for us shivering children, so father lifted Georgia and me on to a log, and mother tucked a buffalo robe around us, saying, "Sit here until we have a better place for you." There we sat, snug and dry, chatting and twisting our heads about, watching.*

The men constructed tents on each side of the creek, with poles propped diagonally against a tree. Canvas, quilts, and buffalo robes were draped over the wood. They erected three such shelters several hundred yards apart: George Donner's tent sheltered five children, ranging in age from three to fourteen; Jacob Donner's tent contained seven children, ages three to fourteen; a third wigwam was for the single men.

At the beginning of the entrapment, there were fifty-six people at the lake camps and twenty-five at Alder Creek—a total of eighty-one. Only forty-six would live to see the California settlements: twenty-six children, eleven women, and nine men.

At Truckee Lake Camp

"The misery endured during those four months … in our little dark cabins under the snow would fill pages and make the coldest heart ache," wrote Virginia Reed. On November 20, 1846, Patrick Breen made his first entry into a diary that became a daily chronicle of the events at the mountain camps until his rescuers arrived on March 1, 1847. His terse comments describe people who are struggling desperately for their lives.

> *Friday Nov. 20th 1846: came to this place on the 31st of last mo 1th. … we now have killed most part of our cattle having to stay here untill next spring & live on poor beef without bread or salt it snowed during the space of eight days with little intermission, after our arrival here.*

On November 29 Patrick Breen killed his last oxen. Two weeks later the Murphys, who lived next door to the Breens, were almost out of provisions.

In mid-December the senior Graves fashioned fifteen pairs of snowshoes and started across the mountains with fourteen others. Mary Murphy, the thirteen-year-old sister of three members of this Expedition of Forlorn Hope reported to her relatives back east:

> *They took food for only six days. But it was not until 33 days later that they reached the first settlement in California—Johnson's Ranch on the Bear river 40 miles north of Fort Sutter. My two sisters and four others managed to live through the terrible ordeal, but my twelve-year-old brother and seven others perished in the snow.*

By Christmas Eve, five men at the lake and at Alder Creek had died from starvation. Patrick Breen wrote in his diary:

> *Thurs. 24th [December, 1846] ... poor prospect for any kind of comfort spiritual or temporal ... may God help us to spend the Christmass as we ought considering our circumstances. Friday 25th ... offerd. our prayers to God this Christmass morning the prospect is appaling but hope in God Amen.*

Amid the privations, a semblance of the Christmas spirit survived. Patty Reed wrote about that spirit in a letter to C. F. McGlashan, the historian of the Donner party.

> *Christmas Eve came, no stockings to hang, no Santa Claus to come down our chimney in that cold yes starving camp. No Papa to come home to his little ones and bring all he could get to please his wife and children. ... Christmas morning came, you could not hear that happy sound "Merry Christmas" ring through the hall. ... Our breakfast was ready, a pot of glue. ... It was stewed ox hide, but we were pleased to have even that to eat. But as soon as we had gone through this ... our poor Mother's face began to brighten up and she would get a bucket of snow, melt it and heat it, carry it out of the cabin door and pour it on the snow at the corner of the cabin ... until she had melted away the snow, away from the hidden treasure.*

Her half sister, Virginia, revealed the surprise waiting for the children.

> *My mother had determined weeks before that her children should have a treat on this one day. She had laid away a few dried apples, some beans, a bit of tripe and a small piece of bacon. When this hoarded store was brought out, the delight of the little ones knew no bounds. The cooking was watched*

*carefully and when we sat down to our Christmas dinner, mother said
"Children, eat slowly, for this one day you can have all you wish." So bitter
was the misery relieved this one bright day, that I have never since sat down
to a Christmas dinner without my thoughts going back to Donner Lake.*

Mary Murphy, in a cabin half a mile away from the Reeds, did not have such
happy memories.

*Christmas we had a meal of boiled bones and oxtail soup. After supper
Mother was barely able to put the babies to bed, and later on that evening
with brother William reading her favorite psalm from the Good Book, she
became bedridden and seriously ill.*

A week later, Patrick Breen made this entry in his diary.

*Thursday 31st Last of the year, may we with Gods help spend the comeing
year better than the past which we purpose to do if Almighty God will deliver us from our present dredful situation which is our prayer if the will of
God sees it fiting for us Amen. ...*
   *Jany. 1st 1847 We pray the God of mercy to deliver us from our present ca-
lamity.*

On January 4, 1847, Virginia Reed, her mother, and two of their hired help-
ers made a second futile attempt to cross the Sierra Nevada. Tommy Reed was
left with the Breens, Patty Reed stayed with the Kesebergs, and Jimmy Reed
remained with the Graves. "It was difficult for Mrs. Reed to get away from the
children," wrote Patrick Breen in his diary.

On January 8 they returned to the lake camp, having failed to find the trail
on the other side of the pass. "The greatest wonder is how they were ever able
to retrace their steps," mused fourteen-year-old John Breen, "as the snow fell
several feet while they were gone." Patty Reed was taken in by the Breens;
Mrs. Reed and her other three children stayed at their own cabin.

The next day Mrs. Reed was back at the Breens' cabin with Virginia, whose
toes were frozen. Soon afterward she and her four children were living in one
end of the Breen cabin. Virginia Reed explained why her family had to find a
new shelter.

*We now had nothing to eat but raw hides and they were on the roof of the
cabin to keep out the snow; when prepared for cooking and boiled they were
simply a pot of glue. When the hides were taken off our cabin and we were*

left without shelter Mr. Breen gave us a home with his family, and Mrs.
Breen prolonged my life by slipping me little bits of meat now and then
when she discovered that I could not eat the hide.

The Breens still had a store of beef, but the Reeds had to kill their favorite
dog for sustenance. "We had to kill little cash ... and eat him; we at his head
and feet & hide & evry thing about him," wrote Virginia Reed to her cousin.
"O Mary I would cry and wish I had what you all wasted."

In late January, Patrick Breen began to record a litany of deaths in his diary:
the names of starving infants, exhausted mothers, and despairing men. His
two oldest sons, John and Edward, assisted with most burials. John Breen remarked later, "Death had become so common an event that it was looked
upon as a matter of course, and we all expected to go soon."

Eleven-year-old William Murphy witnessed the death of his fifteen-year-
old brother on January 31.

When my oldest brother, on whom my mother depended, was very weak and
almost at death's door, my mother went to the Breens and begged a little
meat, just a few mouthfuls—I remember well that little piece of meat! My
mother gave half of it to my dying brother, he ate it, fell asleep with a hollow
death gurgle. When it ceased I went to him—he was dead—starved to death
in our presence. Although starving herself, my mother said that if she had
known that Landrum was going to die she would have given him the bal-
ance of the meat.

John Breen helped to bury the boy in the snow.

I was there to help Mrs. Murphy bury her son Landrum. I made a grave in
the snow, and she and I laid him in and covered him with the snow again. I
then got some wood, as they had very little fire and no one in the house was
strong enough. ... They were so light from starvation.

The Breens and the Reeds were the only families that suffered no loss of life
during the four-month ordeal. They derived their strength from each other's
company (there were two mothers to share the burden of caring for the children), from continued vigilance, and from their prayers. They never lost
hope. Virginia Reed remembered:

I never think of that Cabin but that I can see us all on the ground, praying.
... I can see my Mother planning and wondering what else she could do for

her children. We used to take the bones, heat them up and boil them and boil them over and over again. … The long sleepless nights, the cold dark days we passed in that little Cabin under the snow, but some pleasant hours, too, all were not dark. We used to sit and talk together and some times almost forget oneselfs for a while. We had a few books, I read them over and over. I read the "Life of Daniel Boone" while there.

The Breens were the only Catholic family in the Donner party, and prayers were said regularly in the cabin, both at night and in the morning. The only light came from little pine sticks that were split like kindling wood and constantly kept on the hearth. The Reed children were fond of kneeling at the side of Patrick Breen and holding the sticks as candles so that he could read his prayers. "All of us that were out of bed," wrote Patty Reed in a letter to McGlashan, "would kneel to hear and feel … God have mercy!" On a cold February night, Patty's half sister, Virginia, made a vow.

We had all gone to bed—I was with my mother and the little ones, all huddled together to keep from freezing—but I could not sleep. It was a fearful night and I felt that the hour was not far distant when we would go to sleep—never to wake again in this world. All at once I found myself on my knees with my hands clasped, looking up through the darkness, making a vow that if God would send us relief and let me see my father again I would be a Catholic.

A week later, John Breen encountered the unexpected kindness of a stranger.

About this time an incident occurred which greatly surprised us all. One evening … I saw an Indian coming from the mountain. He came to the cabin and said something which we could not understand. He had a small pack on his back, consisting of a fur blanket, and about two dozen … California soap-roots. … He appeared very friendly, gave us five or six roots, and went on his way. Where he was going I could never imagine.

On February 18 Mrs. Breen and Mrs. Reed, standing on the rooftop of their cabin, saw seven men approaching in the snow. They first thought they might be Native Americans but then heard the welcome cry "relief." The next day Patrick Breen recorded the good news in his diary: "Froze hard last night 7 men arrived from California yesterday evening with som provisions but left the greater part on the way … to day clear & warm for this region some of the men are gone to day to Donnos Camp."

At Alder Creek Camp

At Alder Creek, death had come early. Somewhere around the winter solstice 1846, Jacob Donner, the oldest of the Donner brothers, died, leaving Aunt Betsy to take care of seven children. Tamsen Donner stood by her as best she could.

No special Christmas memories are recorded by the Donner children. Eliza Donner remembered that during the most bitter winter weather, the little ones were kept in bed; her place was always in the middle, where her older sisters, Frances and Georgia, snuggled up close, sharing their warmth. But one happy incident stayed in her mind. It happened after one of the first big winter storms.

> *The snow bank in front of the cabin door was not high enough to keep out a little sunbeam that stole down the steps and made a bright spot upon our floor. I saw it, and sat down under it, held it on my lap, passed my hand up and down its brightness, and found that I could break its ray in two. In fact, we had quite a frolic. I fancied that it moved when I did, for it warmed the top of my head, kissed first one cheek and then the other, and seemed to run up and down my arm. Finally I gathered up a piece of it in my apron and ran to my mother. Great was my surprise when I carefully opened the folds and found that I had nothing to show, and the sunbeam I had left seemed shorter. … I watched it creep back slowly up the steps and disappear.*

By the middle of January, the snow was twelve to fifteen feet deep around the tents, and nothing could be seen except some coils of smoke that found their way through the tent openings. Georgia Donner wrote:

> *It rained and snowed so hard that the few animals we had were covered by the snow, and very few were found by feeling for them with a long pole having a sharpened nail fastened on one end of it. Families shared with one another as long as they had anything to share, making each one's portion very small. The hides were boiled, and the bones were burned brown and eaten. We tried to eat a decayed buffalo robe, but it was too tough and no nourishment in it; some of the few mice that came in camp were caught and eaten.*

Some days they could not keep a fire. Many times during the days and nights, they had to shovel snow from the tents so they would not be buried alive. Their beds and the clothes they wore stayed wet for weeks. "Very few can believe it possible for human beings to live and suffer the exposure and hardships we endured there," wrote Georgia Donner.

As George Donner, the patriarch of the family, was growing weaker, his children spent more time in the snow above the camp. Often their mother would join them and sit on a tree trunk. Sometimes she wrote in her diary; sometimes she sketched the mountains and the treetops. "While knitting and sewing, she held us children spellbound with wondrous tales of Joseph in Egypt, of Daniel in the lions den, of Elijah, healing the widows son, of Samuel, and of the Master who took young children in his arms and blessed them," recalled her daughter Eliza.

John Baptiste Trudeau, the sixteen-year-old teamster, tried to keep the children's morale up. Eliza wrote:

> *Frequently, when at work and lonesome, he would call Georgia and me up to keep him company, and when the weather was frosty, he would bring "Old Navajo," his long Indian blanket, and roll her in it from one end, and me from the other, until we would come together in the middle, like the folds of a paper of pins, with a face peeping above each fold. Then he would set us upon the stump of the pine tree while he chopped the trunk and boughs for fuel. One of his amusements was to rake the coals together nights, then cover them with ashes, and put the large camp kettle over the pile for a drum, so that we could spread our hands around it, to get just a little warm before going to bed.*

It was painfully quiet in the mountains, and the children felt lonesome. As time went by, exhausted by starvation, they lost all inclination to play. Eliza remembered that the last food she saw in the tent before the arrival of the relief party was a thin mould of tallow her mother had pried out of the trimmings of some dried beef.

> *She had let it harden in a pan, and after all other rations had given out, she cut daily from it three small white squares for each of us, and we nibbled off the four corners very slowly, and then around and around the edges of the pieces until they became too small for us to hold between our fingers.*

THE FIRST RELIEF PARTY

By the time the seven men of the first relief party reached the mountain camps, six children had perished: Lemuel Murphy (twelve), who was cannibalized by the desperate members of the Snowshoe party that attempted to cross the mountains in mid-December, and, at the Truckee Lake camp, his brother Landrum Murphy (fifteen), his niece, Catherine Pike, and three other infants—Margaret Eddy, Lewis Keseberg Jr., and Harriet McCutchen.

On Washington's Birthday, February 22, 1847, the rescuers started out across the mountains with twenty-three people from the lake and Alder Creek camps. Among them were the children whose parents thought they were strong enough to cross the mountains. From the lake camp came two of the Breen children, Edward (thirteen) and Simon (nine); the four Reed children, ages thirteen, eight, five, and three; two of the Murphy children, Mary (thirteen) and William (eleven), and their niece, Naomi Pike (three); three of the Graves children, William (eighteen), Eleanor (fifteen), and Lovina (thirteen); and little Ada Keseberg (one). From the Alder Creek camp came the two oldest daughters of George Donner, Elitha (fourteen) and Leanna (twelve), and their cousin, William Hook (twelve), a stepson of Jacob Donner. The three youngest children were carried. The other children walked as best they could. Leanna Donner later wrote in a letter to C. F. McGlashan:

And never shall I forget the day when my sister Elitha and myself left our tent. Elitha was strong and in good health, while I was so poor and emaci-ated that I could scarcely walk. All we took with us were the clothes on our back, and one thin blanket, fastened with a string around our necks, an-swering as a shawl in the daytime, and which was all we had to cover us at night.

At the lake, William Murphy, who was to join the relief party with his sister and niece, was solicitous about the family members left behind.

When the rescuers decided they would carry out Naomi Pike, and that my sister Mary and I should follow, stepping in the tracks made by those who had snowshoes, strength seemed to come, so that I was able to cut and carry to my mother's shanty what appeared to me a huge pile of wood. It was green, but it was all I could get. We left mother there with three helpless little ones to feed on almost nothing, yet in the hope that she might keep them alive until the arrival of the next relief.

The relief party left the lake on a bright sunny morning. Some of the chil-dren were in good health, whereas others were so emaciated that they could scarcely walk. "I was one of the poorest in the party," wrote Leanna Donner, "and not one in the train thought I would get to the top of the first hill." She continued:

*We left the cabins marching along single file, the leader wearing snow shoes,
and the others following after, all stepping in the same track the leader
made. I think my sister and myself were about the rear of the train, as the
strongest were put up front. My sister Elitha and I were with strangers as it
were, having no Father, Mother or brothers, to give us a helping hand, or a
word of courage to cheer us up.*

Leanna and Elitha Donner *did* reach the top of the mountain, but Patty
and Tommy Reed gave out. Near the pass, it became evident to the rescuers
that they were not strong enough for the crossing. They informed Mrs. Reed
that her daughter and youngest son would have to be sent back to the cabins
at the lake to await the next expedition. Virginia Reed described the parting
scene in a letter to her cousin: "Martha said well ma if you never see me again
do the best you can."

The Reed children were taken back to live with the Breens. Four days later,
on February 26, 1847, Martha (Patty) celebrated her ninth birthday. Meanwhile, in the Sierra, her mother and the two other Reed children trudged on
through the snow. Virginia Reed had vivid memories of their journey.

*I think my little brother James was the smallest child that walked across. ...
Poor little fellow, he would have to place his knee on the hill of snow between
each step of the snowshoes and climb over; he was too small to reach from one
step to the other. We were, Mother and I, very much afraid that he would
give out. We had talked the matter over and had desided what we would do;
we encouraged him in every way, kept telling him that every step he took he
was gitting nearer Papa. The man told him that he would buy him a horse
in Cal, and he would not have to walk any more. At night we would go
asleep with out clothes all dripping wet from dragging over the snow all day.
In the morning they would be frozen stiff as a board. ... I only wonder that
we did not freeze to death.*

The dazzling reflection of the snow was trying to the children's eyes; William Murphy became snow blind. Still they travelled on, single file. Each
child had an allowance of only one ounce of smoked beef and a spoonful of
flour twice a day. Leanna Donner remembered:

*Each day allowances were cut short and shorter, until we received each for
our evening meal two small pieces of jerked beef, the pieces not being larger
than about the size of the Index finger. Finally the last ration was issued in
the evening, for the evening and the next morning meal. I received my por-*

tion with the rest, but I was so famished that I could not resist the temptation to eat all I had (my two meals at one time). Next morning, as a matter of course, I had nothing for breakfast. Now comes an incident I shall never forget. My sister seeing my distress, looking at the others eating their morsel of meat (which was more precious than gold or diamonds) divided her picnic with me; how long we went on without food after that I do not know.

When they started to ascend the pass, little Ada Keseberg gave out, and her exhausted mother, unable to carry her, offered twenty-five dollars and a gold watch to anyone who would take the child. They progressed slowly over the pass and approached the place at which food had been cached, only to find that wild animals had devoured it. They sent four men in advance to reach the next cache and, if it still contained food, to bring it back. The weakened children dragged on through the snow with the remaining three men and four women. Then, Ada Keseberg died.

When they came to Bear Valley, they finally found a cache of food that had been left by the relief party. William Hook, Leanna's cousin, climbed up a tree during the night and feasted on the food with a voracious appetite. The next morning, when his companions were about to leave camp, he was found dying.

They had left the lake camp on a Monday. Five days later, on a Saturday, they met James F. Reed, who was leading the second relief party up the mountain. "O Mary you do not nou how glad we was to see him again," wrote Virginia Reed to her cousin. Later, she would recall:

My mother dropped on the snow. I started to run to meet him, kept falling down, but finally was folded in my dear Father's arms once more. "Your mother, my child, where is she?" I pointed towards her. I could not speak. ... When my father heard that Pattie and little Tommie were still in the mountains, he could hardly stop long enough to speak to us. He was so much afraid something would happen, or they would die before he could reach them.

They camped that night and ate the sweet bread James Reed had baked for them. Virginia rejoiced.

We were out of the snow, could see the blessed earth and green grass again. How beautiful it looked. We stayed a day or so, gitting the horses and mules ready to ride. Just think of it, to ride. No more dragging over the snow, when we were tired, so very tired, but green grass, horses to ride, and plenty to eat.

Eighteen-year-old Billy Graves remembered:

> *We were taken on horseback to Johnson's ranch, the first settlement in California; here we were left to look for ourselves, but the people were very kind to us and we got along very well; but our flesh swelled up as if we had been stung all over by bees, and it was equally as sore.*

One of the orphaned survivors who stayed at the ranch was Mary Murphy, who wrote a letter to her "dear uncles, aunts and cousins," on May 25, 1847.

> *William, Simon, Naomi and myself came through, but as for me, I have nothing to live for ... a poor orphan, motherless, and almost friendless ... you have been the companion of all my thoughts. Now just think of me in a strange country and to think on my poor mother and brother that are dead—their bodies to feed the hungry bears and wolves—for there was no burying them, the snow was so deep. ... I hope I shall not live long for I am tired of this troublesome world.*

No such depressing thoughts were on Virginia Reed's mind as she rode off to new adventures in California.

> *One day, I was riding along, feeling just as happy as a bird out of a cage when a young man that had been riding along with me for a day or so (he told my mother he would take care of me) startled me by saying "Little one, I want you to make me a promise" "Make you a promise? What is it?" "It is this, I want you to promise me, if I wait a year or so, that you will be my wife." I never fell off the mule, but think of it, I was riding along on an old mule when I received my first proposal. I laugh even to this day when I think of it and I sometimes imagine I must be a thousand years old now, it does not seem to me that I ever was a Child, and yet in many respects I am a Child even now. ... Well such is life. ... I commenced laughing and said, "I am going back to Springfield to go to school three or four years before I marry anyone."*

THE SECOND RELIEF PARTY

Meanwhile, in the mountain camps, four more children had died in late February and early March: Four-year-old George Foster and three-year-old James P. Eddy at the lake camp; four-year-old Samuel Donner and three-year-old Lewis Donner at the Alder Creek camp. James F. Reed found his two children alive at the Breens' cabin. Patty was sitting on the top of the snow-covered roof. She saw her father in the distance and rushed to meet him, but she stumbled and fell in his arms, weakened from hunger. Tommy was inside the cabin, a mere skeleton. He barely recognized his father.

Patty was assigned the task of giving each person a piece of the sweet bread her father had baked. Eliza Donner, who, with her older sisters Frances and Georgia, had walked from Alder Creek to the lake cabin, remembered:

> *Mr. Reed's little daughter Mattie appeared carrying in her apron a number of newly baked biscuits which her father had just taken from the hot ashes of his camp fire. Joyfully she handed one to each inmate of the cabin, then departed to join those ready to set forth on the journey to the settlement.*

The second relief party left camp on March 3, 1847, with seventeen persons, including fourteen children: Patty and Tommy Reed; the five remaining Breen children, ranging in age from one to fourteen; the four remaining Graves children, ages one to nine; and the remaining children of Jacob Donner, seven-year-old Mary and five-year-old Isaac, as well as his stepson, fourteen-year-old Solomon Hook. The four youngest children had to be carried.

Things went well the first two nights on the trail, but on the third night a terrible snowstorm began that lasted two nights and two days. It claimed the life of little Isaac Donner. He died during the night, lying between his sister Mary and Patty Reed.

When the storm ceased, the four relief members continued with only three children, two of which were Reed's. They left behind the elder Breens and their five children, Mrs. Graves and her four small children, and little Mary Donner, who had burned her foot by the campfire and could not walk. The Breens had refused to accompany the weakened rescuers, hoping another relief party would arrive soon. They had a three-day supply of wood but no food.

Mrs. Graves and her son Franklin died during the first night after the relief party had left. The others huddled around a fire pit that had descended to the level of the earth, more than twenty feet below the snow. Fourteen-year-old John Breen later wrote:

> *I remember the time that I fell into the hole in the snow. … I was about dead at that time. The reason that I fell was that I fainted or became stupefied from weakness, and as I sat on a log my mother told me that she thought I was dieing. She had a few ounces of lump sugar in her packet, and she put a small piece in my mouth which she saw appeared to revive me. She had some difficulty in putting the sugar in my mouth as my jaws were set like a visor as she said.*

Lacking food, the desperate people in the camp consumed the bodies of Mrs. Graves and the two children, Franklin and Isaac.

James F. Reed, with three other men from the second relief party, arrived at the main camp in Bear Valley exhausted and starving but without loss of life. Little Patty was the weakest of the arrivals. She had refused to allow her father to carry her until she collapsed. They wrapped her in a blanket, and Reed carried her on his back, warming her with the heat of his body. Unbeknownst to him, he was carrying another "person" as well, a small wooden doll the child had hidden in her ragged clothing. Years later, Patty Reed recalled her arrival at Bear Valley and her first supper, seated by a warm fire.

Then, she took "Dolly" from its place of conselement, and o, what a pleasant little hour she had, a little girl with her "Dolly," and yet, what had she not gone through, but how happy she was at that camp of plenty. She knew Mama, Sister and Brother had plenty to eat and drink and her new friends had told her what good generous people they would meet, and that they were well cared for.

The children remaining at the Starved Camp were carried out a week later by a very large man named Stark, who was fondly remembered by John Breen: "He would laugh and say it was no trouble to carry the children that they [were] so thin that they were very light, that we would soon be out of the snow when we would have enough to eat and take a long rest."

At Bear Valley a third relief party had been organized. A party of seven men left for the mountains on March 11. The children who had been brought down from the camp were transported by horses or mule to Johnson's Ranch. John Breen, who had just turned fifteen, described his arrival in the Sacramento valley.

It was long after dark when we got in the valley, at Johnson's ranch, so that the first time I saw it was earlier in the morning. The weather was fine, the ground was covered with fine green grass and there was a very fat beef hanging from the branch of an oak tree. The birds were singing from the tops of the trees above our camp and the journey was over. I stood looking at the scene and could scarcely believe that I was alive.

THE THIRD RELIEF PARTY

When the third relief party arrived at the lake in mid-March, two of the fathers among the rescuers, William Eddy and William Foster—survivors of the Snowshoe party—learned that their sons James Eddy and George Foster had died and had been cannibalized. Still alive at the lake cabins were widow Murphy, her son Simon, the three daughters of Tamsen and George Donner, and Lewis Keseberg, whose two young children had perished.

Tamsen Donner refused to leave her ailing husband at Alder Creek camp; Mrs. Murphy and Keseberg were too weak to travel. The rescuers left them some provisions and took the last four surviving children, ten-year-old Simon Murphy and the three Donner girls—six-year-old Frances, four-year-old Georgia, and three-year-old Eliza. Also with them went young John Baptiste Trudeau, who was barely able to walk.

Georgia Donner recalled the leave-taking: "As we were ready to start, Mrs. Murphy walked to her bed, laid down, turned her face toward the wall. One of the men gave her a handful of dried meat. ... She seemed to realize they were leaving her, that her work was finished."

Eliza Donner remembered that her older sister Frances was wearing a pair of her mother's shoes because her own had been eaten by their starving dog. This proved to be a trial for the young girl. Frances Donner never forgot that long walk.

> *I started with shoes that were too large for me and they would come off in the snow when I pulled my feet out after sinking down in the soft snow. Mr Thompson, he was the Gentleman that took charge of me to assist me out to Cal, got tired of pulling them out so often, so at last he left them were they pulled off. Then I travelled in my stocking feet for a time. Then he took his muttins and made me a pair of moccasins and he went bare handed.*

Hiram Miller, one of the rescuers, coaxed the little Donner girls across the mountain pass with promises of a lump of sugar with the evening supper at the campfire. Frances, the oldest, was "very tired, but the sugar was something to climb for, so I got my price." Eliza, the youngest, who had been carried most of the day, wanted the sugar so much she agreed to walk.

> *When we children were given our evening allowance of food, I asked for my lump of sugar, and cried bitterly on being harshly told there was none for me. Too disappointed and fretted to care for anything else I sobbed myself to sleep.*

They resumed their trip the next morning, with Eliza being carried on the back of Mr. Miller in a blanket, Indian fashion. The next evening they camped at the crossing of the Yuba River. Eliza remembered, "We were happy until the arrival of the unfortunates from Starved Camp, who stretched forth their gaunt hands and piteously begged food."

The third relief party arrived in the Sacramento valley without loss of life. At Sutter's Fort, the three Donner girls were given to their half sisters, Leanna and Elitha, who had come with the first relief party one month earlier. They were washed, combed, and fed. The next morning they started out, hand in hand, to explore their new surroundings. They watched mothers sitting on the doorsills or on chairs near them, laughing as they talked and sewed, and little children at play, singing their dolls to sleep.

Near one of the buildings, a freckle-faced boy with very red hair whispered to Eliza:

> *See here, little gal, you run get that little tin cup of yourn, and when you see me come out of Mrs. Wimmer's house with the milk pail on my arm, you go round yonder to the other side of the cowpen, where you'll find a hole big enough to put the cup through. Then you can watch me milk it full of the nicest milk you ever tasted. You needn't say nothing to nobody about it. I give your little sister some last time and I want to do the same for you. I hain't got no mother neither, and I know how it is.*

As a sixty-eight-year-old grandmother, Eliza cherished that memory: "I never saw him again, but I have ever been grateful for his pure act of kindness."

On May 16, 1847, Virginia Reed, faithful chronicler of the journey, sat down in her new home in Napa Valley and wrote a long-overdue letter to her cousin Mary in Springfield, Illinois.

> *O Mary I have wrote you half of the truble we have had but I hav Wrote you anuf to let you now that you dont now what truble is but thank the Good god we have all got throw and the onely family that did not eat human flesh we have left everything but i dont cair for that we have got through with our lives but Dont let this letter dishaten anybody.*

EPILOGUE

Of the forty-one children in the Donner party, fifteen died—fourteen in the mountains and one, the infant Elizabeth Graves, shortly after arriving at Sutter's Fort. Twelve of the fifteen children were below age five, and ten were boys. Among the twenty-six child survivors were fourteen orphans from the George and Jacob Donner families, the Graves family, and the Murphy family. Only the Breen and Reed families incurred no loss of life.

Most of the child survivors led long and productive lives, especially the narrators of this awesome tale. The first to marry, at age fourteen, was Mary Murphy. In June 1847 she wed William Johnson, co-owner of the ranch that had played such an important role in the rescue missions. The letter she wrote to her relatives in the East shortly before her marriage made it clear that she was reluctant to marry. Her husband drank and abused her frequently. She obtained a divorce and later married Charles Covillaud, founder of Marysville, which was named after his young wife.

Her brother, William G. Murphy, worked on a California ranch then attended law school in Missouri; he returned to the West, practicing law in Virginia City. He rejoined his sister and her family in Marysville in 1866; by 1880 he had become the city attorney and the father of seven children.

William Graves became a blacksmith in Calistoga. An articulate man, he wrote a series of articles about his adventures for the *Russian River Flag,* a newspaper published in Healdsburg, California.

In January 1850, at age sixteen, Virginia Reed eloped with John Murphy and, true to the promise she had made in the dark days of the mountain camp, converted to Catholicism. "I was married twice," she wrote, "first by the Lieutenant Governor, and then again in the Catholic Church." Her stepfather, a staunch Freemason, was unhappy about the "popery" of the Murphys but forgave all when Virginia presented him with his first grandchild. The couple settled near their parents in San Jose and had nine children.

Virginia's account of the journey was first published in the *Illinois Journal* (December 1847). She wrote a longer report in July 1891 in *Century Magazine* that was published in book form under the title *Across the Plains in the Donner Party, 1846.*

Martha (Patty) Reed married Frank Lewis in Santa Cruz on Christmas Eve 1856 at age eighteen and became the mother of eight children. Like her half sister Virginia, she became a lifelong friend of the editor of the *Truckee Republican,* C. F. McGlashan. McGlashan corresponded with and interviewed most of the child survivors, wrote articles about the fate of the Donner party in his newspaper, and eventually published *History of the Donner Party.* When told Patty had been only eight or nine years old at the time of the ordeal, John Breen wrote to McGlashan, "She had a wonderful mind for one of her age. She had, I have often thought, as much sense as a grown woman."

Georgia and Eliza Donner, the orphaned children of George and Tamsen Donner, were taken in by a Swiss couple, Christian and Mary Brunner, at Sutter's Fort. The two Donner girls moved with the Brunners to Sonoma and spent seven years with them. Frances Donner, their older sister, lived with the Reed family. At age fourteen their older half sister Elitha married Perry

McCoon, the rejected suitor of Virginia Reed. He was killed by a runaway horse, and she subsequently wed Benjamin Wilder of Sacramento County. In 1854 Elitha and her second husband gave Georgia and Eliza a home and a proper education.

Eliza Donner married Sherman O. Houghton in October 1861 at age eighteen; the couple had six children. Eliza's husband represented the new state of California as a senator in the Forty-second and Forty-third Congress. Her family returned east for four years to live in Washington, D.C., before settling down in San Jose. Although Eliza Donner had been only four years old when she survived the ordeal, she was a keen student of the Donner party, and she eventually published a book entitled *The Expedition of the Donner Party and Its Tragic Fate*.

John Breen went into California's goldfields, returning after a year with a fortune of $16,000 in nuggets. In 1852 he married the daughter of San Juan Bautiste's first postmaster and built a fine adobe house within sight of his parents' house. He raised ten children. He and his younger brother Edward, another child survivor of the Donner party, became prosperous ranchers with reputations for honesty and integrity. John was interviewed by Eliza Farnham in 1849, and she published his account of the ordeal in the snow in her book *California, Indoors and Out* (1856). In 1877 John Breen wrote his "Pioneer Memories."

Eight of the women were still alive at the seventy-fifth anniversary of the crossing of the Donner party in 1920. Among them were four Donner daughters (Leanna, Elitha, Frances, and Eliza); two Reeds (Virginia and Martha); Naomi Pike, a granddaughter of widow Murphy; and Isabella Breen. The high-spirited Virginia Reed died one year later, in March 1921, in her eighty-eighth year. Her sister Martha died ten years later, in 1931, at age ninety-three.

Isabella Breen, at age one, was the youngest of the children to survive that wintry ordeal. She lived to age ninety. Interviewed shortly before her death in 1935 in San Francisco, she said, "I suppose I had the smallest chance of them all to survive, and now I am the last to be living. How strange it seems to me!"

The tiny doll Patty Reed carried all the way from Illinois to California is on display today at Sutter's Fort State Historic Park in Sacramento—a silent witness of one of the greatest tragedies to befall an emigrant party on the way to California.

Patty Reed's Doll (courtesy Sutter's Fort State Historic Park, California Department of Parks and Recreation)

Rescue in the Snow

I N 1846, while the Donner party was trapped in the Sierra Nevada, the United States had gone to war with Mexico. In 1847 only ninety wagons headed for California, as the skirmishes between U.S. forces and Mexican troops continued. But 1848 brought events that would drastically change the magnitude of subsequent migrations. The war with Mexico ended, California and the Southwest became U.S. territories, and James Marshall discovered gold at Sutter's Mill.

News of these events was slow to reach the East, but when it did, the trickle of emigrants to the West became a mighty stream. Around thirty thousand people went to California during the Gold Rush of 1849. Approximately fifteen hundred children and teenagers headed for the diggings with their parents.

Most took the route along the Truckee River into California. Everyone dreaded the forty-mile desert called the "Sink of Humboldt." Fourteen-year-old Sallie Hester made the trip from Bloomington, Indiana, accompanied by her parents, two teenage brothers, and eleven-year-old sister. On September 7 she wrote in her diary:

> *Our journey through the desert was from Monday, three o'clock in the afternoon, until Thursday morning at sunrise, September 6. The weary journey last night, the mooing of the cattle for water, their exhausted conditions ... and the weary, weary tramp of the men and beasts, worn out with heat and famished for water, will never be erased from my memory.*

In addition to the Truckee route, another forty-mile desert stretched southwest from the Humboldt sink to the Carson River, but it provided a slightly easier trail over the Sierra Nevada. Sarah Royce, with her husband and two-year-old daughter, Mary, travelling from Iowa to Weaverville, California, was among the last emigrants on the Carson route in fall 1849. "Rain fell heavily," Sarah wrote in her recollections, "and soon the mountains were blocked by snow. Only one company came through after us." But rumors of a faster, easier way convinced thousands of others who were at the end of the 1849 migration to turn north when they reached the Humboldt River and to head for Peter Lassen's Ranch at Deer Creek, about one hundred miles north of Sacramento.

The previous summer, the owner, a Danish immigrant who was a Mexican citizen, had led a party of ten wagons from Missouri across portions of the Applegate Trail toward Oregon and then turned south to find a shortcut to his ranch. He had led them into dead-end canyons and nearly impassable lava beds but was rescued by a group of gold seekers from Oregon who broke trail, enabling him to finally reach his destination.

Shortly after his arrival, Lassen dispatched agents to divert some of the forty-niners onto his "cutoff" and to set up signboards with the reassuring message that the gold diggings were near. Between seven thousand and nine thousand emigrants took his advice, hoping to avoid the prospect of a desert crossing. Instead, they only succeeded in exchanging one desert for another and added two hundred difficult miles to their journey, travelling north almost to the Oregon border. Hermann B. Scharmann from New York City travelled on that infamous trail, accompanied by his wife, two-and-a-half-year-old daughter, and two sons, eleven-year-old Hermann and fifteen-year-old Jacob.

As soon as we left the Humboldt River we came into a new desert, seventy miles wide, although it had been represented to us as only thirty. ... Even though we exerted all our strength, we took a day and two nights to cross the first part of the desert, where nothing but volcanic mountains on all sides could be seen. Both in front and in back of us was a long train of wagons, so that at least I had company in my misery. Now we came to a place where we saw a neatly arranged row of wagons. All of them were empty and abandoned. In order to save as much as possible, the owners had unharnessed the cattle and driven them on rapidly. Those who had no families took their bundles on their shoulders and proceeded on foot.

On the road over which I had travelled during the day I had counted eighty-one shattered and abandoned wagons, and 1,663 oxen, either dead or dying. Toward midnight ... my son halted, and joined his mother, who was weeping, mingling his tears with hers. The two leading oxen, had lost their last ounce of strength and fell down.

*"Yes," my son said to me, "if you and I were alone, we would do as the
other travellers did, take our knapsacks on our backs and go on foot."*

Nearby, in the mountainous terrain between the Pitt and Feather Rivers on
the Lassen Trail, Oliver Goldsmith and a comrade from Michigan (from the
company of the Wolverine Rangers) came upon a widow.

*After a night of terrible wind, we made a short cut from the road, and going
along the edge of a hill, saw a wagon under its brow; hearing noises that attracted our attention, we went closer and listened. We saw a woman on her
knees, weeping and praying, three young children were with her, each having
on its back a pack as large as it could carry. The packs were made of shirts,
the lower part tied into a bag shape with a string, the sleeves securing the
burden to the little bearer's body. We saw that one child was too small to
travel very fast and waited for them to come into the road, when we told the
woman we would keep with her till we met a wagon or some one who could
help her.*

The father of the little family and one son had been killed in their sleep by a
tree that fell on them during the storm, and passing emigrants had extricated
the bodies and buried them.

Catherine Haun, a young bride from Iowa on her way to California, recorded two other deaths—that of a mother and her newborn infant—on the
same trail.

*Mrs. Lamore suddenly sickened and died, leaving her two little girls and
grief stricken husband. We halted a day to bury her and the infant that had
lived but an hour, in this weird lonely spot. ... The bodies were wrapped together in a bed comforter and wound, quite mummyfied, with a few yards
of string that we made by tying together torn strips of a cotton dress skirt. ...
Every heart was touched and eyes full of tears as we lowered the body,
coffinless into the grave. There was no tombstone—why should there be—
the poor husband and orphans could never hope to revisit the grave.*

The hardships of the trail were aggravated by the fear of marauding Indians. Eleven-year-old Henry Ferguson was one of eight children who left Jasper County, Iowa, with their family in April 1849 in search of riches in California. In September they took the Lassen cutoff at the Humboldt River.
Henry remembered:

Our journey continued down the Pitt River, turning to our left unto what is now Lassen County, California near the present site of Susanville, coming onto the headwaters of the Feather River. On this particular occasion we struck camp very early; finding good feed and plenty of fish in the river, and small game being plentiful, brother John and I took our rifles and went hunting down the river from the camp. All at once we came upon a fresh camp where some wagons had stopped a day or so ago, and near their camp was at least a dozen fresh Indian scalps, the blood hardly dry upon them. They had piled them one on the other to almost a foot high. Now if you imagine we sat down and examined them carefully and counted them, you are away off. We ran to the camp, gave the alarm and in a short time were up and away going until late in the evening as we found that we were in the vicinity of a dangerous tribe of Indians.

In the California settlements fears of an imminent repetition of the Donner tragedy had mounted. The military governor, Major General Persifer F. Smith, authorized $100,000 in emergency funds, augmented by public subscriptions, for relief activities and assigned Major D. H. Rucker to direct the rescue operations.

By mid-September, Rucker had relief teams of civilians and soldiers on each of the three overland trails: the Carson, Truckee, and Lassen routes. He ordered his personnel to backtrack along each of these major access routes to California, to dispense provisions and animals when needed, and to ensure that all emigrant families in the rear would be able to cross the Sierra before the onset of the winter snow.

Among the latecomers on the Carson Trail was Sarah Royce with her husband and two year old daughter, Mary. In her "Pilgrimage Diary" she described the encounter with Rucker's men.

Presently at the head of [a] steep incline appeared two horsemen. ... As they came nearer we saw that each of them led by a halter a fine mule. ... Our little Mary was up in the front of the wagon, looking with wonder at the approaching forms. As they came nearer, they smiled, and the forward one said (to my husband), "You and your wife, and that little girl, are what brought [us] as far as this. ... We belong to the Relief Company sent out by order of the United States Government to help the late emigrants over the mountains. We were ordered only as far as Truckee Pass. When we got there we met a little company that had just got in. ... There was a woman and some children with them; and that woman set right to work at us fellows to go on

*over the mountains after a family they had met on the desert. ... She said
that there was only one wagon, and a woman and a child in it; and she
knew they would never get through them canons and over them ridges without help. ... And she kept at me so, I couldn't get rid of her. You see I've got a
wife and a little girl of my own; so I felt just how it was; and I got this man
to come with me and here we are, to give you more to eat, and let you have
these two mules, and tell you how to get right over the mountains, the best
and quickest way."*

The Royces left their wagon behind and packed their belongings on one
mule. Sarah rode on the other, with Mary in front of her. Her husband
walked beside them. Sarah remembered:

*At first I was rather akward, and so afraid Mary would get hurt, that at un-
even places in the road I would ask my husband to get up and take her, while
I walked ... but on the second day of our new style of travelling I rode
twenty-five miles. ... A week later, we crossed the highest ridge, viewed the
"promised land," and began our descent into warmth and safety. ... I
laughed at my little one's upturned face, as she lay back against my arm,
while I leaned forward almost to the neck of the mule, tugging up the hardest places.*

Although she had abandoned almost all her earthly possessions, Mrs. Royce
managed to bring to California her Bible, her Milton, a tiny lap writing desk,
and *Little Ella*, a book she had picked up among the objects left behind by the
emigrants in the Nevada desert. "I thought it would please Mary," she wrote
in her diary, "so I put it in my pocket ... and more than one pair of young eyes
learned to read its pages in after years."

Relief activities on both the Carson and Truckee routes were successfully concluded before the snow came, but the fate of the emigrants on the Lassen Trail
grew more desperate each day. John H. Peoples had been assigned to head the
relief effort on the northern route. Major Rucker joined him, and both men,
despite severe attacks of typhoid, labored doggedly to get all stragglers into
safety. Among emigrants in the rear of the northern route were the Alford
family from Illinois, the Ferguson family from Iowa, the Scharmann family
from New York, the St. Louis Company from Missouri, the Wolverine Rangers from Michigan, and the Washington City and California Mining Association.

Bogged down on a snowy ridge above the Feather River, the captain of the latter company, J. Goldsborough Bruff, volunteered to remain with his company's wagons while his men pushed on. He gave them his saddle horse and his share of the remaining provisions, hoping to rely on game for his own subsistence. Lingering at his camp day after day, he chronicled the fate of the successive waves of emigrants that passed his "lodge in the wilderness" on the Lassen Trail in fall and winter 1849. A gentle, caring man, his diary entries show the compassion of a father who missed his own children, a little boy and girl, thousands of miles away in Washington City.

> **September 30.**— *Much scurvy among the emigrants, a little girl's mouth badly affected with it.*
>
> **October 2.**—*Some small boys, not over 10 years of age, were leading jaded animals up. A man had a baby in his arms, and in the midst of the thick dust, was urging up his team. ... One wagon, with women and children in it, when near the summit, became uncoupled, and down hill it ran—stern-foremost, with great rapidity. The women and children screamed.*

Meanwhile, Major Rucker was approaching Bruff's camp.

> **October 5.** *Started at sunrise and travelled over a very hilly and rough country, met a great number of emigrants on foot, who said that they had lost their animals, also some thirty wagons, many containing families, some few of whom were entirely destitute of provisions. Issued pork and bread to Mr. Stephen Pine and George R. Bell for their families, also to Mr. William Shang with a family of nine children.*
>
> **October 8.** *Met 27 wagons on the road and found 200 encamped in the valley, with [a] great many families; a great many of the emigrants were sick with scurvy and diarrhea ... also found the man to whom I loaned the mule, and gave provisions a few days back to bring his family in. He had his wife who was sick with the scurvy riding the mule with a child in his arms, and leading the animal by the bridle, with a little boy by his side.*
>
> **October 12.** *Left camp this morning at 9 o'clock, crossed the right branch of Feather River, and after travelling one half mile came to a large emigrant camp of 56 wagons with many families. Immediately after I halted at this place I was surrounded by a great number of persons, all asking for provisions, saying that they were destitute, out of money, and had borrowed from*

*their friends until they could loan them no longer. I killed a beef and issued
a portion to them, with some bread. … After we started we were stopped six
or seven times in the road, and asked for provisions; gave some to Mr. L. G.
Coldwell and his family of six children.*

By mid-October Bruff had plenty of company. He noted in his diary: "On
our camp ground was an ox wagon in which was a widow with eight children.
She buried her husband on the Platte. There were two other families, with
several children." Bruff also took time to pay tribute to his new neighbor.

*October 14. A considerable camp of emigrants there, with women and chil-
dren—and on a neighboring hill Maj. Rucker, U.S.A. was camped, with his
wagons, provisions & men, of the "Relief party," sent out by Gen. Smith. The
Major commanded the expedition. … We proceeded together to the Major's
tent, and I was introduced to him—found him to be a very friendly man
and a perfect gentleman. He was surrounded by begging emigrants, men,
women & children. The Maj. had to serve out beef, pork, flour, bread, etc.
as judiciously as possible. … It was one of the most delicate, and troublesome
duties ever entrusted to any one!*

A few days later, at the close of day, over a ridge above the Feather River,
Bruff overtook a small family. He noted in his diary:

*A few miles back, on the heights, a father with 2 children, a boy & a girl,
were driving a lot of lame oxen along. The children were very small, and the
little girl said to her brother, "Never mind, Buddy, t'aint far to grass and
water."*

Meanwhile, Major Rucker pushed on, although he was so sick with fever
that he could not stay on his horse and had to ride in a wagon. Soon after leaving Bruff's camp, he met the Ferguson family and gave them some beef,
bread, and rice for their eight hungry children; a mile later he saw the wagon
of widow Ely and supplied her and her six children with bread and pork.

The next day Rucker was prostrate with fever and decided to rest. On October 17 he started again toward the rear of the emigrants and came upon the
Scharmann family, which had run out of provisions. Hermann Scharmann
later paid tribute to the indefatigable major in an article he wrote for the *New
York Staats Zeitung.*

*The humane captain … evidently saw through his field glass that we …
were in need of help, and so he rode swiftly toward me. We certainly were in*

a bad way; my wife and I were walking next to the two-wheeled cart which our three oxen, as weak as ourselves, could scarcely drag; my youngest son rode on the emaciated pony which was proceeding with careful steps, and held his little sister in front of him. ... The captain took my oldest son with him and gave him seven pounds of crackers and twelve pounds of pork, since we did not want to wait for the slaughtering of the ox. I cannot let this opportunity pass by without publicly thanking the California Government for its humane action.

Two days later, disaster struck the St. Louis train—the last company in the rear, with twenty-five women and children. All of their cattle were stolen by Indians, and their captain sent an urgent note to the relief party. John H. Peoples, to whom the ailing Rucker had delegated the responsibility of contacting the remaining emigrants on the Lassen Trail, came to their rescue immediately. Here is an excerpt from his report to Rucker.

Early the next morning (on Oct. 23rd) I dispatched five men to hurry them into my camp, advising them by letter that I had a sufficiency of provisions, and enough of wagon room to take in the twenty-five women and children. ... About 10 o'clock the same morning the ... family train came in and knowing that they were fickle-minded, I ordered the women, children, and sick men to get into my wagons ... and start with me at 1 p.m. All agreed to it, but the men quarrelled, and having the women and children with me, I did not care how the rest got along, well convinced that they would not stay far in the rear of their families and at 2 p.m. I started my trains, and made 7 miles before night. ... The emigrant wagons all came in before ten o'clock, and at 12 o'clock at night, the Indian fires blazed up simultaneously from every elevated point. Believing they intended to make a grand and last effort to drive off our stock ... and seeing them plainly around the nearest fire to us, I sent out a party to attack them and drive them off.

The next morning ... after urging the men to abandon their teams, without success, I told them that I should move on with the women and children, as fast as my mules could travel. A few took my advice, and two or three wagons were left behind, but the majority seemed determined to get in with mining tools, cooking utensils, beds, etc. or die with their wagons.

Frustrated, Peoples moved on with the women and children. At Bruff's camp, meanwhile, there was a steady procession of wagons of every kind, oxen, horses, mules, bulls, cows, and people—men, women, and children, all packed—dusty in face and dress, many thin from hunger as well as anxiety. Bruff offered his hospitality to the weary pilgrims: a warm fire, fuel, cooking utensils, and a comfortable bed in his wagons.

His diary entries for the last week of October convey the increased distress of the stragglers on the Lassen Trail.

> *October 26.—A wagon with 3 yoke of oxen, with 3 women and several children, among them a lady with a sick infant, 9 mos old, from Illinois, short of provisions, came up and camped.*
>
> *October 27.—2 ox wagons ... came up. Among these Mr. Tyler, wife and infant. Mr. T. buried his aged parents and child on the Platte.*
>
> *October 28.—Lady, belonging to one of the partis here, was asking for beans, said that her child craved some—poor thing, about 5 yrs. old, was very pale, thin & weak; the lady said he was taken sick. ... The widow with 8 children I saw at Maj. Rucker's camp on the 14th was here also. She had a son in most deplorable condition—emaciated, feeble, and as ragged as a beggar ... he could scarcely speak, and had to be led about.*

One who *did* speak to Bruff was a handsome little boy named Billy, six years old, the age of Bruff's son with the same name. The little pilgrim amused him with his volubility and intelligence. Said he:

> *My father has a red horse—he was a race horse, and he could run fast if he was poor! and he had a sore back, but he died when we struck Goose Creek, and I saw him, poor fellow,—dead! On Pitt river, the Indians stole all our cattle, but we got 40 head back again—My uncle is only a boy, but he aint afraid of Indians—He took a pistol and chased one Indian, and made him drop his blanket; and the Indians fired plenty of arrows at him, but none of 'em hit him. Father has a sword, and 2 holster pistols, and a double-gun besides, and I guess if he had gone after 'em, he would have killed nearly all of 'em! I ain't afeared of the Indians, I aint got no gun, nor pistols; but I've got a knife—here it is (producing a small pocket-knife) and I could kill one with that. I am a great hand for walking; I walked all day yesterday—last night; and when we camped here—on the hill, I said I was'nt tired and was'nt! We left 3 steers here for 2 men to take care of for us and they are going to send up from Lassen's for them—they just now branded 'em. At home in Burlington (Ioway) we had as nice a house as you ever saw; there 'aint any much better; but I guess all the house we'll have in the Diggings, will be our*

tent—Well, I dont care much, so we dont stay too long. At our house at Bur-
lington, we had a nice yard, and plum trees, and peaches, and gooseberries:
and we could go a little ways, and get blackberrys & grapes, and all them
things. Oh, how I miss em!

Soon after Bruff's encounter with Billy, a Prussian, his family, and a friend
passed by his lodge in the wilderness. Bruff described them as an "odd party."

First came a pony, heavily packed with bedding, etc. and a couple of bales of
dry-goods, the beast was very poor and driven by the Prussian; next a cow,
packed with sundries,—driven by the Prussian's friend; then a very poor,
and heavily packed steer, laden with provisions, frying pan, camp kettles,
platters, axe, etc.—driven by the old man's son—a smart handsome boy,
about 12-years-old, and he had an infant tied on his back—Indian fashion.
An old woman brought up the rear, with a bruised face.

The next day the Ferguson family came to his camp. Young Henry Ferguson, age eleven, remembered:

About October 31, around nine o'clock in the evening ... we reached what is
known as Bruff's camp. Our friend Alford's team travelled faster than ours
and they came to the camp earlier, having picked the camping place and se-
lected a site for our tent.

Seeing the camp lights seemed to cheer us and father yelled like a Western
Indian as an expression of pleasure at nearing the camp. It was answered by
our friends, the Alfords, who on the day's journey had killed three deer, and
when we arrived had cooked for us a nice venison supper which we much
enjoyed.

About midnight, in gloomy darkness, the storm broke upon us, hurricane
like winds twisting the trees in its fury, and breaking off near the ground the
great black oak tree under which our tents and also the tents of our friend
Alford were stretched. The body of the tree fell across our tent in which were
four young children, and the top of the tree fell on the Alford tent, killing the
old man and his oldest son [William, age nineteen] instantly, and fatally in-
juring the younger son [Lorenzo, age fifteen] and their hired man, a Mr.
Cameron, who both died the next day. ... The great concussion and falling
tent poles left three of our children badly hurt, but none fatally so, but no
one can imagine a darker scene than came upon us.

Bruff's diary entry gives another eyewitness account of the accident.

> *I ... had slept soundly till abut 1 o'clock this morning when we were awak-*
> *ened by a man, crying at the top of his voice,—"Hallo, here! turn out and*
> *assist, a tree has fallen on a couple of tents, and killed and wounded several*
> *persons!" We promptly turned out in the rain, lit a lantern, aroused our*
> *friends and proceeded to the fatal spot. About 100 yds in rear of my tent, a*
> *large oak tree, decayed near the ground, became heavy with the moisture,*
> *and probably a gust of wind assisted, and it fell, partially over a tent close to*
> *its base, and directly across—another tent, 20 paces further, in which lay 4*
> *men side by side. Whilst extricating the tent from over these unfortunate*
> *men, some attended to the tent at the foot of the tree; it was soon cleared*
> *away, while a little girl within, was crying, saying her stomach was hurt,*
> *and another that her feet were hurt. These two were slightly bruised and*
> *sprained, while several other little children, with them, escaped any injury.*
> *A large limb of the tree had first struck the ground, twisting the lower end of*
> *the tree over, so as merely to knock over the tent & slightly hurt the children;*
> *while the same cause, projected the body of the tree, across the tent of the*
> *men. The old man and one son died in half an hour after the accident. ...*
> *About one hour after dark, the second son died.*

Of the Alfords, only the mother and two grown daughters were left, bereft
in a moment of all their male help—father, brothers, and the sweetheart of
one of the daughters. Bruff helped bury the dead and summoned one of the
doctors who had come up from the settlements to tend to the injured little
girls.

It had begun to snow steadily, and the government relief party was trying to
hurry the rear of the emigration train toward the settlements. Wrote Peoples
to Rucker:

> *For the first time some of the inactive emigrants began to fear and to feel*
> *that there was danger, and the change in their conduct was palpable. ...*
> *During the 31st, the snow continued to fall ... with such fury, as almost to*
> *blind us, and for fear of a heavy storm I kept my men and provisions in the*
> *rear of the family wagons. The snow continued to fall during the night and*
> *on the morning of the first of November. ... It cleared up in the afternoon*
> *... but the next morning (Nov. 2) it was coming down heavier than ever.*
> *   On the 3rd I laid by in the valley to make arrangements to get every body*
> *with me, and the morning of the 4th, having dismounted all of my party, I*

had ... all the healthy women mounted on mules. During that day, I made arrangements to take on three other families which I found ... and thus left Feather river valley, with every woman, child and sick men. ... After making eight or ten miles toward the settlements, the storm increased, and the snow became so deep that I was convinced of the impossibility of the women and children standing the trip in.

Finding a few abandoned tents and empty wagons, Peoples ordered a halt, deposited the women and children and their bedclothes; took all of his provisions from the mules, killed the last beef, and built a large fire. He left one of his men to attend the emigrants and told them to be of good cheer until he returned from the settlements with more help.

Meanwhile, at Bruff's camp the procession of stragglers continued. His diary entry on November 4 reads:

2 ox wagons passed; 2 women and a little girl; on foot, called to warm their feet at my camp fire. I had just prepared my dinner, of roast venison & coffee ... and invited them to partake which they did. ... One of these ladys had a very appropriate volume in her hand—"Pilgrim's Progress."

The neighboring camp had visitors, too: a mother with two little girls and a three-week-old infant. Bruff accompanied the party to their wagon and campfire, carrying the baby boy under his poncho to protect him from the snow; he was followed by the little girls, who cried because they were cold and wet. When he returned to his own lodge, he found some new visitors.

On returning to camp, I found there Mr. and Mrs. Jenkins, their daughter Alice ... her little sister, 2 brothers—smart boys, probably 12 & 14 years of age. ... They were all wet, cold, tired, hungry, & disheartened. I bade them be seated by the fire. ... The mother sat, with her elbows on her knees, and her face in her hands, weeping. Alice sat, close to her, with her little sister in her lap, looking very pensive into the fire. The old man stood opposite, sighing and despondent, while the 2 brave little boys were endeavoring to cheer them up, and to encourage them.

Night cold and stormy. And in this night-storm there arrived more wagons, with women and children. Their situations were indeed pitiable. The distress and suffering in the rear must be very great at this time. I trust that there are but a few there, and that they will be along, with Peoples, in a few days.

Bruff was not the only one who worried about the fate of the rear of the emigration train. William Swain, a member of the Wolverine Rangers from Michigan, was also moved by their desperate plight. His diary entry on November 6 reads:

Many of the emigrants were palsied by that terrible disease, scurvey. Here, too, were females and children of every age. Here might be seen a mother, wading through the snow and in her arms an infant child closely and thickly wrapped with whatever would secure it from the storm, while the father was ... exerting himself to the utmost in getting along his team, wagon, and provisions—the last and only hope of securing the life of the family. There might be seen a mother, a sister or a wife, winding along the mountain road, packing blankets and other articles, followed by children of every age, each with some article on his back or in his hands, hoping thus to enable the teams to get along by lessening the load.

On November 13 Peoples sent a reinforcement of six men, two wagons, and six yoke of oxen to bring in the women and children he had left in the snow. That same night, Bruff had more visitors at his camp.

An elderly man, young man & wife, with 2 children, and a very long cart drawn by 1 yoke oxen, came up to camp. I invited them to warm & dry themselves. ... Their children were crying for food. While these people were sitting in my lodge, drying themselves, the husband said to me "Stranger, I thought I was pretty rugged, but this little girl is just as rugged as I am!" (slapping her on the shoulder); she replied, "Well I be!"

A week later, on November 21, the government relief party passed Bruff's tent with two wagons filled with women and children. A small boy jumped out of one of the wagons and ran toward the campfire, crying, wanting to warm his feet. One of Peoples's men caught him after a small scuffle and put him back in the wagon, and they proceeded on their final journey to the settlements. But Bruff was not alone for long.

Soon after, there came up a tall hearty good-looking man, with his 2 daughters, about 10 and 11 years of age; looking quite hale. The little girls had frock coats of their father on, and each carried on her back a very heavy pack, strapped across the breast in the manner of a knapsack. ... The girls were quite pretty, and one had her naked toes protruding through her broken shoes; their hands were naked, and dripping wet. ... As I had discov-

ered, in one of the wagons given to me, some articles of clothing, probably forgotten by the owners, I appropriated such things as would answer to alleviate the destitute travellers. So I gave each of the little girls a pair of yarn gloves, fine yarn socks, and a coarser pair to draw over their shoes. They dried & warmed themselves, shouldered their packs and proceeded.

Major Rucker, hearing about the relief party's suffering, headed back to Lassen's ranch. He arrived there on November 24 and discovered that many of the stragglers had made it there but that Peoples was in the hills again, looking for others. On November 26 Peoples arrived at the Davis ranch with the last of the emigrants. Major Rucker wrote in his report to the military governor, General Persifer Smith:

A more pitiable sight I never beheld as they were brought into camp; there were cripples from scurvy and other diseases, women prostrated by weakness, and children who could not move a limb, all helpless as infants; in advance of them were men mounted on mules who had to be lifted off the animals, so entirely disabled had they become.

Peoples expressed less compassion for the men than for the women and children. He wrote in his report to Major Rucker:

I must take occasion to remark that had the men of the rear emigration thought less of their property and more of the lives of their families, I could have brought them all to the [Sacramento] valley before the storm. ... I am now well convinced that had there been no relief party, and some one ... to assume command of men, women and children, that most of them would have perished in the snow.

With justifiable pride, Peoples commended the conduct of the men under his command.

They did everything that men could do to facilitate the progress of the family train; and although not one of the party had a dry blanket, or dry clothes for half a month, there was no complaint, but the harder the service, the greater their exertion. At every river or slough they stood ready to wade over, with the women and children in their arms, and even after reaching the settlements, many of them took the money out of their own purses, and gave to the destitute.

But Major Rucker gave credit where it was due. In his final report on the "rescue in the snow" he wrote:

> *To Mr. Peoples, who had command of that party, too much praise cannot be awarded for the perseverance and energy he displayed in bringing in the rear emigrants under such trying circumstances, and for the faithful manner in which he performed all duties devolving upon him.*

Two families managed to reach Lassen's ranch without the aid of People's relief party: the Fergusons, with their eight children—three of them badly hurt—and the Scharmann family, which lost the youngest of their three children near the end of the journey.

The Ferguson family had left Bruff's camp two days after the falling tree had killed four members of the Alford family and injured three of their own children. The oldest girl, age nine, had serious internal injuries and could not be moved for several days. They finally managed to travel eight miles south, below the snowbelt, to a place called Steep Hollow.

Some of their cattle died as they camped there, but they also had a stroke of good luck: A man who had left a wagon at Steep Hollow came back from the settlements with two yoke of strong oxen. He suggested that the Fergusons might put some of their belongings into his empty wagon and travel with him to the settlements. The parents accepted the offer, packed some clothing and bedding into the man's wagon, and took their younger children, leaving eleven-year-old Henry and thirteen-year-old John behind to guard their abandoned wagon and tent. Their father hoped to return in two weeks to fetch the boys and the wagon. Henry later wrote about the adventures of the two young brothers in their mountain camp:

> *Our living was very scant, having really nothing to eat except for what we could kill with our guns. We were almost afraid to venture away from our camp as the country was infested with large grizzy bears, and we could see their tracks around the waggon in which we slept, every morning.*
>
> *Some of our experiences while we boys were left to care for the waggons: We were compelled to eat woodpeckers, so we thought a soup made of them would be fine. We cooked them and made a search in the waggon for something to thicken the soup, and all we could find was a half pound of dried peaches so we cooked them in the broth and proceeded to eat, but in a short time two boys were about as sick as they could possibly be, throwing up all that was in them, and suffering horribly.*

Pressed by hunger, they made another effort to get meat. Armed with their rifles, they ventured a mile from their camp, and John succeeded in shooting a deer.

We took the liver and cooked it on the old camp stove lid, and when half done began to eat like hungry wolves. Soon to our astonishment the animal heat in the liver brought back the same sickness we had experienced when eating the woodpecker soup. ... But the night soon came and we being tired were soon wrapped in the quiet slumber which belongs to a boy's life and knew nothing until the new day came, bringing us renewed energy and a new sense of hunger, which we soon satisfied with a fine meal from the loin of our venison. The deer found in these mountains were very small but by eating sparingly and saving our supply, it lasted for three or four days.

Two long, lonely weeks passed. Finally, after the heavy rain had ended, their father reached them by horseback, bringing a loaf of bread their mother had baked from old, lumpy, wormy flour. "With all its faults, it seemed the most precious morsel of bread we had ever tasted," remembered young Henry. The roads were still too muddy to move the wagons, so the boys remained for another week in the mountain solitude. Wrote Henry:

Supplied with this small ration of bread and the meat we succeeded in shooting, we stayed and watched the waggon which contained all our earthly belongings, until at the end of another long week father came again, bringing plenty of teams to take our waggons to the settlement which was only twenty-five miles away from us, yet almost impassable because of the awful mountain roads.

The Fergusons' ordeal ended in the last week of November 1849. Wrote Henry:

The place we wintered was near the great Lassen Ranch in Lassen County. Here we found a gentleman by the name of Mr. Deuton, who was a cattle raiser and had many head of cattle scattered up and down the Sacramento River. He lived in a great Adobe house with his family, and allowed us to occupy a small house near them. ... As Father was handy with tools he helped Mr. Deuton in many ways, and he in return gave us shelter and all the meat we wanted. Here we spent our first California winter.

Three weeks earlier, Hermann Scharmann Sr. had arrived at Lassen's ranch as well, riding ahead of his wife and children. He bought just enough supplies to keep his family alive and then hurried back to meet them. Only three days had gone by, but when he retraced his steps, he found his family in a heart-rending plight.

When I inquired after my two-and-a-half-year-old daughter, mother and sons began to cry. Amidst tears they told me that my darling little girl had died. ... I tried to speak words of comfort and hope while my own heart was almost breaking.

Scharmann brought the rest of his family to Lassen's ranch, pitched a tent, and remained there for five weeks. Rainy weather and his wife's deteriorating health made travel impossible. Emigrants were pouring in from all sides; prices rose, and everyone spent his or her last cent. Many of the travellers suffered, as did Scharmann's wife, from constant diarrhea, and a number died from it; few bothered with their well-being. Scharmann was dismayed.

Nowhere else have I ever seen such absolute heartlessness as among these crowded sufferers. But Mr. Lassen surpassed all the others in this respect. He, a fifty-year-old bachelor, short and fat, was possessed of an unrestrained desire for gold.

By mid-December 1849, the Scharmann family finally established their first claim, near Bidwell's Bar. Each day eleven-year-old Hermann and fifteen-year-old Jacob worked with their father at placer mining on the Upper Feather River. Each night they returned, exhausted, to their "home"—a sheet of canvas stretched on piles—where they slept on the ground wrapped in their ragged blankets.

Shortly before Christmas, both parents fell ill with scurvy, so the two boys prepared a feast for them as best they could. On Christmas Eve they rode to the nearest town, Marysville, about ninety miles away, and spent their small savings of gold dust, worth around ten dollars, on a can of peaches—"the most desirable thing in the storekeeper's stock."

As dawn was breaking on Christmas morning, they reached their camp by the river. Jacob had brought a branch of pine he had plucked on the homeward journey. "It is our Christmas tree," he said. The boys set it up in the earth that formed the floor of their home and decorated it with some bits of ribbon and cloth. His brother, Hermann, wrote, "We sat before it trying to think it was glorious, all covered with baubles, and loaded with sweets and packets of good things."

They then went about preparing the Christmas dinner. Jacob fried flap-jacks and made coffee; Hermann mixed flour and water for the biscuits, using gunpowder as a substitute for salt. When everything was ready, they set an empty box between the pallets on which their parents lay and presented their gift.

But then came a crushing disappointment. Their parents could not eat the peaches nor the meal that had been prepared with so much care. They urged the boys to eat their share instead. Hermann remembered:

So we sat down and divided the peaches. I am afraid that most of the flap-jacks and biscuits were wasted. Our hunger and the rare treat before us made us forget the sorrow of the futile gift and we ate until not a trace of syrup was left inside the can.

Meanwhile, at Bruff's camp no more visitors came to the lodge in the wilderness. But Bruff was not alone on Christmas Day: With him was his friend Poyle. Bruff's journal entry on December 25, 1849, reads:

Well, here's a Christmas for us, under werry *peculiar circumstances. ... In the afternoon we cleared off the snow and got a hind quarter [of an ox carcass]. ... Roasted a piece and dined heartily, and with more satisfaction than many in better circumstances. After dinner, we smoked our pipes. ... I spoke of merriment, mince-pies, egg-nogg, turkey, &c and he, of roast surloin, plum pudding, punch, ale &c. ... We cut up some running geer of a wagon, and had a lively fire. "Well," says friend Poyle, "Cap, we are both philosophers, and may we not have some sort of a Christmas here?" "Yes," I replied, "but how?—Why," rejoined he "we can each sing a song, and tell a story; and then take a pot of coffee, and call it ale, egg-nogg, or what you please."—"'Nough said," and at it we went;—each sang 2 or 3 songs, and related several anecdotes, then smoked our pipes again, and thus enjoyed ourselves.*

Pilot Knob (Lassen Trail) (D. Appleton Co., New York, 1872)

4

The Kindness of Strangers

Here was a child with the two men at Deer Creek camp that Christmas—a frail, curly-haired boy named Billy Lambkin. Bruff had found the little waif some weeks earlier in a deplorable condition. He wrote on November 16, 1849:

> *There is an inhuman wretch camped here, by the name of Lambkin, as perfect a misnomer as was ever bestowed on anything. The emigrants who traveled along with him, were all familiar with his notorious character ... and related the following: That L. left a reputable wife in St. Louis, whom he had long abused, then stole the only consolation she had remaining, a tender boy, about 4 yrs. old, and with some woman came off on this journey. ... His little boy he treated in the most brutal manner, suffering it to want for every thing, and ... beating him most unmercifully. I heard the poor little fellow crying ... and went up to quiet him. He was laying on damp blankets and endeavoring to pull a wet buffalo robe over him, but it was too heavy for his feeble strength. He complained of hunger & cold; I asked him where his father was? He lispingly replied, "I don't know."*

Bruff covered the boy with some dry blankets and went in search of the father. He found him at the neighboring camp by a large fire, laughing and talking, unconcerned about the fate of his son. Bruff had a few rough words with him and offered to take care of the boy. To his astonishment, the offer was accepted.

> *Late in the afternoon ... Lambkin brot his little son William to my lodge & said if I wanted him I could take him, as he was going to the settlements for*

provisions, and would return in a few days. .... Considering it a humane ac-
tion to take care of the child as well as I could ... I made the boy a comfort-
able bed in a dry wagon.

Bruff did the best he could with his limited supply of mildewed bread and a
few day's rations of venison. For five days the father loitered around the camp,
offering Bruff no provisions for his son. He finally moved on with his cart and
oxen, never to return. Bruff noted in his diary:

While this unfeeling wretch was going off, his little son cried for bread. ... I
gave him a spool of cotton to play with, and while unwinding it, he seemed
to be reminded of his home, of his mother ... saying "Mother's cotton, Moth-
er's scissors, Mother has bread, and Mother has cake, and Mother has tea."
Poor little creature! abandoned in the wilderness by his father.

During the next month, Bruff and his companion tried as best they could
to alleviate the child's suffering. They shortened their own rations in order to
sustain him, giving him the largest share of the food. Often, the two men
went to bed hungry while the boy was still eating his piece of meat. Bruff worried constantly about the child's health. On December 16 he wrote:

We are much concerned about the boy; he is pale, very weak, complains of
pains, and bled at the nose and ears last night. We have continued to give
him the larger share of the food, such as it is, and he eats with good appetite.
... He seems to be indolent ... and I am compelled to take him by the arms
& walk him rapidly, to—and fro—, through our lodge for exercise.

During the week before Christmas, as heavy snow fell, the lodge in the wilderness became increasingly damp and cold. The boy cried a great deal, and
Bruff tried to make him as comfortable as he could. "He sat all day by the fire,
with things to play with," he noted in his diary. "To-night I wrapped him in a
coverlid, and carried him to the wagon, and there secured him comfortably."

On Christmas Day the men gave the largest piece of beef they had roasted
to the boy as a special treat. He ate it "like a young wolf." "The child is doing
well," noted Bruff with evident relief. The next day his diary tells of some
mischief the boy engaged in.

The poor little fellow had been so brutally treated by his father, and probably
with a tincture of his father's composition, that he is exceedingly stubborn
and artful. While we were present, he would feign perfect inability to stand

or walk. ... Yet finding things on the floor that we knew were out of his reach when we went out, we watched, to ascertain if he possibly could move about; and judge our astonishment, to-day, to see him climb up in a chair ... get something down from a hanging shelf, and when he heard us, he ran quite sprightly, and seated himself by the fire!

On New Year's Eve, as the damp snow was making life in their tents and wagons miserable, Bruff and his companion decided to move the boy to the log cabin of the Roberts family—half a day's walk from their own camp. They arrived at the cabin in the evening and enjoyed freshly baked rolls with a fine meal of venison. But the night was not a pleasant one for them. Bruff's diary entry on January 1, 1850, tells the tale.

The day commences with [a] snow storm. ... The Roberts family and myself, and the child, ill all last night, with violent pains & heat in the stomach and intestines. ... Our being simultaneously attacked with these violent symptoms, caused me to apprehend that we had been poisoned. ... I heard Mrs. Robert's say that the substance she put in the bread, to lighten it, she thought was baking soda ... but from its character, and the effects of the bread on us, was convinced that the substance was caustic soda!—and threw it away.

Billy Lambkin did not recover. "We done all we could for the poor little sufferer," wrote Bruff on New Year's Day, "but by 11 A.M. he was extricated from all the hardships of life. ... I procured a piece of white cotton, stripped the boy, washed him with snow, and tied him up in the cloth, and secured the tent to prevent the wolves carrying him off." The next day, Bruff placed Billy in his final resting place.

At 10 a.m. I cleared away the fire, in front of my tent, within 5 feet of it, and assisted by young Roberts, dug a grave on the spot, and buried the boy. I then piled stones on the grave, procured a small piece of plank, made a head board, and sat up, with this inscription:—

WILLIAM
Infant Son of
LAMBKIN
an Unnatural Father,
Died Jan. 1, 1850

Seven-and-a-half-year-old Emma Griffis was luckier than Billy Lambkin. She was kidnapped twice within the span of a month but was safely restored to her parents by a lone gold prospector who doggedly pursued the child, her abductors, and her roving parents. The miner's name was Warren Saddler. He tells his tale in a journal he kept while digging for gold on the American River, where he first met the little girl and her family in spring 1849.

> *Some time about the first of May. ... I packed my tools, blankets and provisions ... and put out ... following the river and up the north fork ... as far as a place called Barne's Bar, It was not long before I had a spot picked out, a claim staked off, and set into work. While I was cleaning out the rocker and panning down my gold to clean it from the black sand, there came down the mountain a family, a man, his wife, and a little girl about seven years of age, with their luggage packed on mules and camped near where I was working.*

The parents had company once or twice a day. Two "rough-looking" men took their meals with them and continued to "hang on" when the family moved to another site on the Bear River—within speaking distance of the prospector. He wrote in his journal:

> *Their little girl [was] playing about their tent and often came near my camp when I was cooking my meals, but never had any thing to say. ... One night ... I heard ... loud talking ... saw one of the men run out of the tent ... swearing ... and pulling a pistol from his bootleg. ... Crack went the husband's rifle, and ... the ball struck him on top of his head. ... In the morning ... the dead man was not there. ... What became of him, I don't know.*

Three days later Saddler staked another claim on the Yuba River, where he met the woman of the shooting party. Much distraught, she told him the second man had run away and had either murdered or stolen her daughter. They had spent a good deal of time and effort trying to find him but had lost his trail.

Two weeks passed, and no one saw the kidnapped girl. Saddler pulled up stake again and moved back to the American River. There, he chanced upon a tall thicket of chaparral that hid a Native American settlement with a row of dirt mounds. To his surprise, he saw a little white girl near one of the huts. His curiosity overcame his fear of the Indians.

> *I sat out for the camp. ... The little girl stood watching me. ... As soon as I spoke to her, before answering, she turned towards the Indians to see if they*

gave her any sign. … By this time the whole camp, old and young, had turned out, standing around and running their eyes from my head to foot, then at the child. At this, she got a little frightened, and placed both her arms around my body, which made the chief give a hearty laugh. I asked him, if the child could go with me to my camp not far away. He nodded his head in consent. … The Indians pressed a little to one side to make a passage way, and let her pass. … As she came near … she made a grab for me. I put my arms around her, seeing she had become much frightened and … the crowd let us pass.

When they arrived at Saddler's camp, he questioned the child about the events that had led to her abduction. She told him the companion of the man who had been shot at Bear River asked her to go with him to a nearby store so he could buy her some cake and "other nice things." She went with him but soon discovered they were heading for the woods. They had travelled several days before they came to the Indian camp—Emma on his mule, and the man walking behind her.

Saddler promised the girl he would take her back to her mother if she would run away from the man she was staying with. He described her reaction in his journal.

This pleased her so well, she jumped about and clapped her two little hands together, and said, "Yes! I will go with you." All this time she had been carry-ing her little hat in one hand, and I leading her by the other, but when she let go my hand, and threw down the hat to clap those two little dirty hands together, and looked at me … with that shining brightness that was in her eyes, it showed her little heart was … hoping once more to see her mother. … I started back to the Indian camp holding her by the hand, while she skipped along by my side.

There the prospector told the chief about the kidnapping. "Captain Lew-is," as he was called by the child, warned Saddler that the abductor had gone to the settlements in the Sacramento valley to get some fresh mules and that he would return in the morning. He promised to keep his men in camp until the child was safe. He would give him a signal when the time was right to take her out.

He picked up a stick, then asked me to let him take my knife. … He shar-pened the stick and stuck it in the ground near the entrance [of his mound] and told me if the child brought me that stick to take her and go quick.

The prospector returned to his camp but was awakened early the next morning by drunken noises that came from the Indian camp. The white man had returned, carrying a hatchet, two large pistols, and a large butcher knife—he was ready for a brawl. Events moved swiftly. Saddler wrote in his journal:

I saw the white man running toward the Indians with his butcher knife in his hand. ... He stumbled and fell, but managed to get up on his feet again. The chief came out to try and quiet him. But the white man was so enraged, he took after the Captain with his hatchet and was about to bury it into his head; but was prevented by an Indian firing his gun, and killing him almost instantly. That ended the row.

Saddler hurried to the camp to fetch the little girl. She took her hat—her only possession—and mounted his mule. The Native Americans gave them some venison and showed them a trail that went to the Sacramento valley. Off they went, as fast as the prospector was able to carry his heavy pack.

The child, being cheerful and happy, gave me encouragement. At first, not a word was spoken by either of us, and she, all the time was punching the mule. ... Finally she turned ... around in her saddle, looking back at me. Then she laughed and took her little hat and swung it several times over her head, and sang out on the top of her voice, "I am going to see my mother again tol—lol—lol! tol—lol—lol! I'm going to see my mother again!" She kept saying these words over and over ... fairly making the words ring with her voice. ... It seemed strange to me, to have such happy company, after travelling alone so long. ... I was proud of her courage and steady mind, for so young a person.

They travelled steadily, over high hills and through deep, dark ravines and thickets of small underbrush, and camped in desolate places, living on venison, tea, and crackers. On the fifth day they could see herds of wild cattle, elk, antelope, and deer—all feeding quietly on the plains. The next day the sun was pouring its heat down on the weary travellers. The prospector continued to carry his heavy pack on his back for three hundred miles. He noted in his journal:

The child must ride. She had no shoes, and if she was to travel on foot, her little feet would soon get sore. She would often jump off the mule and walk by my side for several miles ... which made time pass away much more

pleasant for me. But she, like all children, would get tired and sleepy travel-
ling on foot in the heat. … All I could do was to stop the mule and help her
on the saddle, and fasten the strap, and say to her, "Sleep riding." She would
soon fall asleep, then I would walk by the side of the mule so as to keep watch
she did not slip through the strap and fall. The sight of the poor child lashed
to a sweaty mule and riding in the broiling sun made me feel bad.

They travelled for eight and half more days until they reached the Sacramento River and crossed it on a ferry boat. Saddler obtained some provisions
for himself and his mule and bought "cake and other little things" for Emma.
As they were sitting down to eat, a woman approached them and offered to
watch the little girl so the prospector could take care of his other errands.

Saddler consented and, upon his return, found that Emma had enjoyed
herself so much in the company of the woman that he made an offer to her.

Things looked so much more comfortable to what we had been used to along
the route … I thought it would be better to leave Emma there with the
woman till I could go up and have her father come down for her. After talk-
ing to the woman a short time, I made a bargain for her to keep the child for
that length of time and I would be back in four or five days. … I paid her
what she charged to keep the child till I returned.

Saddler would soon regret this decision. When he returned four days later
with Mr. Griffis and two pack animals, the woman had disappeared. "We
went over to the slough where I had left Emma with the woman," he wrote in
his journal, "and there was no tent, woman or child to be seen anywhere. …
We searched all day around the outskirts of the city, inquiring at every tent;
but could not get any trace of them."

They hunted for two more days without success, and by then Emma's father had become discouraged. He saddled his mule and horse and started for
home. When he left the prospector, Saddler assured him:

I will—if need be—spend a year's time, and all the money I have, and all I
can borrow from my friends to find the child. The first time she was stolen
from you and carried off over three hundred miles and left in camp with a
party of Indians, and I took the responsibility to bring her back to you. And
this time she was … stolen from me, and now I wish to see the thing
through.

Early the next morning, Saddler started on another search for the child. He crossed the Sacramento River and took the road to Marysville. There, he learned from some emigrants who had camped near the trail that they had seen the woman and the missing child in a Mormon train, heading for Salt Lake City. Saddler pushed on, crossed the Yuba River, and encountered their fresh trail near the Feather River crossing. He noted in this journal:

In the morning of the forth day [after I had left Sacramento] I came up to them and found ... they had all their wagons placed in a circle with the tongues run under the back axle so as to close them up and make a corral to live in, and keep out stock. I moved around in front of their camp and the first person I saw was little Emma standing on the tongue of their wagon. I moved along within the circle as close as I could to where she was standing, and as soon her eyes rested on me and she saw who I was, she moved her two little hands over head and clapped them together and jumped down from the wagon tongue and ran and caught hold of my leg, and hung on it so tight it was impossible to get off my mule. About that time, I heard the woman, under the cover of their wagon, speak, and I knew her voice. I asked her to come out. She said, no, she was afraid I would shoot her.

Saddler placed the child on his mule, stayed close behind the animal, and slipped through the openings between the wagons. The woman stayed under the wagon cover and offered no resistance; neither did the men who had begun to crowd around. Not a word was spoken as Emma and her protector made their exit.

They pushed along as fast as they could and camped away from the road. The child was sleepy but was pleased to see her old friend again. He wrote in his journal:

I had only a few drops of water in the canteen that I gave Emma. ... She was so tired she could hardly speak, but told me that she had been walking all day and her feet were aching hard. ... She said they gave her plenty to eat, but she cried all the time she was with them, because she did not want to go with them.

It took them nearly a week to get back to Marysville. There they met two kind strangers who took pity on the prospector and the tired little girl: A woman took Emma in, bathed her, and dressed her in a pretty new outfit. A man who was going to Sacramento gave them a ride in his wagon, with Saddler's mule hitched to the rear. They arrived in the city in two days.

The prospector bought new provisions, and the next morning, before the sun was up, he and the child were on the move again. They were heading for the north bank of the American River where Emma's parents had previously staked a claim. On the evening of the third day, they arrived at the place where the Griffis's tent had stood, but there was no trace of either the father or the mother. Saddler described the reaction of the little girl.

> *The child began to cry. … I reached up … to help her off the mule, the tears were streaming down her cheeks … she had lost all hope. … I told her I thought we could soon find them camped in another place. She said, "No!" She was tired … and wanted to lie down, and asked me to unroll the blankets. … Then she wanted me to lie down by her. As I raised up to leave for a few minutes, she said again, "Don't leave me! Do come and lie by me." … I was not gone for more than five minutes, and when I returned I … found she was sound asleep. … If I ever felt bad in my life it was while sitting and gazing on that sleeping disappointed child.*

In the morning, the prospector found the tracks of her parents' wagon and traced them to the main road. Emma asked him, "What are you going to do now?" When told they would continue the search for her parents, she cried out, "No, no! You stop and go to work mining and I will live with you. I am so tired of travelling." But then she changed her mind, took his hand, and smiling, said, "Yes! I will go with you."

They were soon joined by several miners who had known the Griffis family and had heard about Emma's having been kidnapped. Her parents had told them they had given up looking for her and were moving south, near Stockton, to find a ranch they might farm. As they were preparing to leave, the miners were busy collecting money for the prospector and the child. Saddler was moved by the outpouring of goodwill.

> *They insisted in my taking it; said in case I should loose my mule or have any unexpected bad luck, the money would help. … so I consented to take it and told them in case I did not succeed in finding Mr. Griffis, the money would go towards taking care of the child. At that moment, one of the party … sang out, "This is right, and the child must have a purse, too." He took my gold pan and turned it bottom up, and took out of his shirt pocket a small gold scale and placed the scales on the pan, then took weights enough to make two hundred dollars … each miner giving what he pleased till the weights were balanced. … Emma was already sitting on the mule when they handed her the purse. … She gave it a toss to me and said, "You take it and*

take care of it for me!" ... I started up the mule and we all bid each other good-by.

They travelled for eight days through rugged country, crossing three major rivers and innumerable creeks. "Emma stood it like a lump of iron," Saddler wrote in his journal. "She found no fault even when we were obliged to cross the rivers hanging on to the mule's tail and being towed across through deep water. She ... would hang to her grip like a little lobster."

One night, when they had camped near a ford across the Mokelumne River, they found a small strip of board lying in the dry grass. It had been part of the cover of a candle box, and on it were several items written with a pencil and nearly rubbed out. At the top was Mr. Griffis's name—the list of articles was a bill of goods he had bought. "We looked each other in the face, but did not utter a word," wrote Saddler. "We were so glad to once more get square on their track that we were unable to speak."

It took them another week to find Emma's parents. They stopped for several days at the ranch of one of the prospector's old friends, who volunteered to ride out into the valley to inquire about the Griffis's whereabouts. With renewed hope, Emma and Saddler continued their search. At sunset the fourth day, they came upon a partially enclosed ranch and the little girl spotted a familiar animal. Wrote Saddler:

Emma, riding on the mule ... happened to spy a horse standing inside this corral. She stopped ... and sang out, "Oh, there is papa's horse!" ... He was much thinner in flesh than when we last saw him ... but it was the same horse. ... Emma's little face showed that her heart was glad. She then began looking about on all sides of us ... saw nothing, and turned to me and said, "Oh now where is mamma?"

They went to a nearby tent and were greeted by a stranger—a tall, "rough-looking" man. He had bought the horse from Emma's parents but knew nothing more about their fate except that they had gone further south, intent upon settling on a ranch. Disappointed, the girl and the prospector moved on, travelling for two more days, taking a zigzag course, asking every person they met whether he had seen Emma's parents. Finally, they had a stroke of good luck. A stranger who stopped at their campfire for a cup of coffee had seen the Griffis's mules and a tent they had recently set up in the foothills.

That night at their campground, the two weary travellers were surrounded by a pack of wolves who ventured close to their fire. As darkness fell, they had another visitor: a large grizzly bear, who came near enough so they were face-to-face with him. Noted Saddler in his journal:

> *It was a star-light night and the old rogue seemed to be watching us while we were watching him. He sat still and made no more moves. ... We sat on the blankets watching the fire burn and listened to the wolves who were keeping up their terrible yells. ... Finally Emma said, "Here take your gun!" She turned back to the fire while I moved along towards "the cat," as Emma called him. ... He moved away without ... even the sound of a growl.*

The next day they travelled until nearly noon, when they sighted a tent. Emma's eyes were riveted on it. Not a word was spoken. Then she spotted a cream-colored mule, her favorite animal. It raised its head, saw the child, and came running toward her, dragging a long lariat. Saddler described the encounter.

> *Emma ... had turned deathly pale again. I saw ... she was prepared for another disappointment. ... But she held on the rein of the hackamore with a firm grip. So I knew she was not going to faint and fall from the saddle. ... We had only a few rods to go before reaching the tent. ... We heard a good deal of rattling of tin-ware and knocking over of stools before the door opened. ... Two persons, a man and a woman, appeared ... nearly frightened out of their senses. They did not recognize me or their child. Emma was sitting on the mule and never spoke a word. I reached up, took her from the mule ... sat her down on her feet in front of her mother ... and said, "Here is your lost child."*

That evening, Mrs. Griffis cooked a special supper, and Warren Saddler was the honored guest. Emma urged him to stay with her family for two nights. He consented but was surprised to hear her say the next day, "When you do go, I want to go to the mines with you. I have seen my mother now and want to go back. ... I don't want any body to take better care of me than you do."

It took the prospector a long time to convince the girl that she was better off remaining with her parents than suffering the hardships of a miner's life. They talked all day, at supper, and through the night; when Saddler left on the third day, after having given Emma's "gold purse" to her mother, there was much sadness. He wrote in his journal:

*I bid them good-by and took Emma's little hand while large tears rolled
down her checks to think she was to be left. I also felt bad to leave her as I
had her in my care so long and got much attached to her. But she was in her
mother's care now which was a great relief to me. I had done what I had un-
dertaken to do, so I had no further responsibility resting on me.*

By the time Emma Griffis was safely back with her parents, another kidnapping had taken place—this time on the high seas. Eliza Farnham, a young
widow, had left New York on May 19, 1849, on the ship *Angelique,* with six-
year-old Charles, three-year-old Eddie, and a young woman whom she had
engaged as a nurse for her sons. With her also was a friend, Miss Sampson.

She was on one of the ships that departed from Atlantic ports almost daily
from the moment President Polk had announced that "California's mines are
more extensive and valuable than was anticipated." The trading route around
the Horn offered a tried-and-true passage to the Pacific, although it was no
less tiresome than the overland crossing.

Eliza Farnham was heading for California to claim not a stake in the gold
diggings but rather some land her lawyer husband had bought in the Santa
Cruz valley north of Monterey Bay. He had died suddenly on September 13,
1848, on one of his forays out West. The fertile land now belonged to the
young widow and her two boys, and she was on her way to take possession of
their inheritance.

After a few days at sea, the passengers began to become sick from the foul
water. Eliza wrote a petition to Captain Windsor requesting a stop at a nearby
port. The petition was signed by twenty-one of the twenty-two passengers,
including six-year-old Charlie. "As this paper had been drawn up by myself,"
wrote the widow, "and was sent in my handwriting, it greatly increased the
anger he had all along felt toward me, and which I had never allowed him to
dissipate by abusing me, as he had the rest of the [female] passengers."

During the first week of October, after a voyage of nearly five months, they
sighted the harbor of Valparaiso. The teenage girl who was nursemaid to the
two Farnham boys informed Eliza that she planned to marry the ship's steward in the port, and the young widow set about to find a Chilean nurse who
might be more dependable. Mrs. Farnham described her encounter with the
ship's captain.

*The captain had been informed in the consul's office ... that I had made
such an arrangement, and he expressed no objection to it. ... The woman
was on board the vessel, and seen by him engaged in my rooms twenty-four*

hours before he sailed. [But] when he came on board the last time ... He inquired who that woman was, and ... I replied that she was my servant. "Have you a passport for her," said he. "No," I replied, "I was told I needed none." "Then she must go ashore," he said. "I should subject myself to a heavy penalty to take her without one. ... Put her into the boat and send her off."

Eliza Farnham was not easily intimidated. She told the captain she would go with her servant to the consul's office to get a passport or something equivalent. To this the captain replied that he was going to sea and would not wait for her if she was not back on time.

The determined widow wasted no time. She hastily pulled ashore and stopped for only a moment at the consulate, where she learned that the captain had no authority to demand any papers and had simply tricked her to vent his anger. Within less than an hour, she returned to the pier. When she arrived, the boatmen told her the ship had moved to the other side of the promontory where the tide seemed more favorable.

The men moved the rowboat around the point. Eliza could now look out to the open sea. There, already halfway below the horizon, was the *Angelique* on her way to San Francisco. Her two little boys were aboard. She was stunned by what she saw.

I did not really doubt that a few minutes more would place me beside my children. ... But at this moment I saw the vessel. ... She stood before my straining sight ... with a fresh, steady breeze filling her sails. ... The hope with which I first caught sight of her died ... in a moment, and a sickening, terrible conviction that she was gone, settled down on me like the chill of death.

Eliza had to wait for a month for another vessel that would carry a woman passenger. Finally, the American ship *Louis Phillipe* from Baltimore came into port, and her captain graciously offered Eliza accommodations with several married couples. On November 9, 1849, exactly a month after she had watched the *Angelique* carry her children away from her, the young mother began her journey to California to find them.

The voyage took thirty-eight days. When they neared San Francisco, the Golden Gate was invisible behind sheets of rain. The fog was so thick that the captain did not try to enter the bay for a week. Before daybreak on Christmas Eve, Eliza was awakened by shouts from the crew: San Francisco was on fire. By the next morning, Christmas Day, 1849, most of the fire had been put out, but the fog had closed in again. The ships outside the Golden Gate had to stay there for two more days. Eliza later reflected on the long wait.

> *That was the sorest trial of all. … I could better have born twenty days at sea, than those nine days; but they came to an end at last, and we dropped anchor somewhere off North Beach, on the tenth evening, after it was too late to see anything but two or three straggling lights shining dull through the fog that never cleared and the rain that never ceased pouring. This, then, was California, but I was too much engrossed in thinking of my dear children, and what had been their fate since they were parted from me, to entertain a thought of the wonderful country … before me.*

The following morning they discovered that one of the ships anchored in the bay was the *Angelique*. Eliza Farnham set out in a boat provided by Captain Brathane and was taken to the ship in the early afternoon. She wrote of her reunion with her children: "I found them still on board of the vessel, where the indefatigable Miss Sampson, who had chiefly taken care of them, aided by some of their fellow-passengers, still remained awaiting my arrival."

Miss Sampson had refused to leave the ship until the children's mother claimed them. Shocked by Captain Windsor's conduct, several other passengers, both men and women, had offered to help her and had done all they could to ease the loneliness and bewilderment of the two young boys. The older boy, Charlie, was in good health and spirits, but three-year-old Eddie was feeble—the sudden and prolonged separation from his mother had taken its toll.

"We went on shore almost immediately," wrote their mother, "if that be properly be called shore where tall men were wading in water to the tops of boots above their knees, and where … floundering along with a strong man at each elbow, we seemed to be almost submerged in a sea of mud." They stayed in San Francisco for six weeks and then took a boat down to Santa Cruz. Accompanied by Miss Sampson and her two children, Eliza Farnham arrived at her ranch on Washington's Birthday, 1850. It had taken her nine months to reach her new home.

Good-Bye Death Valley

O N March 7, 1850, ten emaciated argonauts stumbled into the compound of the del Valle ranch, north of present-day Newhall, near Los Angeles. Among them were four children, two boys and two girls, ranging in age from two to eight. They were the last of the forty-niners who had managed to come out alive from the "jaws of hell."

Their tale began five months earlier, when they were among nearly a thousand emigrants who had arrived at the Mormon settlements at Salt Lake City in late September 1849—too late to attempt to cross the Sierra Nevada. The Mormons had encouraged the emigrants to take a southern route instead, by way of the Old Spanish Trail to Los Angeles.

Over one hundred wagons started south from their rendezvous near Provo, Utah. The train of this "Sand Walking Company" included a microcosm of the United States: people of English, French, and German descent; Catholics, Protestants, Mormons. There were single men, like the "Jayhawkers" from Illinois, and the "Bugsmashers" from Georgia and Mississippi—including several young African Americans, who had taken an oath of allegiance to their group for mutual protection. Among the families with children were the Arcanes, French immigrants from Chicago; the Bennetts, headed by a trapper and lead miner from Wisconsin; the Briers, a Methodist minister and his family from Michigan; and the Wades, who had been employed at the royal court in London before they immigrated to the United States.

All had been forewarned by their Mormon guide that the advantages of the southern route—no snow, no major mountain ranges—would also entail some disadvantages, among them scarcity of both water and forage for their animals. Young John Wells Brier, age six at the time of their departure, gave an account of the first month of their journey.

Leaving Death Valley—The Manly Party on the March After Leaving Their Wagons (The Pacific Tree and Vine Co., San Jose, California, 1894)

On September 30, 1849, our party of 105 wagons left the rendezvous on the bank of a stream flowing into Utah Lake. … Captain Hunt, who had contracted to conduct us to Los Angeles within nine weeks for a thousand dollars, was our leader. While the teams were fresh and the credit of Capt. Hunt was unimpaired, we were in excellent spirit, but … the train had been loaded for expedition rather than comfort, and no provision had been made for leisure. The leading thought had been to make it as easy as possible for the teams; and when they began to wear a jaded look, when five weeks of the nine had passed with no more than a third of the distance covered, the spirit of discontent grew towards open revolt.

The Captain was taciturnity itself. If he possessed the knowledge of a guide, he seemed to be wanting in the tact of a leader. This may be the fancy of a child, for I confess that I was afraid of the silent man, and wondered if he ever loved anybody, and if he slept on horseback.

We had journeyed into the Great Basin. … A party came into our camp at Iron Buttes, who were on a … march to California, guided by a chart, furnished by a Utah chief, Walker. It was a most inviting trail, dotted at convenient intervals with springs; and as we were assured that a fortnight would take us to the enchanted shores of Owen's Lake [in California], our affections were immediately alienated from Captain Hunt and the Spanish Trail.

The "Walker cutoff" showed a route that cut three hundred to five hundred miles from the emigrants' journey to the gold fields, a route that went due west, with water holes, along the mountain ranges. Not everyone took the map at face value. William Lewis Manly, a friend and scout of the Bennett family, remembered:

A great many were anxious to get the opinion of Capt. Hunt on the feasibility of the new route for he was a mountain man and could probably give us some good advice. He finally consented to talk of it, and said he really knew no more then the others about this particular route, but he very much doubted if a white man ever went over it, and that he did not consider it at all safe for those who had wives and children in their company to take the unknown road.

But the Reverend John Brier, a circuit-riding preacher with a flair for oratory, convinced most of the emigrants that they should take the shortcut. His son John recalled:

There were perhaps five hundred people within the circle of our wagons. In the mass meeting, the new departure was discussed, and my father was one of the most enthusiastic advocates. The guide very consistently opposed it. "Gentlemen!" he exclaimed with characteristic brevity, "All I have to say is, that if you take that route you will all be landed in Hell!"

On November 4, 1849, the train divided, and all but seven wagons headed directly west into unknown territory. After three days of easy travel, they encountered "Mount Misery" (straddling the present-day Utah-Nevada border), a long, deep chasm that stopped the oxen in their tracks. Seventy-five wagons turned back to rejoin Hunt's train along the Old Spanish Trail. They arrived in Los Angeles, without mishap, seven weeks later.

INTO THE JAWS OF HELL

The Bennett, Arcane, Wade, and Brier families, with four women—one pregnant—and eleven children, ranging in age from two to fourteen, decided instead to cast their lot with the adventurous single men who were determined to follow the cutoff. They detoured north around the chasm and continued west. Young John Wells Brier described the next stage of their journey.

> *When the train was once more set in motion, ax-men led the way. A rough and hazardous track was exposed, to follow which tested to the utmost the discipline of the oxen and the will of the drivers. Evening closed about a camp pitched among the bog lands of the Muddy, a sluggish stream issuing southward from Mountain Meadows.*
>
> *Relief from anxiety assured to the camp a night of perfect rest, and the oxen, renewed by abundance, were ready for the long climb and trackless way inviting to purer air and a wider view. The grade was easy, however, and near the summit, in an old Indian cornfield, the camp circle was formed and the cattle were relieved of their yokes. There was a light fall of snow and the cold was penetrating, but soon great fires, fed by greasewood, shot into lofty spires, imparting warmth and radiating cheer during the preparation of the evening meal. … The men circled about the greasewood fires and sang the old songs, some of which were parodied in a manner to turn regrets to laughter. I well remember the chorus of "Carry me back" and that of "Oh, Susanna" accompanied by the strains of Nat Ward's fiddle.*

The wagons headed northwest across the Muddy to the White River, looking for the mythical east-west dividing range, along the base of which they expected to find the cutoff. But as the days passed, it became clear that no such range existed. Turning southwest into a barren valley, they pursued another illusion—the mirage of a vast lake that proved to be only a few muddy alkaline pools. With the aide of a captured Piute Indian, they finally found good water near the foot of the Timpahute Range. John Wells Brier remembered:

> *We journeyed fifty miles with the Timpahute, and descended into the first real desert I had ever seen, and saw here, for the first time, the mirage. We had been without water for twenty-four hours, when suddenly there broke into view to the south a splendid sheet of water, which all of us believed was Owen's Lake. As we hurried towards it, the vision faded, and near midnight we halted on the rim of a basin of mud, with a shallow pool of brine. From this point I remember little of our westward course across the great desert until we rested at the mouth of a deep-walled fissure, and two Indians were brought into camp, captured at the extremity of the cleft. Questioned by signs as to the directions of the great water, they pointed to the southwest, and one*

of them led two of our young men to a beautiful mountain spring. During
the night both escaped.

They moved on over treeless hills and barren valleys. Their weakened oxen
crawled at an ever slower pace. The Brier family finally burned their wagons
and loaded their few remaining supplies onto their forlorn animals. Young
John Wells Brier vividly remembered "the abandonment of our wagons, the
drifting sand, the cold blast from the north, the wind-beaten hill, the burning
of wagons as fuel, the forsaking of nearly every treasured belonging. ... The
walking, now made necessary, was hard upon the women and children, but
the short rations were more trying for all."

On December 2, 1849, after camping together for the last time on the
shores of Papoose Dry Lake in southwestern Nevada, the weary travellers split
into two parties. The Bennetts and Arcanes, with their teamsters, went south,
followed at a distance by the Wade family. The Briers and the Jayhawkers
continued their westward course. Juliette Brier, John's mother, gave an account of what happened to her family on the next part of the journey.

We reached the top of the divide between Death and Ash valleys, and, oh,
what a desolate country we looked down into. The next morning we started
down. The men said they could see what looked like springs in the valley.
Mr. Brier was always ahead to explore and find water, so I was left with our
three boys to help bring up the cattle. ... I was sick and weary and the hope
of a good camping place was all that kept me up. Poor little Kirke (age 4)
gave out and I carried him on my back, barely seeing where I was going, un-
til he would say, "Mother, I can walk now." Poor little fellow! He would
stumble on a little way over the salty marsh and sink down crying, "I can't go
any farther." Then I would carry him again, and soothe him as best I could.

The boys would ask for water, but there was not a drop. Thus, we stag-
gered on over the salty wastes, trying to keep the company in view and hop-
ing at every step to come to the springs. ... Night came on and we lost all
track of those ahead. I would get down on my knees and look in the star-
light for the ox tracks and then we would stumble on. There was not a sound
and I didn't know whether we would ever reach camp or not.

The Arcanes and the Bennetts, on their course due south, fared no better
than the Briers. Wrote Manly, who scouted daily for water:

The party kept rolling along as fast as possible but the mountains and valleys
grew more barren and water more scarce all the time. ... Our oxen began to

look bad, for they had poor food. They moved slowly and cropped disdain-
fully the dry scattering shrubs and bunches of grass from six inches to a foot
high. … No one knew how long before we might have to kill some of them to
get food to save our own lives. … Mrs. Bennett and Mrs. Arcane were in
heart-rending distress. The four children were crying for water but there was
not a drop to give them, and none could be reached before some time. …
The mothers were nearly crazy, for they expected the children would choke
with thirst and die in their arms, and would rather perish themselves than
suffer the agony of seeing their little ones gasp and slowly die.

In mid-December, the Bennett-Arcane train found some relief for the children's hunger. They stopped for nine days at a hastily abandoned Native
American village, devouring the winter's store of squash they found there and
fattening their oxen on the stubble in the cornfield. The Piutes would later
trail them across the Armagosa desert, seeking revenge by trying to take their
oxen, but to no avail. It took both trains nearly three weeks to cross the
Armagosa and to reach Furnace Creek Wash on the present-day Nevada-Cali-
fornia border.

Just before Christmas the Brier family arrived at the rim of Death Valley.
Young John Wells Brier picks up his family's trail.

After many days of bitter travel, we reached the Amargosa and camped in its
dry channel, counting ourselves fortunate to find a muddy pool of water.
The end of the next day (December 23) found us, with our canteens empty,
at the summit of a pass where there was no water, no grass, no fuel—nothing
but a low plant, mottled with pale red and purple, that rattled desolately in
the north wind. Early the next morning (December 24) from the top of a
neighboring crag, my father looked across the furrowed hills into a deep val-
ley reaching westward to a lofty mountain range, and in it, seeming scarcely
two leagues away, a beautiful oasis of grass and spring water. All that day we hur-
ried toward it hardly able to keep pace with the eager animals down the well-
beaten Indian trail, and it was past midnight before we reached the oasis.

THE FIRST CHRISTMAS

IN DEATH VALLEY

John's mother, Juliette Brier, later gave a memorable account of the Christmas
spent at Travertine Springs, near present-day Furnace Creek Inn.

About midnight we came around a big rock and there was my husband at a small fire. "Is this the camp?" I asked. "No, it's six miles farther," he said. I was ready to drop and Kirke was almost unconscious, moaning for a drink. Mr. Brier took him on his back and hastened to camp to save his little life. It was three o'clock Christmas morning when we reached the springs. ... We found hot and cold springs there and scrubbed and rested. That was a Christmas none could ever forget.

My little ones had no thoughts of Santa Claus that year. The men killed an oxen for our Christmas, but its flesh was more like poisonous slime than meat. There was not a particle of fat on the bones, but we boiled the hide and hoofs for what nutriment they might contain. We also cooked and ate the little blood there was in the carcass. I had one small biscuit, but we had plenty of coffee, and I think it was that which kept us alive.

Music and singing? My, no! We were too far gone for that. Nobody spoke very much, but I knew we were all thinking of home back east and all the cheer and good things there.

Young John Brier remembered, "The men wanted something to remind them of other days, and my father gave them a lecture on education. It was grave and humorous." It was intended, his mother explained, to lift his sons' spirits.

One member of the audience was not impressed—William Lewis Manly, who was scouting ahead of the Bennett-Arcane party and who had arrived at Travertine Springs the evening of December 25. He later wrote in his autobiography:

As I recollect this was Christmas day and about dusk I came upon the camp of one man with his wife and family, the Rev. J. W. Brier, Mrs. Brier and sons. ... When I arrived at his camp I found the reverend gentleman very cooley delivering a lecture to his boys on education. It seemed very strange to me to hear a solemn discourse on the benefits of early education when, it seemed to me, starvation was staring us all in the face, and the barren desolation all around gave small promise of the need of any education higher than the natural impulses of nature. None of us knew exactly where we were, nor when the journey would be ended, nor when substantial relief would come.

That night, one of the members of the Jayhawkers, who had also camped at Travertine Springs, asked Mrs. Brier, "Don't you think you and the children had better remain here and let us send back for you?" "No," she said, "I have never been a hindrance. I have never kept the company waiting, neither have my children, and every step I will take will be toward California."

The next morning the "company moved on over the sand to—nobody knew where"—the Briers in the rear, with their small children having but one day to recuperate. A reconnoitering party found the wagon tracks of some of the Jayhawkers who had proceeded them, and the Briers decided to follow those tracks. Nearly opposite their encampment a trail mounted to the Panamint Range, where a valley, rich in grass, offered an easy descent into the Wild Rose and Darwin canyons and opened up a way to Watkins Pass. But the Briers did not know this and moved northwest instead. Young John Wells Brier remembered:

> *On this day two of the men came upon an old Indian in a depression, with the sand packed about him, but his head left exposed. One of them mistook him for a wolf, and was about to shoot him, when the other exclaimed— "My God! it is a man!" He was released from confinement, and we watched him catch beetles for food, and visit the near spring for drink, though his eyes may have been dead for a quarter of a century.*

Manly, meanwhile, guided the Bennett-Arcane party into the Travertine Springs camp the Briers had left the day after Christmas, where they rested until January 6, 1850. They did not want to abandon their wagons as the Jayhawkers had done and decided instead to head south across Death Valley to the base of the Panamint Mountains.

Unbeknownst to both the Brier and the Bennett-Arcane parties, the Shoshone Indians were watching their arrival and departure. George Hansen was a small boy at the time. He was born about 1841 and was "in his tenth summer and about as tall as a wagon wheel" when he saw the first white people in Death Valley. He ran from the sight, which terrified him, and thus won his tribal name, "Bah-vanda-sava-nu-kee" (the Boy-Who-Runs-Away). As an old man he still remembered the incident.

> *A strange tribe of other people … came down Furnace Creek, some walking, slow like sick people and some in big wagons, pulled by cows. They stopped there by the water and rested. When other Indians saw them, they ran away and told all other Indians at other camps. Our people were afraid of these strange people. They were not our kind and these cows my people had never seen before.*

Never had they seen wagons or wheels or any of the things these people had; the cows were spotted and bigger than the biggest mountain sheep, with long tails and big horns. They moved slow and cried in a long voice like they were sick for grass and water.

Some of these people moved down the valley, some moved up, and they stopped at Salt Creek crossing. When it came night, we crawled close, slow, like when trailing sheep. We saw many men around a big fire. They killed cows and burned the wagons and made a big council talk in loud voices like squaws when mad. Some fell down sick when they ate the skinny cows. By and by they went away, up that way where Stove Pipe hotel is now. They walked very slow, strung out like sheep. Some men helped other men that were sick. ... As they went they dropped things all along the trail, maybe they were worthless things, or too heavy to carry.

After they go, we went to that place at Salt Creek and found many things that they left there. When they burned the wagons some parts did not burn. That was iron, and we did not understand this.

Those people who went down the valley to Bennett's Well stayed there a long time. They had women and children. By and by they went away, all went over the Panamints and we never saw them again.

ESCAPE FROM DEATH VALLEY

The Briers, on their northwest course, united their fortunes with those of the Jayhawkers. Young John recalled that "my mother was the only woman in this company. There were three children of us, the youngest four years and the oldest eight. We went without other food than that supplied by our few emaciated oxen for six weeks."

Some Jayhawkers had been reluctant to accept the Briers into their company. L. D. Stephens, one of the young men, remembered:

Rev. J. W. Brier and his family came up to us and wanted to travel with us. At first we objected as we didn't want to be encumbered with any women [and children], but we hadn't the heart to refuse. So they joined the Jayhawkers and the little woman proved to be as plucky and brave as any woman that ever crossed the plains.

Juliette Brier, age thirty-five, earned the Jayhawkers' respect and affection. One of them observed that in walking nearly a hundred miles through barren desert and sharp-edged rocks, she frequently carried one of her three children on her back, carried another in her arms, and held the third by the hand. She later described the vicissitudes her party encountered during the last week of 1849.

> *A march over twenty miles of dry sand brought us to the foot of the Pana-mint mountains with hope almost gone and not a drop of water to relieve our parched lips and swollen tongue. The men climbed up to the snow and brought down all they could carry, frozen hard. Mr. Brier filled an old shirt and brought it to us. Some ate it while hard and relished it as though it was flowing water, but enough was melted for our frenzied cattle and camp use.*
>
> *We went on over the (Towne's) pass through the snow into what they named Panamint Valley, and found a deserted Indian Village among the mesquite trees. We were rejoiced by seeing hair ropes and bridles and horse bones, thinking we had reached civilization. The men ahead, however, could only report more sand and hills. After two days here we struggled away into the desert carrying all the water possible. We grew more fearful of our provisions and watched each mouthful, not daring to make a full meal. Cof-fee and salt we had in plenty. The salt we picked up in great lumps in the sand before coming over the last mountains. Our coffee was a wonderful help and if it had given out, I know we would have died. New Years Day (1850) was hardly noticed. We spent it resting at the head of Panamint Val-ley.*

On January 6 two of the Jayhawkers decided to strike out on their own. They took with them their supply of flour, which until then had been shared by the entire company. Juliette Brier made twenty-two little crackers from some dough before they left and put them away for her children for an emergency. "This was our last bite of bread," she remembered.

Now began their race with death, a race they had to run each day. Young John Wells Brier described the next part of their arduous journey.

> *Steering north of west we drove across the shifting dunes for twenty miles to the pass between the Panamints and Telescope Peak. All this I can distinctly and accurately recall. Twenty miles across the naked dunes, the wind driving the sand like shot into the face and eyes; a raging thirst, for we had found no potable water in the Valley of Death; the bench lands, thickly strewn with basalt boulders; the snow-line, to which my father mounted, returning with all the snow he could carry, which we melted for man and beast; the field of snow that we crossed, the cattle eating it to assuage their thirst; the midnight*

march down the long and irregular ravine; the arrival at an Indian village
among the mesquite groves, in which only one of the villagers remained, an
aged squaw, who scolded us in a language we did not understand.

By this time the physical condition of the party had deteriorated badly. It
had been weeks since they had escaped the "death hole of sand and salt," and
more hostile terrain lay before them. Mr. Brier, who had always been "active,
enterprising, and irrepressible," could do no more than stagger on with the assistance of two sticks. Two members of the Brier party succumbed—Mr. Fish,
who lay unburied where he had fallen, and Mr. Isham, his mouth and throat
so dry and parched and his strength so drained that he was unable to swallow
a single drop of the coffee that Juliette Brier had prepared for him.

Young John Brier picked up their trek through the Panamint desert.

Toward evening of the second day [of our crossing] we approached a narrow
fissure, with perpendicular walls a thousand feet high. Its floor was of level
sand, and rose steeply at the upper end. As we approached the end of the
dreary chasm the thirsty cattle sniffed the air and broke into a trot. But the
water proved to be only a slow trickle, which, in a hour, yielded enough for a
ration of coffee before sleeping.

The next day ... at the end of a most discouraging afternoon we suddenly
emerged upon a scene as wonderful as it was unexpected—a great body of
water shining only a few miles across the desert. Again it was the mirage, but
we did not discover this for many hours. Long past midnight we came up to
it, and found only a basin of slime.

Juliette Brier, driving the emaciated oxen *and* holding on to her three young
sons, vividly recalled the agony of that trek.

It was always the same—hunger and thirst, and an awful silence. ... Our
greatest suffering for water was near Borax Lake. We were forty-eight hours
without a drop.

My husband tied little Kirke to his back and staggered ahead. The child
would murmur occasionally. "Oh father, where's the water?" His pitiful de-
lirious wails were worse to bear than the killing thirst. It was terrible. I seem
to see it all over again. I staggered and struggled behind with our other two
boys and the oxen. The little fellows bore up bravely and rarely complained,
though they could hardly talk, so swollen were their lips and tongues. John
would try to cheer up his brother Kirke by telling him of the wonderful wa-

ter we would find and all the good things we could get to eat. Every step I ex-
pected to sink down and die. I could hardly see.

By now the entire party was desperate. As one after another of those searching for water returned unsuccessfully, death from thirst seemed certain.
Juliette Brier, praying for delivery, was still confident that water would be
found. As she attempted to reassure her children, one of the members of their
party, Deacon Richards, rushed into camp with the news that he had discovered a stream, which they named Providence Springs. They camped there for
two days, during which they killed an ox and "jerked" the meat.

Despite this brief respite, the next days were among the worst of the journey as the group struggled through the Argos Mountains and across the El
Paso Range and pressed on toward the Mojave desert, where Joshua trees were
growing in the dusty soil. Young John Brier remembered:

We went along an Indian trail into a defile in one of the branches of which
my elder brother lost his way. He corrected his mistake in time, and was met
by his agitated parents, driving his oxen and whistling in absolute uncon-
cern. … My mother was nearly distracted with fear of his capture by Indians
before he again joined us.

They pressed on southward. Once into the Coast Range, they found grass
for forage and water. But some of the emigrants had endured beyond the limit
of survival. At one abundant spring, a man named Robinson lay down to nap,
"weary-like," as Juliette Brier observed, "and his life went out." She continued:

Sometimes we found water and grass in plenty, but never a thing to eat. And
the silence of it all! "Oh!" I thought, "if I could only see something to show
the end of our journey." But I didn't dare speak of it for fear of alarming the
children.

  But I never lost hope. I couldn't give up. We needed all our hope and faith.
I knew before starting we would have to suffer, but my husband wanted to
go, and he needed me.

Deliverance finally came. On February 4, 1850, a group of wide-eyed Jayhawkers beheld the sight of a vast herd of cattle and an old Spaniard and some
Native American vaqueros galloping up on fine horses. Juliette Brier described their encounter with the owners of the del Valle ranch.

The Spaniard was amazed at our appearance, I suppose. We looked more like skeletons than human beings. Our clothes hung in tatters. My dress was in ribbons, and my shoes hard, baked, broken pieces of leather. Some of the company still had the remains of worn out shoes with their feet sticking through, and some wore pieces of ox hide tied about their feet. My boys wore ox hide moccasins.

The old man took off his hat, bowed and said in a broken voice, "poor little Padre!" [to Mr. Brier]. He led us up to his house and the old lady burst out crying when she saw our condition. They were very kind and cooked us a grand feast. … It was like coming back from death into life again.

Young John gratefully remembered the Spaniards' hospitality.

The morning of our arrival, the Indians were ordered to drive up a band of horses and mules, that animals might be selected for our journey to Los Angeles. A quiet bay pony was chosen for my mother. Two pillows served for a saddle; and when she was placed in position, I was lifted to a seat behind her. My younger brother was secured at the back by the use of a silk handkerchief.

Twenty miles to Los Angeles. We had walked twice as far within twenty hours, over waterless wastes of sand and stony mesa. This was a pleasure trip! About half way, we halted before a small hacienda, and were saluted by a Senora, who invited us to enter for rest and refreshment. We were glad to accept her hospitality; and she served us with tortillas, milk and cheese. … The remainder of our journey was without incident, and we halted in the evening on a hill overlooking Los Angeles.

The Wade family arrived in Los Angeles one week after the Briers. They had stayed at Travertine Springs with the Bennett-Arcane party and moved south with them at the beginning of the new year. Manly observed in his report on their escape from Death Valley that "Mr. Wade, his wife and … children who did not mingle with our party, but usually camped a little distance off, followed our trail, but seemed to shun our company."

This "distance" might have been a result of traditional English reticence or even a bit of snobbery. Wade had been a coachman to the king of England and his wife a governess to the children of the French ambassador at the British court. More likely, however, the distance was a practical matter of survival. Following in the wake of the Bennett-Arcane party saved the Wades from having to scout and allowed small water seeps, exhausted by the others, to refill.

The Wades had to meet the needs of a thirsty throng of three adults (the parents and a teamster who drove their wagon) and four children: fourteen-year-old Henry, eleven-year-old Charles, nine-year-old Almira, and five-year-old Richard. They also had four oxen to care for.

Fifty-year-old Henry Wade was more experienced than the other emigrants in the care and handling of dray animals and wagons. He took the lead in searching for a wagon pass further south. Instead of crossing the Panamint Mountains, he and his family went to Saratoga Spring before turning west. In just a week they reached the Mojave River and the Spanish Trail, near present-day Barstow. Almira Wade, his nine-year-old daughter, remembered:

> *A Frenchman was hired for his board to assist my brother Harry, the oldest*
> *of us children, in prospecting ahead, and whenever they could find water or*
> *feed, they signaled our party by a fire, Indian fashion. But we were often*
> *obliged to camp without anything but barren sand. Everyone carried all the*
> *water they could in canteens and powder cans, and drank all the water they*
> *could when leaving a place where they found it. But it was so hot, and our*
> *thirst so overpowering, that the water never lasted long.*

After many hardships, the Wades struck the Mojave River and a trail along its banks that had plenty of grass and water. On January 29 they met a group of miners who were coming from California and who gave them a pail of flour. Soon after, some cattlemen took them to their camp, where they were rendering tallow. The men baked "tortillas"—thin cakes made of flour and water—for the Wade family. They allowed their hungry guests to dip the tortillas in the boiling tallow and to eat as much as was safe for them. "It was the best meal I ever ate in my life," remembered the little girl.

The Wades arrived at Roberts Mill, near Los Angeles, on February 10, 1850, with their wagon intact. The Bennett-Arcane families would take another four weeks to escape from Death Valley.

By the end of the first week of the new year, the wagons of the Bennett-Arcane party were wending their way slowly from one spring to the next along the foot of the Panamints until they reached a small water hole south of what today is Bennett's Well. Seeing a pass at the head of the canyon to the west, they decided to take their wagons over it. They struggled for two days pulling the wagons up the canyon before they realized they could not get through.

They returned to the water hole and debated long into the night about what they should do next. Manly, their scout, remembered:

*We had a few small pieces of dry bread. This was kept for the children giving
them a little now and then. Our only food was in the flesh of the oxen, and
when they failed to carry themselves along we must begin to starve. Mr.
Bennett spoke and said: "Now I will make you a proposition, I propose that
we select two of our youngest, strongest men to ask them to take some food
and go ahead on foot to try to seek a settlement, and food, and we will go
back to the good spring we have just left and wait for their return."*

Twenty-nine-year-old Manly and twenty-five-year-old John Rogers were
selected, and they consented to go. The following day, January 15, 1850, they
started off on foot for the settlements, taking with them about ten days' rations of beef jerky, a couple of spoonfuls of rice, and about as much tea. "This
seemed like robbery to the children," observed Manly. They were also given
around sixty dollars in coin with which to buy food to bring back. The rest of
the party—men, women, and children—moved several miles north to the
fresh grass and springs at Bennett's Well to await the return of "the boys."

Manly and Rogers were gone twenty-six days, and they covered about five
hundred miles on their rescue mission to the ranches in the San Fernando valley. Travelling light and moving fast, they caught up with some of the Jayhawkers at Indian Wells, passed the rest near Red Rock Canyon, and reached
the San Fernando Mission on the eleventh day of their journey. They spent
the night there and were treated with kindness.

The next day, January 26, they reached the del Valle adobe. There, with the
aid of Tejon rancher Darwin French, they bought three packhorses, a little
one-eyed mule, and sacks of beans and wheat for their return trip. Manly remembered with special affection the Spanish señora who helped them pack
their supplies.

*She put me in mind of my mother, only she was of dark complexion. ... She
came in with a small child by her side and pointed to it and to us and then
held up her hand and shut it one finger at a time. I now understood that she
had been told that we had children back in the mountains. To answer her, I
put my hand on my breast, and then held it up, keeping my thumb down.
By this she understood that there were four children. ... When we got ready
to start ... the woman came out with four oranges in her hand and pointed
to her child and by signs gave us to understand we must take the fruit to the
children and not eat it ourselves.*

When they left the Bennett-Arcane families, Manly and Rogers had hoped
to be back in fifteen days. Now they knew it would take them many more

days to complete the return trip. "We said to each other," wrote Manly, "if no women and children was out there we would not go back." But back they went, trying desperately to make time. In retracing their route, they rode their animals too hard. One horse dropped dead in the Argus Range, and the other two gave out trying to climb the Panamint Mountains. Only the little one-eyed mule, wise to the desert, was unhurt.

Back in Death Valley, the Bennetts and Arcanes were beginning to think waiting was a mistake. They had expected Manly and Roger to return in two weeks, but when three and a half weeks had passed with no sign of the two men, the rest of the group decided they must move on their own. To stay meant they would surely die. By February 9 they had stripped the canvas off their wagons and were making packs and harnesses for their oxen when they heard a rifle shot, which had been fired by Manly. "The boys are coming! The boys are coming!" shouted one member of the party. It was a joyous reunion, lasting late into the night, as the families ate their first real meal in months. But the joy did not last long. Reported Manly:

> When they heard us relate the story of our journey for their relief, they were almost in despair. Said they, "When such men as you and John had all you could do to get out, what are we to do?" The two small children were not able to walk. Mr. Bennett's youngest [Martha, age 4], that a few months before scampered about camp as lively as a quail, was now helpless. It had been sick during our absence. … Her limbs had lost all the flesh and seemed nothing but skin and bones, while her body had grown corpulent and distended, and her face had a starved pinched and suffering look, with no healthy color.

But forge ahead they must. The two families packed everything their oxen could carry and left their wagons and most of their belongings behind. Their final journey was about to begin.

THE LAST TREK

To accommodate the two youngest children—two-year-old Charlie Arcane and four-year-old Martha Bennett—the group took two of their strongest hickory shirts, turned the sleeves inside the bodies of the shirts, sewed up the necks, and then sewed the two shirts together at the flaps, making two pockets. The two smallest children were put in the pockets on each side of a slow and steady ox, facing outward. The two older Bennett children—George (age eight) and Melissa (age five)—were placed on top of "Old Crump" and given a strap with which to steady themselves.

On February 11, 1850, the last trek of the Bennett-Arcane party began. Rogers led the march with his ox and the one-eyed mule; Manly guided the other pack animals; each woman rode on an ox; and Arcane followed, leading Old Crump with the children. They had gone only four miles when Mrs. Arcane's ox began to buck and kick, and Mrs. Bennett's ox joined the rampage. The sight was more comic than tragic, for no one was hurt. Manly observed:

> *Arcane stood holding on to "Old Crump," but the big children jumped off, and Mrs. Bennett snatched the little ones out of the pockets for fear he would get frisky also, and she followed on carrying the youngest, the perspiration running down her face. After this ... we concluded we had better go in camp and repair damages. [On the second day of the trek] the women did not attempt to ride but followed on, close after Old Crump and the children who required almost constant attention, for in their cramped position they made many cries and complaints. ... At the end of the day's march, Bennett took poor little Martha from the pocket and carried her in his arms. ... Arcane also took his child ... throwing away his double barrel gun, saying: "I have no use for you."*

By nightfall the next day, they were nearly out of Death Valley. They camped high in the Panamint Mountains at a spring just short of the crest. From the summit the following morning, February 15, Manly, Bennett, and Arcane took a long look back. Manly observed, "Just as we were ready to leave camp, we took off our hats, and then, overlooking the scene of so much trial, suffering and death, spoke the thought uppermost in our minds, saying:— 'Good-by Death Valley!'"

But their trek was not over. They travelled first along the foot of the highest mountain peak, over bare rocks, and then turned south, entering a narrow canyon where they had to lower both their belongings and the children over a steep precipice. At the end of the first week of their journey, "There was little water left in the canteens, to be given only to the children, who would cry when thirsty," noted Manly, "the very thing to make them feel the worst."

On the eighth day of the trek, camp was made at a salt-water hole. Little Charlie Arcane broke out with a rash all over his body and cried bitterly day and night. No one could offer him any relief; no medicine was left.

During the second week of their trek, the party crossed the large expanse of China Lake valley and reached Indian Wells on February 21. They found water holes and filled their canteens, and their spirits lifted. "All began to talk more and feel more hopeful of getting through," observed Manly. They made camp the next day near Walker Pass and saw the sun rise over a great sea of mountains to the east of Death Valley. On February 25, the fourteenth day of the trek, the group camped in the desert near present-day Mojave. They had walked fifteen to twenty miles each day. Manly noted that the disposition of the children had improved—with the exception of the youngest child.

Arcane's boy Charley still suffered from his bogus measles or whatever else his disorder might be, and Bennett's little Martha grew more quiet and improved considerably in health, though still unable to walk, and still abdominally corpulent. The other two children, George and Melissa, seemed to bear up well and loved to get off and walk in places where the trail was smooth and level. Bennett, Arcane and Old Crump usually traveled with the same party as the women, and as each of them had a small canteen to carry water, they could attend to the wants of the children and keep them from worrying and getting sick from fretfulness. They often carried the two younger ones on their backs to relieve and rest them from their cramped position on the ox. Everyone tried to be just as accommodating as they could and each one would put himself to trouble to relieve others.

By the third week of the trek, the trials of the trail were beginning to take their toll. With one foot plodding after another, each mile became more of an effort. Young Charlie Arcane seemed to grow worse rather than better. His entire body was as red as fire, and he screamed constantly because of the pain of the severe itching. Nothing could be done to relieve him.

The party began their ascent into the foothills southeast of Palmdale. "We breathed with much more freedom," wrote Manly, "when we knew we had at last left the horrible desert behind us." Little Charlie Arcane was beginning to feel better. The change in air and water had begun to effect a cure. He was placed back in his pocket on the faithful ox. Manly noted, "Old Crump bore the same four children, every day, carefully, with never a stumble or fall, as though fully aware of the precious nature of his burden."

On March 7, 1850, the epic trek was over. The group reached the foot of a hill, only a hundred yards from the del Valle ranch. Manly described the reunion with the Spanish señora.

Scarcely had we removed the harness from the oxen when the good lady of the house and her little child came down to see us. She stood for a moment and looked around her and at the ... small children on the blankets, and we could hear her murmur "mucha pobre" [very poor]. She could see our ragged clothes and dirty faces and everything told her of our extreme destitution. She then turned to us, Roger and I, whom she had seen before, and as her

*lively little youngster clung to her dress, as if in fear of such queer looking
people as we were, she took an orange from her pocket and pointing to the
children of our party, wanted to know if we had given them the four oranges
she sent to them by us. We made signs that we had done as she requested,
when she smiled and said "Buenos Muchachos" [good boys].*

The Spaniards invited the Bennett and Arcane families to their house.
There they were given a good supper of tortillas, beans seasoned with pepper,
baked squash, and chili con carne—meat with pepper. "We soon found this
to be one of the best dishes cooked by the Californians," observed Manly. The
children were carefully waited on and were given special attention by the señora. It was late in the evening by the time the feast was over. Manly observed:

*The unaccustomed shelter of a roof and the restless worrying of the children,
who required much attention, for the change of diet had about the same effect on them as on Rogers and myself when we first partook of the California
food, gave them little sleep, but still they rested and were truly grateful for
the most perfect hospitality of these kind hearted people.*

The Arcanes left the party the next day. They made a bargain with the
Spaniards to take them to San Pedro, the nearest seaport, about sixty miles
away and offered them their remaining two oxen for pay. The others departed
on March 10. Wrote Manly:

*Our little train now seemed much smaller. Three oxen and a mule were all
our animals, and the adults must still walk, as they had done on our desert
route. … We put our luggage on the oxen and the mule, loaded the children
on Old Crump as we had done before, and were ready to move again. Our
good friends stood around and smiled good-naturedly at our queer arrangements, and we, now knowing how to say what our hearts would prompt us
to, shook their hands and said good bye in answer to their "adios amigos" as
we moved away, waving hands to each other.*

EPILOGUE

The Arcane family went from San Pedro to Santa Cruz, where Abigail gave
birth to a daughter, Julia, with whom she had been pregnant on their fateful
journey. The little girl lived only nineteen days and died in July 1850—Death
Valley's youngest victim.

Abigail Arcane had two more daughters. The oldest, also named Julia, was handicapped and required extensive care. But her mother never lost her stamina, strength, and determination. Captivated by the beauty of the redwoods, she told her husband: "You can go into the mines if you want to. I have seen all the God-forsaken country I am going to see, for I am going to stay right here as long as I live."

John Baptiste honored his wife's wishes. He opened a gunsmith store in Santa Cruz, and he and his family prospered. Little Charlie became a machinist, owned a bar, and played in a band.

Bennett's attempt at mining failed, and he eventually turned to farming at Moss Landing, near Santa Cruz. The children—George, Martha, and Melissa—all settled in southern California.

With the profit from the sale of the oxen Juliette had herded across Death Valley, the Briers purchased a half interest in a Los Angeles hotel and "a fine old vineyard." Mrs. Brier was in command of the kitchen, from whence no dried beef jerky was ever served. Reverend Brier preached the first Protestant service ever given in Los Angeles. Giving up on the imminent salvation of the townsfolk, the Briers moved north to Marysville and Lodi, where John Jr., the middle son, followed in his father's footsteps and became a minister. Christopher Columbus Brier ran a private school in the San Francisco Bay area, and Kirke White Brier became a principal at Sacramento High School. The indomitable Juliette outlived her husband and all of her children except one son and died in Lodi in 1913—at age ninety-nine. Shortly before she died she wrote, "Life is not unpleasant and I still like to meet friends of Long Ago." Manly, the major chronicler of the Death Valley saga, wrote of her, "All agreed she was by far the best man of the party."

The Wade family mined along the Tuolomne River and eventually settled in Alviso, at the southern edge of San Francisco Bay. There they took up a freighting business and later ran a stagecoach and an inn. The four Wade children—Henry Jr., Charles, Almira, and Richard—who had crossed the plains and desert with their family, and Mary Ann, who was born in California, all married and had large families. The Wades were the only family to bring a wagon out of Death Valley. They used it in their freighting business, and their grandchildren loved to play in it.

Manly tried mining, in partnership with Bennett, moving north from the Merced River to Coloma where the first gold nuggets that brought about the rush of 1849 had been found. While prospecting in that region, his faithful dog, Cuff, who had been with him during the entire trek through Death Valley, disappeared, and Manly mourned his loss.

A few months later, he found Old Crump feeding with a herd of cattle in the San Joaquin valley. The ox, fat and sleek, allowed itself to be petted. Its current owner would not sell it or allow it to be worked, for "he knew the faithful part he had performed in the world, and respected him for it."

Manly returned to Wisconsin for a short time, but the gold fever was still in him. By July 1851 he was back in San Francisco, and he mined, with fair results, in Downieville and Moore's Flat, where he also ran a small store. In 1859 he settled in San Jose. He died in 1903 at age eighty-three.

His companion on the rescue trip, Rogers, tried mining as well and later worked in a quicksilver (mercury) smelter. Its lethal fumes resulted in the loss of both his feet at the instep. A lifelong bachelor, he continued to support himself as a carpenter, mechanic, and farmhand on a ranch near Merced. In 1894 he wrote a brief account of his journey for the *Merced Star*. In 1895, more than forty years after they had last met and one year after he had published his book *Death Valley in '49*, Manly visited "Big John" to rekindle old memories of their journey through hell.

George Hansen, the Shoshone Indian who had watched the group silently as they escaped from Death Valley, lived to be nearly a hundred years old. In February 1940, in an interview shortly before his death, he said:

The hearts of our people were heavy for these strange people, but we were afraid; they had things that made fire with a loud noise and we had never seen these before. After this happened we were afraid more of the strange ones would come.

And they did.

An Ordinary Journey

O N OCTOBER 18, 1850, the sidewheel steamer *Oregon* arrived in San Francisco Bay, draped with hundreds of yards of red and white bunting. From mast to mast hung a sheet of canvas on which was painted in large letters, CALIFORNIA ADMITTED! Facing the other side of the vessel was another sign bearing the message CALIFORNIA IS A STATE!

Congress had approved statehood on September 9, but it had taken forty days for the news to travel from Washington, D.C., to the shores of the Pacific. The young editor of the *Alta California* wrote, "We are now in the Union, thank God! We are in the United States of America once more."

That year, around forty-four thousand people crossed half a continent to reach the Golden State, nearly twice as many as in 1849 when the gold rush had taken off in earnest. In 1852 the number of California-bound travellers was even larger, reaching a high of fifty thousand. Their journey was made easier than those of their predecessors because there were now more military posts and commercial enterprises along the overland routes and more accurate guides to point the way.

Most of the California gold had been depleted by 1853, but about twenty thousand emigrants were still heading west, many to join relatives—fathers or brothers—who had gone out earlier. Overland travel by families became rare between 1854 and 1858. Reports of hostilities against wagon trains had increased, and there was intermittent warfare between Plains Indians and soldiers of the U.S. Army. When the skirmishes abated in 1859, there was an upswing in overland traffic to the thirty-first state in the Union.

THE OVERLAND ROUTE

Most emigrants in the 1850s followed the tried-and-true Platte River Road. Conscientious travellers bought a popular guidebook by Franklin Street, *Cali-*

California Emigrants: The Last Day on the Plains (courtesy Bancroft Library, University of California–Berkeley)

fornia in 1850, to obtain a "concise description of the overland route from the Missouri River, by the South Pass, to Sacramento City, including a table of distances from point to point." It is interesting to compare the accounts given in Street's book with the observations of the children who travelled along that road.

> For those who design procuring their outfit at some point on the river, ST. JOSEPH is the most suitable.
>
> —GUIDEBOOK

> *We expect to remain here several days, laying in supplies for the trip and waiting our turn to be ferried across the river. As far as the eye can reach, so great is the emigration, you see nothing but wagons ... a vast army on wheels—crowds of men, women, and lots of children.*
>
> —Sallie Hester, age fourteen, 1849

> From ST. JOSEPH the road runs through the bottom, which is covered with a dense growth of cotton-wood and other timber. It is very crooked, and in some places extremely muddy.
>
> —GUIDEBOOK

The first part of [the route] is beautiful and the scenery surpassing anything of the kind I have ever seen—large rolling prairies stretching as far as your eye can carry you. ... The grass so green and flowers of every description from violets to geraniums of the richest hue. Then leaving this beautiful scenery behind, you descend into the woodland which is ... interspersed with creeks.

—Elizabeth Keegan, age twelve, 1852

288 miles. FORT KEARNEY.—The Fort is situated near the head of Grand Island. From Fort Kearney you will travel most of the way near the banks of the [Platte] River on a good road.

—GUIDEBOOK

I had never seen a soldier before and thought they must be wild men. I was more afraid of them than I was of the Indians.

—Florence Weeks, age eight, 1859

468 miles. ASH HOLLOW.—About twenty miles above ASH HOLLOW, you will come in sight of COURT HOUSE and CHIMNEY ROCK.

—GUIDEBOOK

At noon we camped in sight of the Court House Rock. ... By the aid of our spy glass we can plainly see the cracks and crevices in ... [its] walls.

At noon [next day] we were nearly opposite the "Chimney Rock,"... on the south side of the River. ... Near this we found some wild southern wood ... also some beautiful carnations and roses.

—Eliza McAuley, age seventeen, 1852

604 miles. FORT LARAMIE.—The best way here is to cross the Laramie River about one mile below the Fort and go up the valley of the Platte.

—GUIDEBOOK

A short distance away we can see the Fort, and yesterday morning I went to visit it. Saw several large white houses, which made me think of home, as it has been a long time since we had seen any. The trees, too, looked very nice and cool.

—Maria Elliott, a teenager, 1859

By the time they reached Fort Laramie, the emigrant children and their families had traveled one-third of the distance between their departure point on the Missouri River and their destination—California. They now began their ascent into the Black Hills, "sixty miles over the worst road in the world," as Sallie Hester wrote in 1849.

786 miles. INDEPENDENCE ROCK.—This rock stands on the north side of the river, and is so close to the bank that there is but room enough for wagons to pass. It is ... a singular curiosity.

—GUIDEBOOK

A party of fourteen of us went to visit Independence Rock. ... It is one solid mass of granite, rather steep, but we ascended it without much difficulty. Found many names and dates inscribed upon it; one written in 1849. But we wrote our names on a piece of paper, and put it under the edge of a large rock on the top. It is the grandest sight that we have seen yet. ... Found near the top a large natural basin of water in the solid rock, where we bathed our heads, and washed our face.

—Maria Elliott, 1859

791 miles. DEVILS GATE.—This is a place where the river passes between perpendicular rocks, four hundred feet high.

—GUIDEBOOK

Several of us climbed this mountain—somewhat perilous for youngsters not over fourteen. We made our way to the very edge of the cliff and looked down. We could hear the water dashing, splashing and roaring as if angry at the small space through which it was forced to pass. We were gone so late that the train was stopped and men sent out in search of us.

—Sallie Hester, 1849

886 miles. SUMMIT OF THE SOUTH PASS.—The country westward from here has the appearance of a vast plain, which you will find very barren, being void of almost every kind of vegetation.

—GUIDEBOOK

Ate luncheon on the South Pass of the Rocky Mountains. Altitude seven thousand, four hundred feet, but the ascent is so gradual, that one scarcely knows when one is at the summit. The headwaters of the streams flowing eastward to the Mississippi and those flowing westward to the Pacific are but a few feet apart.

—Eliza McAuley, 1852

1,009 miles. FORT BRIDGER.—The fort has a very handsome location in a valley formed and watered by three small streams. Road very hilly and rough from here to the City of the Great Salt Lake.

—GUIDEBOOK

The flag impressed me more than anything I saw there. This was the third Fort we passed through.

—Florence Weeks, 1859

1,128 miles. CITY OF THE GREAT SALT LAKE.—The city is situated 22 miles from the lake, and three miles from the mountains that enclose it on the east. It is very handsomely located.

—GUIDEBOOK

We camped for a week near Salt Lake City. It was a beautiful city. … Every block had a stream of clear, sparkling water running around it. We purchased fresh vegetables there, and they were the best we had every tasted. On the 24th of July the Mormons celebrated. There was a grand parade through the streets, and Brigham Young and his many wives were in the procession. … I saw Brigham Young's home—several buildings joined together. Each wife had a separate home where she lived with her children. We saw Salt Lake at a distance, and when the sun shone on it, it looked like a lake of gold.

—Mary E. Ackley, age ten, 1852

The last third of the journey—from the Great Salt Lake, along the meandering Humboldt River, across the forty-mile desert and the summit of the Sierra Nevada—was the most daunting part of the overland trek.

1,428 miles. HUMBOLDT RIVER—This river you will find very bad fording, being deep and its banks steep and miry.

—GUIDEBOOK

When we reached the first crossing of the stream, all stood aghast. It seemed impossible that any wagon could cross over the rocks, but what could we do? We just had to cross over, so the men mustered up courage and made the attempt. I watched one wagon cross. As many men could get hold of the wagon went into the stream and literally carried the wagon over the rocks. The poor oxen fell down time and again before they reached the other side. Each wagon went through the same trial until all had crossed. It took us the whole day to go four miles.

—Mary E. Ackley, 1852

1,736 miles. SINK OF HUMBOLDT.—When the river is up it spreads out in sloughs … but all sink away in the sand and are lost. … The first thirty-five miles of the desert, you will find the road mostly good, but the last ten miles is extremely sandy, it is best to cross as much of it as possible at night.

—GUIDEBOOK

Many teams go in this desert but few come out of it. We had great difficulty to get across. … The mules we had in our carriage gave out when we were about ten miles in. … We had to take a yoke of oxen out of a large wagon which so weakened the others that when we were within about twelve miles of being across we were compelled to leave the carriage behind.

—Elizabeth Keegan, 1852

1,912 miles. FOOT OF THE FIRST RIDGE OF THE SIERRA NEVADA.—You now commence ascending the mountains, which is about one mile to the summit, and most of the way extremely steep.

—GUIDEBOOK

This is the way it was managed: A dozen yoke of oxen were hitched to one wagon, and with hard pulling they reached the top. After all the wagons were over, we took lunch on top of the mountains, and then prepared to go down, which was more dangerous than going up, for in places the mountain was very steep. One yoke of oxen was hitched to a wagon, and one at a time went down. Heavy chains were fastened on behind the wagon and as many men as could catch hold of the chain did so, and when the wagon started they pulled back to keep the wagon from running down the mountain and killing the oxen. We were an exhausted community when we camped that night—the women and children as well as the men—for we had to walk all the way.

—Mary E. Ackley, 1852

1,923 miles. SUMMIT OF THE SIERRA NEVADA.—Near the summit are immense banks of snow. … You will now find the road very hilly.

—GUIDEBOOK

The crossing of the plains is nothing to the crossing of the mountains. Some of them are so high and steep you would scarcely think if you turned your cattle loose they could … get up. … After you cross the last of the mountains you descend into the Sacramento valley long looked for by the weary emigrant. The heat can scarcely be endured, particularly so on first coming down from the mountains. It is very cold on them. One night it froze so hard that the water in the bucket had half an inch thick of ice on it.

—Elizabeth Keegan, 1852

COVERED WAGON LIFE

Life on the long overland journey had a certain rhythm that needed to be attuned to the terrain and the climate. The overlanders began their journeys in the spring as soon as the prairie grasses could provide forage for their grazing animals—usually in mid- or late April. They followed the life-sustaining rivers that angled westward from the Missouri in the summer and crossed the mountains before the first heavy snow. To accomplish this feat, they had to establish a routine of daily travel, with regular times for meals and rest.

The emigrants would rise at four or five o'clock in the early morning, pull down their tents, load their wagons and fix breakfast. By seven o'clock they were ready to roll. At noon they stopped for an hour's rest. In the late afternoon the trail captain would give the signal to stop for the night. Wrote Mary Ackley:

We traveled about twelve miles a day, and then we stopped for the night. All the wagons were drawn up in a line, and then the tents were pitched behind them, forming a street. Then preparations began for supper.

Sallie Hester noted in her diary:

We have a cooking stove made of sheet iron, a portable table, tin plates and cups … knives and forks … camp stools. We sleep in our wagon on feather beds; the men who drive for us [sleep] in the tent. We live on bacon, ham, rice, dried fruits, molasses, packed butter, bread, coffee, tea and milk as we have our own cows. Occasionally some of the men kill an antelope and then we have a feast.

Children cherished this routine. They were part of a travelling community of family, friends, and neighbors and had their chores and assigned duties—

their company depended on them. "Gathering buffalo chips [for fuel] was Ester's and my job," wrote Florence Weeks. "We were rather finicky about it at first, but found they were as dry as a chip of wood. We had a basket with a handle on each side to carry them."

Another chore for children was cooping up the fowl when the train set out in the morning, letting them out at each campsite to feed, and cooping them up again for the night. Children were out early, gathering fresh eggs or drawing buckets of water from springs and rivers. Boys with hunting dogs and fishing rods would set out to enlarge the standard menu of bacon and salt pork, flapjacks, and dried fruit. Elisha Brooks, age eleven, recommended that last item only for its economy: "You need but one meal a day; you can eat dried apples for breakfast, drink water for dinner, and swell for supper."

Fourteen-year-old Rebecca Nutting remembered, "How we did relish the fish and venison and Buffalo steaks. We had fine home cured bacon, but we got tired and needed a change." And Maria Elliot liked to gather the berries that grew by the riverside. "They are the richest wild fruit I ever saw," she wrote in her diary.

Teenage girls like Maria helped their mothers with the baking and cooking. "The boys are stealing the cookies as fast as she can bake them," noted Eliza McAuley. Occasionally, Mother Nature interfered with the preparation of a meal. Wrote Eliza:

> *When we stopped to make camp, it was pouring rain. ... For two hours it hailed and rained and blew a perfect gale. When it slacked up a little we got out the provision box and ate a cold supper. Then each one rolled up in a wet blanket and slept until morning.*

Regardless of the weather—rain, hail, or dust storm—at night, boys as young as eleven or twelve took turns standing guard. Elisha Brooks remembered:

> *One of my brothers and I were standing our watch one night in one quarter of the field at a little distance from the camp; the cattle had laid down to rest; and by eleven o'clock all had become quiet. ... My head fell to nodding drowsily as I reclined against my resting pony, when suddenly an Indian yell rent the air, and wild, rushing, leaping shadows went hurtling by with shrieks and tumult awfully appealing. Our skeleton beasts sprang up and away like a whirlwind ... until the sound died in the distance, and silence fell upon us again.*

Each day, most emigrant children on the overland trail cared for their stock of cows, oxen, horses, and mules. During the twelve to twenty miles of daily travel, many youngsters rode their ponies ahead of the train. Sometimes they would choose a camping place; at other times they would help drive the cattle. Girls, too, would drive stock when their fathers or older brothers were too tired or too sick to do so. Wrote Eliza McAuley on July 4, 1852:

Made eighteen miles today and camped on the Big Sandy. Had to drive the cattle six miles toward the hills for grass. It has been so windy and dusty today that sometimes we could scarcely see the length of the team, and it blows so tonight that we cannot see the tent or get any supper, so we take a cold bite and go to bed in the wagon.

The young travellers had great sympathy for the animals that carried their families and their belongings across thousands of miles of difficult terrain. When their oxen and horses suffered, the children were in anguish as well. Wrote Mary Ackley:

I must pay a tribute to our wheel oxen, Dick and Berry, who drew the family wagon all the way across the plains. They were gentle, kind, patient and reliable. I loved them and my heart often ached for them when they tried to hold back the wagon on a steep hill, and sometimes the wagon would strike them in spite of the driver's carefulness, and the dumb animals gave no sign of distress, although I knew they suffered.

And Florence Weeks remembered:

We had a horse we called Muggins, the homeliest piece of horseflesh I have ever seen—a dirty color, great big head, and crooked hind legs. I was riding him one afternoon with sisters Esther and Alice on other horses and we got way behind the train. After a while this old horse started and I couldn't hold him, could only hang on. I thought when he got to the rear wagon he would stop but he kept going until he got up front beside our wagon. I rolled off. I heard the laughs from the other wagons as I passed by. ... Poor old Muggins had lots of horse sense—Mother, Esther and I cried when we had to leave him near the Sink of the Humboldt.

Pets, too, were cherished companions on the long journey—whether a faithful dog or a tame squirrel or even a tame antelope named Jennie. Jennie's owner, Eliza McAuley, recorded the animal's antics in her diary.

We came near losing our pet antelope this evening. As she was frisking about the camp, a man from another camp was about to shoot her, thinking she was a wild one. She ran to another camp where a woman got hold of her and held her, and would scarcely believe that she belonged to me, though the poor little thing was struggling to get away and bleating piteously for me. Finally she got away and came bounding to me and followed me home.

Life on the overland trail was not all tiresome drudgery; it was also filled with adventure and merriment. Music was a favorite entertainment on the trail, when the wagon trains were camped in the evenings or laid over for a Sabbath rest. "Our journey was very pleasant," wrote Mary Ackley. "The young people danced in the evening by the moonlight and the little children, too, had merry times." Observed Maria Elliott:

The boys had quite a joyful time last night. A man from Mr. Feiser's train came over and played the violin and some sang. He is a first rate player. There were fifty-one sitting round to hear the music until quite late. ... [Some time later] we stopped for dinner. ... A company was passing and we heard some very good instrumental music. ... There was a man that played on the flute, and a girl that played on the bass viole. ... They give concerts in the towns they pass through.

There was other entertainment on the trail that drew an appreciative crowd. Reported Eliza McAuley:

We camped here near some good sulphur springs. There are a great many camped here and a merrier set I never saw. Just after dark we were treated to a variety of barnyard music in various parts of the camp. Roosters crowed, hens cackled, ducks quacked, pigs squealed, owls hooted, donkeys brayed, dogs howled, cats squalled and all these perfect imitations were made by the human voice.

Among special occasions for merriment on the trail were weddings and Fourth of July celebrations. Rebecca Nutting witnessed a surprise party for some newlyweds.

David Parker and Catharine Hickman was married. Such a Chivarie as they got that night was enough to awaken the seven sleepers. The newly married couple occupied a wagon for sleeping apartments. The first notice they had of any disturbance was when most of the men and women in the com-

pany took hold of the wagon, the men at the tongue pulling, the women at the back pushing, and ran the wagon a half mile out on the prairie. Then the fun began. Such a banging of cans, shooting of guns and every noise conceivable was resorted to. The disturbance was kept up until midnight.

Maria Elliott celebrated Independence Day in the company of several wagon trains. Her diary entry on July 4, 1859, reads:

I was awakened this morning bright and early by the firing of guns from some distant companies. It seems that they had not forgotten Independence Day [even] if they were far away on the plains, and from home and friends. Got breakfast quite early, but before breakfast the boys fired off some shooters. Had apple dumplings for supper which were very good. We had an invitation … to a Fourth of July dance. … After supper, [brother] Jack played on the violin, and some of the boys sang before retiring.

A favorite pastime of the young diarists on the overland trail was reading. Popular books like *The Life of Daniel Boone, Pilgrim's Progress,* and *Robinson Crusoe* kept them company on the long journey. Sallie Hester and Eliza McAuley wrote frequent letters to their friends, and others sketched some of the scenery along the way.

Maria Elliott worked on her embroidery when she had time to spare, and Eliza McAuley practiced target shooting with her brother's pistol. "I was very expert at missing the mark," she wrote in her diary, "but managed to hit the tree three times out of five."

Fifteen-year-old Mary Margaret Hezlep assembled nine patch blocks for a quilt she had stitched, together with her mother and maternal grandmother, as their wagon train made its long and arduous journey west. "Ho for California" is written on one block; others read "Left Hamilton April 15, 1859," "Seven months on the road," "Crossed the Plains," and "Arrived in California, October 18, 1859."

ENCOUNTERS WITH NATIVE AMERICANS

Of all the exotic sights that attracted the curiosity of the youngsters on the overland trail, the indigenous people elicited the widest range of emotions, from anxiety to ambivalence to genuine affection. First encounters were usually fraught with more negative emotions for the children than were later ones, for they were based on fears of theft or bodily harm to themselves or their animals.

The popular guidebooks fostered some of this anxiety, especially with re-gard to the poorer tribes—the Pawnee in Kansas and eastern Nebraska and the Root Diggers of the Humboldt River region. Joseph Ware wrote in his 1849 *Emigrants' Guide to California*, "In the Pawnee country watchfulness is required to prevent their stealing your stock." Franklin Street warned in his *California in 1850*, "The Digger Indians have been troublesome ... stealing horses and mules."

Occasionally, some of these fears were justified. Wrote Sallie Hester in May 1849:

> *We are now in the Pawnee Nation. ... We are obliged to watch them closely and double our guards at night. They never make their appearance during the day, but skulk around at night, steal cattle, and do all the mischief they can.*

Mary E. Ackley experienced some of that "mischief" in 1852.

> *Long before daylight the camp was astir. The captain and father were sitting by the campfire when the cook was preparing breakfast. They heard some-thing flying over their heads and remarked: "How strange for birds to be fly-ing in the darkness; what could have disturbed them?" And they heard it again and again. Day was breaking and we were ready to start, when to our surprise and horror we found arrows all over the camp. Some had gone through the covers of two wagons, but no one was injured. Several cattle had been killed and father had an ox wounded. ... The supposed birds captain and father had heard were arrows shot by the Indians on the hillside. That was the only time we had trouble with the Indians during the whole trip.*

Once the emigrant children overcame their initial fear of Native Ameri-cans, they recorded their observations much as any self-respecting modern anthropologist would do. Wrote Mary Hite in 1853:

> *Saw our first Indian. We children stayed close to camp but Father said the Indians were civilized. The Indians were nude save for a throw over one shoulder, & a strap around the loins. The leader of the tribe would wear a band of feathers around his head—when a young Indian would kill his first bird, it would be tied to his hair and he would wear it for a few days.*

Maria Elliott reported in 1859:

*We met a party of Indian warriors. They had been making a treaty of peace
with the Sioux. They had their pipe of peace. They were dressed very well;
had capes and coats on and a great many ornaments. Some had beads on
their necks, brass earrings, and finger rings on every finger. Some had tin ornaments for a sash; the tin was round and about two inches in diameter.
They also had feathers on their head. They came up to the carriage and
shook hands with us. Said they were Pawnees.*

If the emigrants took the time to become acquainted with surrounding
tribes, their youngsters usually learned to appreciate their customs. Wrote
Eliza McAuley in 1852:

*While we were getting supper, the Pawnee chief and twelve of his braves
came and expressed a desire to camp with us. . . . It takes quite an amount of
provisions to entertain them, but some willow boughs strewn around the
camp fire suffice them for a bed. At break of day, the Indians awoke us, singing their morning song. The old chief started the song and the others chimed
in and it was very harmonious and pleasing.*

The Native Americans were equally curious about the customs of the emigrants. Maria Elliott reported in 1859:

*There is an Indian village a short distance from our camp. It is quite a small
one, only about twenty wigwams. Had been there only a short time when a
goodly number of the inhabitants called on us. . . . They were very much
amused at our singing, and when we would stop, they would motion for us
to go on. . . . They stayed until dark, when they left for their homes. As I was
writing on the ground, by the side of the wagon, a great number came
around me and stood looking at my writing for a long time. I suppose it was
quite a novelty for them.*

Florence Weeks described a similar encounter with curious members of the
Snake tribe in 1859.

*We had our lunch near where five hundred Indians were gathered and after-
wards Mother was sewing and some of the squaws came to watch her. They
jabbered and laughed. Finally Mother gave one of them a needle and
thread, and she was so pleased, then all of them wanted one.*

Emigrants often accorded their greatest compliments to the Sioux. Ten-year-old Kate McDaniel described her fascination with the young daughter of a Sioux chief who visited her camp in 1853.

> *She was about fifteen years old and ... very beautiful. ... She was dressed in a loose white buckskin gown, soft as silk. ... The skirt came to her knees and she wore long leggings. The bottom of the dress had deep fringes on it. ... I could not keep my eyes off her. ... The old chief was very proud of his daughter and she was a favorite in camp.*
>
> *The little princess, as we liked to call her, let us pet her pony and then she showed us how she could ride and what her pony could do. ... Then [she] jumped into her saddle, waved her hand to us, and with a little giggling laugh, was gone like a beautiful bird.*

The Sioux were equally fascinated with white children. Elisha Brooks reported that "they offered a pony for a boy and two for a girl. ... No mother wished to sell her children at that price, though our teamster tried to dispose of me in this way, claiming that was more than I was worth." In 1853, an Indian tried to buy Mary Hite for three ponies, but her parents thought she was priceless.

The Plains Indians were usually generous to the emigrant families, providing them with information, clothing, foodstuffs, horses, and needed equipment. The Crow were particularly helpful at river crossings, taking women and children over on horseback. Henry Haight observed in 1850:

> *The Green River [was] a large stream ... and very dangerous to cross. ... There were a lot of friendly Indians of the Crow tribe who assisted us very much. ... There was a family, consisting of a man, his wife, and a child. ... The Indians insisted on carrying her and the child across the river behind them, but she was afraid to trust her child with them. Finally, one of the Indians snatched the child, placed it before him on the horse, and landed it safely on the other side. The mother hesitated no longer, but allowed an Indian to take her up behind him and soon joined her child on the other side.*

The Crow were equally solicitous of young Elisha Brooks, who—together with his mother and his siblings, four boys and a girl, ranging in age from four to thirteen—set out in 1852 from Michigan to join his father in California. Near Council Bluffs their hired teamster deserted them, as "the air was thick with tales of Indian massacres, starvation and pestilence." His mother struggled on alone with her children in her covered wagon.

On the Sweetwater River, their desperate little party came across a band of friendly Crow who were moving camp in search of better hunting grounds. They travelled with Elisha and his family for more than a week, marching ahead or on their flanks by day and erecting their tents near them at night to assure their safety. Elisha remembered:

> *We presented a strange and weird scene in camp and a motley and pictur-*
> *esque procession enroute: red men in rich robes of bear and panther skins*
> *decked out with fringe and feathers, red men without robes or feathers, and*
> *unwashed; favorite and actually handsome squaws in elegant mantles of*
> *bird skins, tattooed and adorned with beads; unlovely squaws in scanty rags*
> *and no beads, and unwashed; papooses rolled in highly ornamented cradles*
> *grinning from the backs of their ancestors; toddling papooses with a rag and*
> *unwashed; ponies hidden under monumental burdens; packs of dogs creep-*
> *ing under wonderful loads, and bringing up the rear an old ox team with six*
> *wild, ragged children and a woman once called white and sometimes un-*
> *washed, for we could not always get water enough to drink. We were a Wild*
> *West Show.*

Occasionally, encounters led to bonds of genuine affection between emi-grant children and Native Americans. Eliza McAuley described in her diary her budding friendship with an American Indian and his young son during a week's layover at Bear River.

> *July 21, 1852: At dinner time a very intelligent Indian named Poro came to*
> *our camp. He says he has been to the Missouri River and seen steamboats*
> *and explained by signs what they were like. He seems to understand the cus-*
> *toms of the whites very well. ... In the afternoon he came again, bringing his*
> *little boy, four or five years old. He interpreted a number of Indian words for*
> *us.*
>
> *July 22, 1852: The Indians are very friendly and visit us often. We have en-*
> *gaged Poro to make us some moccasins, or rather his squaw is to make them.*
>
> *July 23, 1852: Poro visited us again today and brought his friend Pavee to*
> *see us.*
>
> *July 25, 1852: This is the most like Sunday of any day since we left home,*
> *and we feel very much at home here. Old Poro came along about ten o'clock*
> *and stayed a long time, teaching us his language. It pleases him very much to*
> *see us try to learn it.*

July 27, 1852: Poro brought our moccasins. They are very neatly made. His little boy came with him. I offered a gay plaid shawl in payment for the moccasins. Poro was quite pleased with it and inclined to accept it, but referred the matter to the boy. He talked to his father who explained that he thought it was very pretty but he could not eat it. He wanted bread and sugar, so we gave him what he wanted.

July 28, 1852: Poro came again today and brought a nice mess of berries. He has been counting the "sleeps" before we go away, and regrets our going very much. He said today "One sleep more and then wagons go away to California," and we have parted with white folks that did not regret [the partings] so much.

ENCOUNTERS WITH SEPARATION,

DEATH, AND PAIN

Sometimes children on the overland trail wandered too far away from their company and faced the terror of getting lost in unknown territory. Elisha Brooks remembered:

In one of the[se] detour camps, a little three year old boy, the only child of his doting parents, was missed at supper time, and we all turned out exploring the country far and near through the dense sage brush that covered all the ground, without finding a trace of him. Soon after dark a terrific storm arose, lasting through the night and destroying all hopes of finding the child alive. However, the search was renewed at dawn, but by nine o'clock, it was decided that he had probably been devoured by the wolves that we had heard in the lulls of the storm, and the company, all but our family, hitched up and drove on...leaving the stricken parents alone in their despair.

In about an hour, a man rode up on horseback inquiring whether we had lost a little boy, as one had been found that morning about two miles away, moaning under a sage brush, nearly dead. It was our missing boy, and the delirious parents took him, and turned their team towards home.

Even more terrifying to children was the possibility of being separated from a parent who was lost on the trail. Mary Ackley wrote about her feeling of desolation when, a few weeks after her mother's death from cholera, her father got lost while searching for a missing ox.

I never felt so miserable in my life. I sat on the ground with my face buried in my hands, speechless. I knew well that if a train did not overtake father the treacherous Indians would kill him. What would become of us children? I heard men talking in low tones, and I gathered from what I heard that the captain intended to send out a posse to search for father as soon as the men had supper. Then I heard cheer after cheer. I looked up and there was big, handsome father riding in front of a pack train.

Death, the ultimate separation experience, was a constant companion on the overland trail—even in the course of an ordinary journey. The mortality rate "on the plains across" little exceeded that of friends, neighbors, and relatives who stayed home. But the travel conditions were such that the emigrant children could come face-to-face with death in sudden and disturbing ways.

One of the youngest child diarists, eight-year-old Florence Weeks, was aware of the finality of death—its irreversible and unbridgeable separation from life. She wrote in 1859: "One had the oddest feeling seeing those graves in such lonely places, but it made no difference to the ones who was gone. It was the thought of going on without them."

Children saw death in many forms, among loved ones and strangers and among their cherished animals. They saw draft oxen and mules left to rot where they dropped. They passed Native American burial places close to the road. Tribes along their route were ravished by the diseases the emigrants brought, and the youngsters often saw the results. Maria Elliott observed in July 1859:

We went this morning to see the skeleton of a papoose, which had been buried in a tree, and had fallen down. It was done up in a red handkerchief, with red and blue flannels, and last of all, a buffalo robe. It was very much dried and shriveled up; I should think it had been dead for quite a while.

Death on the plains from cholera occurred most frequently between 1849 and 1852 and caused even the most robust individual to succumb—often within two days after the illness struck. Sallie Hester wrote in 1849:

We had two deaths in our train within the past week of cholera—young men going West to seek their fortunes. We buried them on the banks of the Blue River, far from home and friends.

Three years later, in June 1852, cholera broke out again among the emigrants travelling along the Platte River. Mary Ackley remembered:

*Mother was among the first victims. We camped alone on the day she was
first taken ill. Our train went on. We heard there was a physician not far
behind us ... and we waited for his train to overtake us in the middle of the
afternoon. He stopped and treated mother, stating that the case was very serious, and advised us to join his train the following day, as they intended to
camp part of the day. We started the next morning, overtaking his train at
noon, and camped on a beautiful spot where wild roses grew in great profu-
sion. On June 24 at 2 o'clock in the afternoon mother died.*

Death seemed especially cruel if youngsters lost *both* their parents to the
raging disease. Bernard J. Reid, a traveller on the pioneer stagecoach in 1849,
saw an emigrant wagon on the Sandy River, apparently abandoned. Near it he
observed a rude headboard indicating the graves of Rev. Robert Gilmore and
his wife, who had both died of cholera on the same day. He approached the
wagon and saw a seventeen-year-old girl, her eyes vacant.

"I learned from her in reply to my questions," Reid wrote in his diary, "that
she was Miss Gilmore whose parents had died two days before; that her
brother, younger than herself, was sick in the wagon, with cholera; that their
oxen were lost." But help was soon on the way: An ox train from Missouri arrived, and their captain volunteered to take the orphaned youngsters and care
for them. The boy eventually recovered.

The death of children, like that of adults, was common enough on an overland journey to be remarked upon by the young diarists. Infants and toddlers
were especially vulnerable to intestinal diseases, such as dysentery and "mountain fever." The former was spread through contact with infected victims,
their clothes, their bedding, or contaminated water; the latter was contracted
from bites of ticks indigenous to an area between Colorado and the Sierra Nevada.

"Brother Jim, four years old, had mountain fever," wrote Mary Ackley in
1852. "When he recovered his hair all fell out." Some children did not survive
the illness. Maria Elliott wrote in her diary in 1859:

May 31: *Mr. Fletcher's child is quite sick. Has been for several days.*

June 1: *Dolly is much worse. ... We had all retired to our wagons, when his
mother gave a scream and we all rushed to her wagon. We found him ... in
the agonies of death. ... We immediately went to rubbing him in brandy
and gave him some to take. ... Applied some warm clothes to his body which
was growing cold. He revived and breathed a little easier.*

June 2*: Little Dolly is no more. … He died at seven. … His parents took his death very hard.*

There were also enough accidents on the overland trail to cause the children anxiety. Most pervasive was the fear of drowning at the frequent river crossings. Reported Sallie Hester in 1849:

Crossed Truckee River three times [today]. Came near being drowned at one of the crossings. Got frightened and jumped out of the carriage into the water. The current was very swift and carried me some distance down the stream.

And Mary Ackley observed in 1852:

We had to cross the Green River which was very swift. … One man started to ford the river in a wagon with two of his children. The wagon body floated off and went a mile down stream before it was rescued. One daughter who was twelve years old, saved herself and the life of her little sister, two years old, by catching hold of the wagon bows and holding her little sister's head above the water.

Poisonous snakes and scorpions were the scourge of the desert crossing on the last leg of the journey. Wrote Maria Elliott:

[Brother] Johnny looked at [brother] Charley's back and found a scorpion which was very poisonous indeed. … The poison was all over his hands. They helped him to Henry's wagon and gave him a shot of a pint of brandy and put a tobacco poultice on the bite. He was crazy for about three or four hours, and then fell asleep.

By far the greatest number of mishaps involving children occurred when they were playing with guns that accidently discharged or were thrown from horses or run over by wagons. Mary Ackley remembered:

My two brothers were playing in the wagon on the bed, the curtains were rolled up and the front wheels went down in a rut which jarred the wagon, throwing brother John [age seven] out. A hind wheel ran over him, breaking one of his legs. … He was confined to the wagon for the rest of the long journey.

Most emigrant travellers on the northern route successfully surmounted the hazards of the terrain and climate and the occasional "sick spells" without

A Pioneer Family on the Overland Trail (courtesy The Denver Public Library, Western History Department, #F12921)

loss of life and property. In the 1850s, the journey from the jumping-off points at the Missouri River to California might last four to five months—considerably less than the time it took to cross the plains in the 1840s but long enough to engender a great feeling of relief when the end of the trail was in sight. Mary Ackley wrote in 1852:

> We passed through Sacramento ... and forded the American River at Lisle's Bridge and camped for the night on the Marysville road. ... Near the camp [we] found a home for us for the winter, and after a five month's journey we were truly thankful we had arrived at our destination.

That same year, twelve-year-old Elizabeth Keegan left her home in Kansas on May 3 and arrived in California September 17, riding horseback all the way. She spoke for all her travel companions, young and old, when she wrote to her brother and sister after her arrival in Sacramento: "No one can picture the feeling of those who have come that wearisome journey, the joy they feel at once more beholding and mingling with their fellow creatures."

Mayhem on the Gila Trail

O F ALL THE ROUTES to California, the southwestern trails through present-day New Mexico and Arizona were the least crowded—only about a quarter of the westward-bound travellers in the late 1840s and the 1850s used the Gila Trail. Traversing the deserts of the southwestern frontier, this route, like the northern ones, took a course determined by available sources of water and accessible passages through the mountains.

Travellers coming from Santa Fe or El Paso entered Arizona south of the rugged Gila Mountains, then went west a hundred miles to the Santa Cruz River. Turning northward, they followed the Santa Cruz for another hundred miles to its junction with the Gila River. Farther west, after the Gila joined the Colorado River, the trail pushed on across the sand dunes, then over the mountains to reach the Pacific Ocean near present-day San Diego.

Many argonauts chose this trail because they were lured by advertisements and newspaper editorials in Missouri, Arkansas, Oklahoma, and Texas which promised that "the journey can be made in about two months with pack mules and in about three months with wagons." The reality was quite different: Like the northern trails, the southwest route was long, wearying, and monotonous. Louisiana Strentzel, a doctor's wife from northwest Texas and the mother of two young children, wrote about their journey shortly after her arrival in San Diego in December 1849.

> *We found that the only way to get through was to travel slowly in the cool of the day, save the animals as much as possible and stop at every little grass we could find. … The dust was almost insufferable; it was generally from six to twelve inches deep. It was almost impossible for our wagons to travel nearer than fifty yards to another.*

Fortunately for the southwestern travellers, there were army forts, such as Yuma, and trading stations and towns, such as Santa Fe, El Paso, and Tucson, which provided respite from sand and rocks and offered opportunities to buy necessary supplies. One advantage for California-bound emigrants on this trail was a general absence of diseases, such as cholera and scurvy. Reported Louisiana:

> *Little Pussy [two-year-old daughter Louise] and Johnny [infant son] have not been sick an hour on the journey … they both look red and rosey and have grown so they cannot wear [any] garment that was made for them when we left home.*

The emigrants enjoyed friendly relations with Native Americans in the Pima and Yuma villages of Arizona and among the Pueblos of northern New Mexico. They visited their homes as they traded for corn and vegetables or fresh horses. Because most of the wagon trains of California-bound emigrants were large, they were not attacked by hostile Indians as they crossed the Southwest.

But there were exceptions: Occasionally an emigrant family travelling alone became the object of an Indian raid. The story of the most famous raid—the Oatman massacre—is told through the voices of the surviving children, Lorenzo and Olive Oatman, and their friend, Susan Thompson. Their trek began like any other "ordinary journey" west.

Royce Oatman and his pregnant wife and seven children headed from Davenport, Iowa, to California on May 8, 1850, in the company of Ira Thompson and his family. At Independence, Missouri, the Oatmans and Thompsons joined several other families, forming a train of around thirty wagons and about a hundred people. They divided into several parties, and Royce Oatman was elected captain of one of the bands.

"Of the three score in our company" remembered his thirteen-year-old daughter, Olive, "quite a number were children. That first week's journey cannot obliterate from memory … our joyful glee, as we romped and danced along the trail of our slow moving teams."

Her friend, seventeen-year-old Susan Thompson, thoroughly enjoyed the first fun-filled weeks of travel.

> *We were a happy, carefree lot of young people and the dangers and hardships found no resting place on our shoulders. It was a continuous picnic, and excitement was plentiful. In the evening we gathered about the campfires and played games or told stories or danced. … My old violin … so many eve-*

nings gave out the strains of "Money Musk" and "Zipp Coon" as the young folks danced in the light of the campfire and the lard-burning lanterns. Often, during the daytime halts, we ran races or made swings. There was plenty of frolic and where there are young people gathered together, there is always plenty of love-making.

The wagons proceeded southwest to the Big Bend of the Arkansas River and encountered only a minor Indian scare. Remembered Olive Oatman:

While our tents were pitched at the banks of the river and our Sabbath service was being conducted ... a band of Indians appeared on the opposite side—singing and dancing in a grove. They were of the Comanche tribe and about them were a number of very beautiful American horses and mules which they had stolen.

The Indians were peaceful, but the wrangling among the travellers, "due to religious penchants and strong prejudices of certain restless spirits in our company," intensified. When the wagon train reached the New Mexican frontier settlements of Moro and Las Vegas, the angry party split into two groups. Thirty-two persons chose the more northerly road westward by way of Santa Fe; Royce Oatman and his friends opted for the southerly route by way of Socorro and the San Pedro and Santa Cruz Rivers. The group was now in Apache country. Susan Thompson remembered a funny incident.

Lucy Oatman and I were like any girls, careless and given to forgetting our household duties, and when, after night-fall, we found that we had forgotten to fill the water buckets for the morning, we concluded the easiest way to avoid a scolding was by slipping down to the river without anyone's knowledge. We were just starting back with our dripping pails when we heard someone coming. We clutched each other in terror, remembering all too late the warnings we had heard of the fearful Apaches. In a moment we were reassured by the sight of a boy who was the worst tease in the company. He, too, had forgotten his pail of water. A time for revenge for many practical jokes had come and with a great crashing of underbrush we rushed at him through the darkness. There was a banging of water buckets, a flying of heels and a volley of blood curdling yells, "The Apaches are coming! The Apaches are coming!" Under cover of the general confusion, Lucy and I and our water pails stole quietly into camp.

Only twenty people faced the most dangerous part of the southern journey, and half of them were children. Oatman led the way with his pregnant wife, Mary Ann, and their seven children, ranging in age from mid-teens to an infant. Following the Oatmans' wagon were seven others, including the Thompsons. The Thompsons' teenage daughter Susan remembered:

I think I shall never forget the scenery in the Santa Cruz Mountains. To me the most beautiful spot in our journey of thousands of miles was found among the stately pines on a mountain where a natural fountain poured its crystal waters into a granite basin fully six feet across. Gathering spruce gum afforded us much amusement, and one day while Lucy Oatman and I had strayed on before the wagons, we heard a great screaming and clamoring behind us. We had always discussed what we would do in case we were attacked [by Apaches] ... but we were called upon to do nothing more vigorous than to pick up the scattered tin dishes, and repack them into one of the overturned wagons.

Because of frequent delays caused by snow storms, supplies were running low. "Our route lay through a wild and mountainous region, with severe ascents and steep declivities, which wore upon our teams with disheartening effect," observed thirteen-year-old Olive Oatman.

The group finally reached Santa Cruz, with the hope of replenishing their provisions. But the Apache had raided the town a short time before and had left no food. The train pushed on to Tucson. Susan Thompson remembered:

From here to Tucson, Arizona, we suffered for bread. Captain Oatman allowed each person but a biscuit and a half per day. We tried to eat hawks and I recall how sick my mother was when she attempted to drink some soup made from coyote meat.

They arrived in Tucson on January 8, 1851: Susan Thompson turned eighteen that day. The mothers and daughters in Oatman's train were the first white women who had entered the village, and the natives urged the "gringos" to remain there to protect the isolated village from Indian raids. Susan remembered a brief encounter with the Apache that turned out to be harmless.

One day I went into the field and found two Apaches, dressed only in breech clothes, untieing my pet calf. Without thought as to my peril, I rushed up to them exclaiming, "If you don't let my calf alone, I'll tell the men in the

*house." They did not know that my mother and I were alone and the ruse
frightened them away.*

After one month's rest, Oatman was determined to press on ahead of the
others. Four families, including the Thompsons, decided to remain in Tucson
for several more weeks, resting and replenishing their supply of cattle. The
Oatman family, together with the Wilders and Kelleys, resumed their journey
westward. Reported Olive Oatman:

*With scanty supplies, a long journey and hostile Indians to content with, our
hearts saddened as we thought of our desperate situation. The next settlements was the Pimo Village, ninety miles distant through the most dismal,
desolate and unfruitful of all the regions through which we had traveled. We
reached the village on the 16th of February 1851, six months from the time we
left Independence, Missouri.*

When they reached the Pima village, Mrs. Wilder was confined because of
childbirth. The villagers warned the emigrants that the next stretch of the
Gila Trail was unsafe. The Wilders and Kelleys decided to remain and "await
future events."

Against the advice of everyone, Oatman and his family moved on. "He resolved to proceed under the protection of God," Olive remembered, "trusting
he might reach Fort Yuma in safety." One hundred ninety miles lay ahead of
them—a weary trek over grassless desert and barren mountains. They
trudged along with their emaciated animals—four cows and two oxen—often
travelling at night when the temperatures had cooled to a "mere" 90 degrees.

Toward evening on March 18, 1851, they reached the Gila River, about
eighty miles east of Yuma. That evening Royce Oatman had a premonition
that something dreadful was about to happen. The family camped on the
summit of a hill and ate their meager meal of bean soup and a few crusts of
dry bread. Oatman had just put the last of their baggage into their wagon
when a group of Yavapai Indians climbed up the hill.

"My brother Lorenzo saw them first," Olive remembered, "and told my father about them." The Indians asked (in Spanish) for a pipe and tobacco and
then for food. Royce Oatman told them they had none to give. "We saw that
they were offended," observed his daughter.

The Yavapais withdrew for a moment for a powwow, and the Oatman family finished reloading their wagon, intent on resuming their journey. The attack was sudden and violent. Brandishing war clubs, the Indians struck down
Royce Oatman, his wife, and five of their children—all but thirteen-year-old

Olive and seven-year-old Mary Ann, whom they hustled aside. Susan Thompson learned the story from Lorenzo Oatman, who survived the attack.

> *As Lorenzo ... sprang to his mother's assistance, it flashed through his mind like a ghastly joke, that the Indians were beating his sister Lucy with gigantic wooden potato mashers and then with a quick slash of a knife in his scalp and the spurting of hot blood, his mind went into darkness. The scorching heat of the next morning's sun awoke him. He found that he had rolled or been thrown to the foot of the hill. Weakened by his injuries and by the remembrance of the nightmare he had lived through, he feared to go alone up to the scene of the tragedy. His only thought was to reach Pima Village or his old friends.*

Lorenzo tramped the desert for three days in the blinding heat, living on mesquite beans a party of friendly Pima Indians had given him. He then met the Wilders and Kelleys, who took the boy to Pima to recuperate. Following his directions, they came to the place that now bears the name Oatman Flats.

At the brow of the hill, they found the mutilated bodies of Mr. and Mrs. Oatman, Lucy, her five-year-old brother, her two-year-old sister, and the infant. Olive and Mary Ann Oatman were missing. There was no way to dig graves in the sun-baked ground, so they placed the bodies beneath a large pile of rocks.

Meanwhile, Susan Thompson and her family were advancing from Tucson in a large company. They passed near the burial site of the Oatman family on their way to Fort Yuma. Susan remembered:

> *For many days the horror of the fate of our beloved Lucy had kept Isabel Lane and me close to the wagons. But one day, being sure we had passed the graves of our friends, we walked on ahead of the train only to suddenly come upon a chip basket which we often helped our companion to fill with kindling. We cast one horrified glance at the pitiful pile of rocks and what they all too plainly disclosed and fled back to our parents and friends.*

By the time the Thompsons finally arrived at Fort Yuma, Susan's father and her little sister, Lucy, were gravely ill. But there was also a happy event. "Another traveller joined us in our pursuit of Gold," reported Lucy. "She was my little sister Gila whom we named in honor of the river near her birth place." At a party given in her honor by an army physician at the fort, Susan Thompson played her first game of cards "with a blase air and a great feeling of dissipation."

From Yuma, the Thompsons began the last stage of their journey. They and their oxen were quickly reaching the limit of their endurance. On their final trek, wrote Susan, "the oxen were so worn with fatigue and lack of water that the only way they could be kept going was by my walking before them, holding mesquite beans just out of their reach."

They arrived at Warner's ranch, northeast of San Diego, to a cordial welcome, and they replenished their empty larder. They settled at El Monte, a station on the stagecoach road between San Bernardino and Los Angeles, and opened an inn. In October 1853 Susan Thompson married and moved to Los Angeles. Lorenzo Oatman made his home with the newlyweds. He spent five years trying to get help for the rescue of his sisters.

The story of the fate of the two captive Oatman sisters rests on the testimony of the one survivor, Olive. She later told her rescuers that she and her sister Mary Ann had been carried away by the Yavapai (whom she mistook for Apaches), under cover of moonlight, across rough terrain, away from the spot at which the massacre took place.

The two young girls were barefoot and were stripped of much of their clothing, and they were soon covered with cuts and bruises from frequent falls over sharp stones and spiny cacti. Seven-year-old Mary was carried like a sack over the shoulder of one of the Indians; thirteen-year-old Olive walked for four days—unaided—until they reached a small village of huts that were half underground, which was surrounded by a rocky range. Olive said:

> *There we were made to stand up in their midst and they all danced and shouted about us. Toward daybreak we were taken to the chief's family, and in their ... hut tried to rest. The next day they showed us how to dig roots and kept us at it.*

The girls soon learned enough of the Yavapai language to be able to communicate with their captors. When their tattered rags fell off, the sisters tied barks around their waists in imitation of the Indian women. After they had been in the camp for about a year, they saw some Mojave Indians in the village who came once a year to trade vegetables for furs. Olive remembered:

> *One day when Mary and I were gathering roots ... we saw in the distance a party coming—an Indian riding upon his horse and a squaw walking by his side. ... We heard we were sold [for the price of two horses, two blankets, and a few pounds of beads] and ... that the party now coming was sent by the Mojave Chief to pay for us.*
>
> *The squaw was his daughter sent to accompany us. ... The chief's daughter showed [us] some kindness. ... We slept beneath her blanket on our jour-*

*ney and were taken to the house of the Chief on our arrival, and she gave us
some cake which was being baked in the sun.*

The Mojave chief adopted the girls as his own children. He allotted each a
blanket, food, a garden plot, and some seed. Both girls were tattooed with the
tribal mark of five vertical lines from lower lip to chin.

In spring 1853, the Colorado River, whose normal overflow irrigated the
garden plots, ran dry, and in the fall famine followed the drought. Olive reported:

*Food of every description was scarce ... and the winter with its rains, winds
and frosts was fast approaching. Feeble as Sister Mary was, we spent whole
days in search of roots and seeds without getting as much as we could hold in
our hands.*

Along with many Mojave children, Mary Ann Oatman starved to death.
"The wife of the chief came and bent over her, the night she died," said her
sister Olive, "and wept bitterly, as did her daughter." Olive's grief at her sister's
death so moved the chief that as a mark of deference he permitted Mary's
burial in her own garden plot instead of requiring cremation, which was the
custom among the tribe. "The Indians dug a grave about five feet deep," observed Olive, "into which we lowered the body, after wrapping it carefully
with the only tattered blanket they had given me to wear."

Early in 1856, the commander of Fort Yuma heard about the captive girl.
Francisco, a Yuma Indian, told him that up the Colorado River, a white girl
was being held by the natives. The commanding officer supplied him with
beads and blankets and directed him "to go for her."

Olive noted the confusion that reigned among the Mojaves when Francisco
arrived. A council was held, and Olive surmised that the Indians would take
her life rather than give her up. She was wrong. Francisco had hinted to the
Mojaves that they would all be killed if they did not release her. Said Olive:

*This frightened them very much, and they ... concluded to let me go if he
would give them his horse, blankets, beads and some money. ... The Chief's
daughter had always given evidence of a strong attachment to me. ... This
daughter, in accordance with my wishes, was sent by her father to accompany me to the Fort.*

Olive reached Fort Yuma on February 22, 1856—five years after the massacre. Upon approaching the whites, she threw herself on the ground, embar-
rassed by her Indian skirt of bark. She would not get up until clothing, bor-
rowed from some of the officers' wives, was brought to her. The girl, when

asked her name in Mojave, eagerly replied, "Olive Oatman." During the next several days, English words gradually came back to her, and she haltingly related the story of her captivity.

Her brother, Lorenzo, heard about her release through the local newspaper. Susan Thompson Lewis remembered:

> *One evening, he came galloping his horse into the yard and waving a copy of the Los Angeles Star in his hand. ... In one corner was a notice asking for communication with the friends or relatives of Olive Oatman. Lorenzo ... and [his friend] Jesse ... started overland at once for Yuma. And there ... they found a frightened tattooed creature who was more savage than civilized and who sought at every opportunity to flee back to her Indian husband and children. ... For, after the famine, Olive became the wife of the Chief's son, and at the time of her rescue was the mother of two little boys.*

Olive and Lorenzo were given a home by Susan Thompson's parents in El Monte, California. Susan remembered that Olive was given to frequent weeping spells. "In time," she said, "we erased the tatoo marks from her face, but we could not erase the wild life from her heart."

After Olive had recuperated, she and her brother were taken to the home of their cousin Harrison B. Oatman in the Rogue River valley in Oregon. In 1857 both attended the University of the Pacific at Santa Clara. In March 1858 they accompanied the Reverend B. Stratton, author of their best-selling biography *Captivity of the Oatman Girls,* to New York. Lorenzo Oatman went to Illinois to raise a family, but he died young. Olive Oatman lectured about her experiences in Rochester, Syracuse, and New York in order to raise funds for churches and to promote Stratton's book.

When a delegation of Mojaves came to New York City, she contacted them. "I learned ... that the Chief's daughter was yet living," she told her lecture audience, "and that she still hoped that I would tire of my pale faced friends and return to her."

Instead, Olive married a white man, John B. Fairchild. She died in Sherman, Texas, in 1903 at age sixty-four. Although she wept for her half-Mojave children and the chief's daughter, who had loved and cherished her, she never saw them again.

Published accounts of the fate of the Oatman family were read widely by California-bound Americans, but they travelled on the Gila Trail anyway. By 1852, ferries on the Colorado River at Yuma had transported thousands of emigrants across the river, first on reed rafts pulled by swimming American Indians and then on barges attached to pulley ropes.

Most of the emigrants on the Gila Trail were unattached young men; few older people or families with small children were seen along that route. One of the few such families in 1853 was that of nine-year-old Maggie Hall, who had left their home in Grayson County in northeastern Texas in April. They had three large freight wagons, with three to four pairs of oxen hitched to each, and a spring wagon, with covered top and rolled curtains and drawn by four mules, for the family. In addition to Maggie, there were her parents, her two younger sisters, Annie and Sallie, an older brother, and a servant-cook named Delia. Her married older sister, Rachel, who was also in the wagon train, adopted a little boy, Frank Burns, when his father drowned on the first part of the journey.

They travelled nearly one thousand uneventful miles simply to get out of Texas, following first the Brazos, then the Colorado, and finally the Pecos Rivers. As they crossed Kiowa and Comanche territory—away from all government protection—there were occasional alarms from the boys who stood guard at night. "Someone would cry Indians," Maggie remembered, "but that scare was groundless and very exasperating. ... It made the women nervous and sick—while [we] small children slept like logs after a day's travel."

The first group of Native Americans they actually met face-to-face were Comanches, "who brought their squaws with them, so we knew that they came in peace," wrote Maggie. After claiming and being given seven oxen, the Comanche camped near their train and spent the night eating. When the emigrants reached the Guadeloupe Mountains, another band of Indians drove off their herd of fine brood mares, valued at a thousand dollars apiece, under cover of night.

They replenished their supplies in El Paso, where they camped on the Rio Grande for two weeks and then slowly trekked through high, rough mountains in Apache territory. The only "wild Indian" Maggie actually encountered—and it must have been a comical sight—was an Apache who came to their camp one night, took one of their ponies, and "rode away with Mother's dress on," observed the little girl. More frightening to Maggie was a stampede of their oxen.

> *The whole train ran away in every direction. ... When it stopped, there were only two out of six oxen left [that pulled the family wagon], one on top of the other, and one's horn broken off. We sat there crying, waiting, everything so still—only night around us. ... It took several days to get the stock together and repair the wagons and yokes.*

They reached the Gila River at a Moncapah village, where their hosts supplied them with beans and melons. Observed Maggie:

> *These village Indians ... were so friendly. ... Until that year very few had seen a white man and none a white woman or a child, and they never tired of watching us and our ways. They were equal to a circus in interest to us. The children wore nothing except beads, the women a bark around their waist. ... They followed us as we travelled—men, women and children.*

They crossed and recrossed the Gila River and passed the place where Olive Oatman's family had been killed—"saw parts of their wagons," remembered little Maggie. At Yuma, her father got his stock across the river, holding on to their horns. "The Yuma Indians were lost in admiration of Pa," remembered his proud daughter, "his size and his feats of swimming."

The worst of the journey through the desert was still ahead. Maggie reported:

> *The oxen began to give up and lie down. ... The last day all oxen were gone but four, and as night came all the water was gone. The sandstorm that ... came ... was a terrible experience. ... Neither horses nor oxen would go against it and the men could not expose their faces. ... The stock huddled together. ... Mother and children stayed in the wagon and we had no supper that night.*

But deliverance was near. The next day they met some men carrying kegs of water, and they gave them some to quench their thirst. The Hall family reached a well before daylight, and nine miles later they came upon a river with plenty of water and feed. "We were full of joy," wrote Maggie. "We had reached California at last!"

The emigrants who followed Maggie's family on the Gila Trail had an easier time, for they no longer had to contend with surprise raids by the Apaches. In 1856 a newly appointed Indian agent, Dr. Michael Steck, began regular distributions of food and supplies to the Apaches. In turn, he gained their promise that the Gila Trail emigrant wagons would be left alone. That promise was essentially kept for nearly five years.

But an occasional train still encountered mayhem and massacres. One of these involved an emigrant party from Iowa that set out for California in spring 1858.

The Brown, Rose, and Jones train left Keosauqua in April 1858. It consisted of three families: Mr. and Mrs. Brown, with five children, ranging in age from two to fifteen; Mr. and Mrs. Rose, with two little girls, both under six years of age; and Mr. and Mrs. Jones, with their sixteen-year-old son, Ed, who was old enough to help drive a large herd of cattle that were to be sold for profit in California. Because of his previous experience on the western trails, Brown was elected captain of the company.

The party chose to take the southern route across the plains, rather than the more travelled northern route by way of Salt Lake City, because they feared the hostile attitude of the Mormons and the Indians in that area. Seven months earlier, on September 11, 1857, a group of zealous Mormons, with their Indian cohorts, had attacked an emigrant train near Mountain Meadows and killed as many as ninety-six persons, sparing only eighteen young children. The memory of the Mountain Meadows massacre was still fresh in people's memories.

So the Brown, Rose, and Jones train went south instead, crossing the Missouri near Independence, and continuing on to Santa Fe. They reached the vicinity of Santa Fe by the end of June and camped for the Fourth of July at the base of the San Francisco Mountains. The men went up the mountain range and brought back some snow for the celebration.

In Santa Fe the families were advised, because of their large band of cattle, to take the newly surveyed "Beale and Whipple" route through northern Arizona instead of the more travelled southern route through Fort Yuma. They would find more abundant feed for their livestock in the virgin country along that road, and they had the army engineers' survey map to guide them. As far as they knew, they were the first wagon train to travel through northern Arizona.

The Zunis, whose territory they crossed, were kind to them. Little Kate, one of the children, remembered a city on a hill, closely built and thickly inhabited by the Indians. To enter their houses, they had to go up a ladder to a flat roof and then down a ladder to the floor. She noted:

> *The man tended the babies, knit, and wove blankets, and the woman ground the corn. … Often, as she ground, she carried a nursing child upon her back, throwing her breast over her shoulder within reach. She chewed constantly what proved to be wheat, and when it had reached a certain consistency she took it out. … The people were exceedingly hospitable, and greeted the newcomer with "eat, eat." I ate heartily of a certain sweet mush they gave me, and I only laughed when I learned that it was a choice dish made of chewed wheat.*

Nothing of special note happened to the party until they reached the banks of the Colorado River, about two hundred miles from Fort Yuma, near present-day Mesquite Flats. Unbeknownst to them, they camped on one of the Mojave's cattle sites.

From the time of their arrival on August 29, they saw Indians coming and going, begging for food and pilfering some. Annoyed, the emigrants stretched a rope across the entrance to their campsite. The Indians were not allowed to enter. Their expressions showed immediately that they were deeply offended by what to them must have been a serious breach of hospitality.

The next day, August 30, no Indians came to the camp in the morning. The Spanish guide who had been hired in Santa Fe sensed trouble coming, but the emigrants did not heed his warning. They went on with their chores and, at noon, ate their usual frugal meal.

The surprise attack came in the early afternoon. Sally Fox had climbed up on a wagon and happened to look out away from the camp. She cried in terror, "The Indians are coming! They are going to kill us!" and jumped to the ground. Her half sister Kate told what happened next.

We children were lazily sitting about on the ground. One sister was stringing beads taken from an old moccasin, and most of the men were sleeping under the wagon through the heat of the afternoon. ... Suddenly there was a dreadful scream; then another and another ... till in one second the air was rent and torn with yells. In ... that second the close chaparral had become black with Indians. ... They wore loin cloths, and some had feathers ... on their head, with ... paint glowing on face and breast.

The women and children, through an air thick with flying arrows, fled into one covered wagon, and there my mother wrapped us all round with feather-beds, blankets and comforters. I do not think I was frightened, not because of any courage, but because of a wild excitement that filled me. I half leaned upon the knee of my sister [Sally]. She says she was conscious of no pain ... felt no sudden pang, but something warm seemed running down her side. ... Looking down, she saw an arrow which had pierced her flesh and protruded its flinty head from the wound. "Mother," she cried, "I am shot," and fainted. My mother drew the arrow backward through the wound.

The Indians, under cover of the fight, had driven the herd of cattle across the river. The emigrants, vastly outnumbered, fought with desperation. The captain of the train, Sally's stepfather, was killed by a shower of arrows. To encourage his warriors on to final victory, the Indian chief stepped boldly into the open and was shot—on the third try—by a preacher from Missouri.

The death of their chief cooled the Indians' ardor. Taking their dead and wounded, they "made off down the river" within an hour. Of the emigrants, two were captured, four were killed, and about a dozen were wounded. As soon as the Indians had gone, a council was held in camp to decide what to do next. The train was still about five hundred miles from California, and the next white settlement, Fort Yuma, was two hundred miles away—through hostile Mojave country all the way. The group decided to turn back, with the hope of meeting another emigrant train. Sally described their departure.

With one wagon so arrayed that most wounded could lie down, and one ... containing all our food, clothing and utensils, we gathered up our few remaining cattle and started back, as we couldn't fight our way over the river and into California. All that my ... mother took for herself and five children, she put into a flour sack, and we always had to go to bed when our clothes were washed.

They left the camp after burying their captain's body in the river wrapped in a blanket with a log chain wound around him. Mrs. Brown, his widow, rode horseback, carrying two-year-old Orrin in her arms. Both were wrapped in a buffalo robe to keep arrows from wounding the boy in case any Indians followed them. When it was dark, they stopped only about a half mile from the camp until the moon rose. They were so still that even their little dog, Pedro, did not bark or whimper. The Mojaves *did* come back to the former campsite that night and held a war dance, but they did not pursue the emigrants. Young Kate picked up the trail of her family.

Then began a weary tramp backward to Albuquerque, over mountains, desert, and plains, every step of which for hundreds of miles we felt was watched from every bush and point. The few cattle remaining to us were those too feeble from the effects of alkali to swim the river; our food was insufficient, we could not find water, our progress was miserably slow.

Her sister, Sally, continued the story of their trek.

My invalid sister and I were hourly expected to die, so weak and feeble was she, and I, too, from my wound. We were almost in despair of reaching civilization, as what cattle we had for food were almost gone. ... We might have starved altogether, had not one evening a number of our cattle that had ... strayed from those taken by the Indians and followed us back, suddenly walked into camp. We rushed to meet them, and … did hug them in our joy; but, alas, they too, had to be sacrificed for food.

After her horse gave out, Mrs. Brown had to walk with the other women across the desert, all the while carrying her two-year-old son. The children would hold on to the wagon wheels when resting, so they could take up when the wheels began to turn again. Little Kate remembered:

My mother sat between the wheels, as I often caught one of the spokes, and other hands grasped the wagon behind to feel its first motion. A nameless dread shook me one night, for one of the young girls had failed to waken, and we had traveled on without her. Oh, horror, if it had been I to open my eyes … and find myself alone in the trackless sand! When she was recovered, I looked upon her with awe because of the experience that had just been hers.

Whenever there was anything to eat, the wounded were helped first. One day Mrs. Brown offered her daughter Sally a tidbit, but the little girl suspected they had killed her pet goat, Vegas, and refused to eat the meat—hungry as she was. The next night she was given a little piece of bacon; it was so precious to her that she kept it in her mouth and went to sleep with it, "like a little mouse owl," her mother observed.

After about a hundred-mile trek back, the party reached Peach Springs Canyon. They were close to starvation. Sally remembered that seven-year-old Julia Brown, who was fond of church hymns, piped up and said, "One thing assures me; the Lord will provide." Her words seemed prophetic, for at about sundown they were met by an emigrant train that, seeing their sad condition, generously shared their own food and supplies with them.

When they heard the story of the Indian attack, the members of both the original group and the emigrant train voted to return to Albuquerque. Sally was deeply impressed by the kindness of one of their leaders, a Freemason, who later brought them safely to California.

We went together, he providing food for all, daily killing his cattle until his huge herd was rapidly disappearing, and the stock of supplies was reduced to giving out beef without salt, and a few crumbs of crackers which Mr. Smith declared the best dish he ever tasted. … Never once did he loose his patience nor his cheerfulness; indeed, he was … always ready with a joke, even on the most discouraging days. My little brother used to call Mr. Smith to such meals as we had, "Smithy, come to beans," and he would always respond with a smile … and came leading the little messenger by the forefinger.

The pure, dry air of Arizona had aided nature in healing Sally's wound, and she was able to walk again by the time they reached Albuquerque. But her two-year-old brother Orrin fell sick and died. Two days after their arrival, a wagon carried him in a little coffin to the small burying ground set apart by the American inhabitants of Albuquerque. His sister Kate remembered:

When our small hillock was made, we stood around it ... we knew, having once left it, we never should see it again. We gathered stones and put upon it, to prevent the digging of wolves; and then, having done all, we looked at each other, dreading to go. We had grown stoical ... and we had each a knowledge of death from having stared him in the face ... but as my mother turned, in the wagon, to look her last upon the lonely hillside, she cried, "Oh, my boy, my boy! How can I leave him there?"

They spent the fall and winter of 1858 at a campsite near what today is the Old Town section of Albuquerque. The Freemasons and the Mexican women who were their neighbors did everything they could for the widow and her little girls. When the wounded had recuperated fully, the emigrant party left in spring 1859, taking the southern overland route through Socorro. Little Kate was entranced by its inhabitants.

We were encamped at the Warm Springs, a little way out upon the hillside from Socorro. The water gushed ... warm ... from a rock in the hill. It had hollowed out a basin for itself. To this basin flocked the women of Socorro when ... washday came—barefooted, and with the bundles of clothes upon their heads. ... They let down their bundles and washed their clothes upon the stones as the Zuni women [had] ground the corn, slapping them and pounding them ... with a soap-root. And then, while they caressed me, and passed me round, it was ... "Ah, the poor little girl, out from the midst of Indians!" and "See the little one!" while half bashful and half charmed I drew away.

As the emigrants crossed into Apache territory, Chief Cochise and some of his warriors suddenly appeared in their camp, as if they had sprung out of the ground. They were entranced by the bald head of Mr. Smith, the leader of the train, who looked to them as if he had been scalped. Smith offered them beads and trinkets as tokens of hospitality, and Cochise was delighted. He bid his warriors to leave, and they disappeared as suddenly as they had come.

The chief stayed, to the consternation of the emigrants, and spent the night in their camp. Young Sally was certain they would all "wake up dead," but he reassured them that he was a "bueno" (good) Indian. As a token of friendship, he gave Mr. Smith a quiver of lion skin filled with arrows. True to his words, he allowed the train to go through his territory undisturbed.

The Arapahos, Zunis, and the Pueblo tribes were friendly to the emigrants, but Sally could not shake her fear of Indians. Further west, on the Gila River, the emigrants came across the grave in the desert that marked the site of the Oatman massacre. Sally misread the inscription on the headstone as "scared" rather than "sacred to the Oatman Family." Her sister, Kate, wondered:

Why had we escaped and they been doomed? I went up the overhanging bluff, and stood among the scattered remnants of their effects. Here lay the hub of a wheel; there a ragged portion of cloth clung to a bush; just beyond, a tin-pan, battered and rusty, half-tipped upon a stone; and each article seemed to whisper into my child-ears their story again.

They pushed on to Fort Yuma, where the children were fitted with new clothes by the storekeepers, who took pity on them because of their ragged appearance. They crossed the California border—where Sally promptly lost her brand-new bonnet—and were graciously received by the padre at Mission San Gabriel. They went on to the old plaza in Los Angeles and camped there overnight. The next day, at San Buena Ventura, they came to the shores of the Pacific. Sally's mother, who had saved every drop of water in their canteen during their trip through the desert, exclaimed, "Thank God, there's enough of it," when she saw the ocean for the first time.

In fall 1859 Sally's family finally arrived at her uncle's ranch at Vacaville, near Sacramento. There, in the Music Room of Harbinson House, is displayed the dress she was wearing when her wagon train was attacked on the Colorado River—with a tear in the upper part, where she received the arrow wound. She never mended the holes.

Shortly after her arrival, Sally planted four black walnuts she had picked up on her trek through Arizona. They grew into shady trees on the emigrant wagon road that passed by her uncle's ranch from the northern goldfields to San Francisco Bay and gave welcome shade to many travellers passing through the hot Sacramento valley.

Sally became a teacher in San Francisco. Once, when she was relating her adventures to some schoolchildren and told them how she was shot and wounded by an arrow, one little boy asked excitedly, "And did you live?" She *did* live a long and happy life, surrounded by her children and grandchildren. Today, the Nut Tree Restaurant, located at the site of her uncle's ranch, still honors her thoughtful deeds.

Sally Allen Fox's Apron and Doll (courtesy the Power family, Nut Tree, Vacaville, California)

8

Seeking the Pot of Gold at Rainbow's End

T HERE IS EVERY CLASS OF PEOPLE here in California, the rich and poor of every nation in the world," wrote twelve-year-old Elizabeth Keegan to her brother and sister in St. Louis in December 1852. "See what gold can do—it brings men from all nations here to this distant shore to make their fortune."

Not only men but women, children, and teenagers flocked to California's mining towns during the years of the Gold Rush. Eleven-year-old Martha Gentry travelled with her family from Linden, Missouri, to California to find their "pot of gold." Her parents moved from one mining camp in the northern foothills to another. She later remembered:

> *It was in Placerville that I found my first nugget. One day a miner gave me and the other children permission to dig on his claim, telling us we could have what we found. Diligently we set out to work, and carefully scooped up the soft dirt and then washed it, just as we had seen the men do so many times. I was the luckiest one of the group, and found a nugget worth five dollars. With this I bought a pair of shoes, of which I was sorely in need, for the moccasins given me by an old Indian squaw were now worn out.*

John Wood, who left St. Joseph, Missouri, in 1850 to try his luck in the mining town of Ringgold, California—a few miles southeast of Placerville— recorded in his journal an encounter he had one day with two little girls. They were carrying dirt in a bucket to their father, who was rocking out the gold.

When he asked them how long they had been at the camp and whether they were alone with their father, one of them replied, "About a month; and mother and [brother] William died on the plains, leaving none but father and us." Said her sister, "I had to drive the ox-team many a day on the mountains." Observed the miner, "To see such … fortitude in little girls, inspired me with new hope and resolution, and now I thought, 'what folly to despair!'"

Like these two girls, sixteen-year-old John McWilliams from Griggsville, Illinois, seemed an unlikely candidate to join the Gold Rush. He had been left a semi-invalid by "hereditary consumption" and frequent bouts of fever and chills. His mother and brother had died of tuberculosis, and he, too, seemed destined to have a short life. But he began to grow at age fourteen and by 1850 had attained the height of 6 feet 1 1/2 inches on a lean 122-pound frame. The boys at home called him "legs-a-might."

They admired his gumption, for young John told his father and his friends that he was going to California or die. Grudgingly, as did many parents during the years of the Gold Rush, his father gave his consent, and on April 9, 1849, John and three other young boys from his hometown left in a wagon. John later discovered that his family had put a shroud in his trunk, so certain were they that he would die before he could return.

Yet, unlike many forty-niners, John was never ill en route and had gained twenty-eight pounds by the time he reached California. The standard items of equipment he and his young companions carried were bacon, coffee, calomel, quinine, gold pans, and a butcher knife. He arrived in the mining district known as Old Shasta, near present-day Redding, California, in October 1849. Remembered John:

> *We had shovels and picks with us, which we had brought across the plains. But we didn't just know how to set to work, and were pretty well down at the mouth, for the California gold diggings of which we had thought so much, didn't look like a bit as we thought they would. In my imagination I thought I was going to dig gold out by the bucket-full.*

As luck would have it, young John met one of his former teachers from Griggsville in a gulch where the "old-timers" were digging. He showed him how to work a rocker, made of a hollowed-out log, and a riddle made of slats to hold the dirt—rocking the cradle with one hand and dipping up water from the gulch with a long-handled dipper in the other.

"It was about as crude a machine as I ever saw in the mines," John observed, "but the first day we tried it we took out about one hundred dollars—the biggest day's wages we made that winter. I suppose there weren't any happier people in California that night than we three boys."

John and his friends stayed by that gulch throughout the winter, building a rough cabin near where they had first camped. Sometimes they made ten dollars a day, sometimes less, for they could work only part of the time because of heavy rain and snow. With hopes of finding a richer lode at another location, they left in the early spring. Others who came after them were luckier than they had been. John wrote wistfully in his *Recollections*:

> *After we left, right where we boys had been working our first claim, one of a party, going along the gulch after a rain, kicked out a chunk of gold which weighed five hundred dollars; and we heard that a negro took out of our deserted claim ... twelve hundred dollars in one day. That's miners' luck.*

Seventeen-year-old Jasper S. Hill joined the Mount Pleasant Mining Company and headed for California—hoping, like John McWilliams, "to strike it rich." On July 28, 1850, he wrote a letter to his family in Iowa informing them that he had moved from the town of Weaverville to the Middle Fork of the American River to "work a claim which is thought to be a very good one. Our company," he noted, "numbers thirteen, all first rate jovial fellows, and several are very good musicians who have their violins with them and thus pass off the idle moments by playing on their instruments while others are singing."

For two months young Jasper picked away in the rocks along the river, getting from fifty cents to four or five dollars a pan. The excitement of "seeing gold in such quantities" wore off, and his next letter, from Sacramento City on October 21, 1850, told of a new get-rich scheme he and his companions had in mind. He reassured his parents:

> *Do not be uneasy about me for there's a chance of making money yet in California as I have learnt the ways & manners of coining money easier than by diggings, and that is speculating on fruit, such as oranges, grapes, watermelons, pears, figs & various other trash, which has been carried on extensively at this point during this summer & fall, and which has made many men fortunes.*

But that fortune did not come to young Jasper, who ended up in Nevada City in December, writing, ever hopeful, in his Christmas letter to his family:

> *So here goes for a pile next spring up on the Feather River. Gilkyson and I both feel like making a pile and returning together next fall. I hope we may*

be fortunate as I know you want me to come home, but I do not feel like coming until I make something to pay for my time and labor.

Occasionally, a lone widow with a brood of children would also try her luck in one of the mining towns that sprang up in the foothills of northern California. Louise Clappe, the wife of an itinerant physician who travelled from one mining camp to another to tend the sick, wrote to her sister in New England about a family she met at Indian Bar in fall 1852.

The most interesting of all my pets was a widow, whom we used to call the "long woman." When but a few weeks on the journey, she had buried her husband, who died of cholera after about six hours illness. ... When I knew her, she was living under a large tree ... and sleeping at night, with all her family, in her one covered wagon ... she had eight sons and one daughter ... the oldest was but fifteen years of age, and the youngest a nursing babe of six months ... She owned nothing in the world but her team, and yet she planned all sorts of successful ways to get food for her... family. She used to wash shirts and iron them on a chair. ... But after all their privations [her children] were—with the exception of the eldest—Hope—as healthy looking a set of ragged little wretches as ever I saw. The aforesaid "Hope" was the longest, the leanest, and the bob-sidedest specimen of a Yankee that it is possible to imagine. He walked about looking as if existence was the merest burden and he wished somebody would have the goodness to take it off his hands.

Fourteen-year-old Rebecca Nutting and her widowed father from Des Moines, Iowa, eked out a living boarding miners in a log house they built in Nevada City. The young girl took care of the cooking and most other chores, for "father's health was very poor." When he recovered, Rebecca's father went to Bear River, about twelve miles from Nevada City, and made arrangements to move there in June 1851 and open a boardinghouse for miners and the sawmill workers at the local lumber mill. Rebecca wrote:

We lived that summer in tents. We had a long shed, made of pine boughs for a dining room. My father had no less than 40 boarders all summer. We had a large room made of boughs for a kitchen. ... Father made up his mind to winter there on Bear River. He built us a house from lumber sawed at the mill. ... On April 15, 1852, George Woodson and me was married. ... Father moved away the next morning after I was married, leaving me a girl of

*little more than 16 years to cook and do the housework for 20 men, some-
times more.*

Her first son, William Henry, was born in 1853 and became the pride of her
life. "He was so much company to me," she wrote, "as it had been sometimes
5 months at a time [that] I did not see the face of a white woman."
Not all young miners came from "the States." There were also immigrants
from Mexico, who had come on creaky oxcarts along the dusty trail from San
Diego to Los Angeles to Santa Barbara and Monterey. Among them was
young Ygnacio Villegas, whose family had settled at San Felipe near the Mission San Juan Bautista and had opened a store and restaurant there in 1851 for
the accommodation of the miners who came north from the Gila Trail.
Ygnacio was eleven then and hungry for reading. "I used to hover around the
wagons, as they camped by my father's store," he remembered, "to see if they
had anything to read. I read *Robinson Crusoe* five times and *Pilgrim's Progress*
several times."
In 1858, when he was in his teens, Ygnacio spent many weeks in a quartz
mine his father had claimed at Yankee Hill, a short distance from the mining
town of Columbia. "I had a wonderful time," he later remembered.

> *There were all told seven men in the company. ... In religious faith the party
> was very cosmopolitan, as it consisted of a Jew, a Protestant and several
> Catholics. ... Our interests were in common: we wanted to rough it while
> digging for gold.*

They built a cabin of rough board, with bunks, and erected a mill that was
run by water diverted from the Stanislaus River and carried in flumes to the
mining camps. Ygnacio was put to work on the sluices. He worked from sunrise to sunset every day, until Saturday noon. On Saturday afternoon he and
his companions did their washing and went into town to buy provisions. Almost everyone, having no home ties, made the saloon their club on Sunday.
Remembered Ygnacio:

> *We went into the saloons to rest ourselves and listen to the excellent music on
> the violin, with piano accompaniment, or went into a French pastry shop
> where we got sweet tidbits of any kind. ... The fandango houses were very
> numerous, and it was amusing to see the contrast on the floor, one would see
> the dandies who ... had ... all the ease and grace of gentlemen, and then the
> clumsy clod-hoppers who came in loaded down with gold dust. While all*

were dressed alike, it was easy even for a youth like myself to pick the sheep from the goats.

By 1859, most of the gold had been extracted from the Sierra foothills. The twenty thousand emigrants who headed from the Missouri River towns of Omaha and Nebraska City to California that year found mostly abandoned placer mines and deserted log cabins that had been taken over by Chinese immigrants.

In May 1859, sixteen-year-old Charles Frederick True went with his family from Minnesota to Placerville. His uncle owned a ranch in California and had written to them about "its wonderful climate, its diversified and beautiful landscape, the fertility of its soil, and its freedom from blizzards, electric storms and tornados."

Near Placerville, Charles saw his first group of "John Chinamen" and watched them work, with bare feet, in the mud and water, digging patiently with their picks and shoveling the dirt into sluice boxes to wash out the gold. One of the Chinese youths observed with regret that his supply of water would soon be exhausted. Then, turning his face upward and looking at the clouds, he cheerfully added, "Pretty soon him rain—him come—and then me washee more gold."

Young Charles found the Chinese miners to be more hopeful than the Americans he met who "for one reason or another" were still living in the log cabins they had built in 1849. He wrote:

All up and down the mining belts of the slopes of the foothills of the Sierra ... were to be found many ... rough log cabins with one small window, one door, a large open fireplace and a chimney made of clay, invariably out of plumb as though liable to fall over. Within these ... interiors, men who in the heyday of their younger lives had come for gold from faraway homes in the "States," spent the brief remainder of their ... lives in idleness, solitude, filth, and wretchedness, rather than return to their former homes in poverty—"dead broke."

But the hopeful still came to California—this time in search of fertile land. By 1859 the state was evolving from a mining community into a wealthy agricultural society. The population shifted from the mining towns of the Mother Lode to rural areas in the Central Valley and along the coastline. The children of the agricultural districts soon outnumbered those in the mining areas by about four to one.

Among those children was eight-year-old Florence Weeks from Centerville, Michigan, who had crossed the plains with her family in 1859 to settle on her uncle's ranch near San Jose. In a diary kept by Florence and her mother, she described the shock of her arrival in California after a four-month journey.

We arrived at Mission San José in the afternoon and stopped there as Uncle Jared had so many friends and we had to be introduced. I can remember sitting in the back of the wagon and looking very seriously at the strangers, who afterward were to become our friends. We then started and drove three and a half miles to the ranch and a sorry looking place it was. The first look we had at it (my sister) Esther and I cried and asked Uncle to turn around and go straight back to Michigan. The house consisted of two shacks separated by a step; and the fields were covered with stubble. In a year's time there was a nice new house built, and so began our strange new life in California.

In 1860 the pace of westward expansion came to be symbolized by the Pony Express, which provided mail service between St. Joseph, Missouri, and Sacramento, California, using a rapid relay of horses and riders. The 1,966-mile gallop took eight to fifteen days, depending upon the weather.

The company purchased only the best horses and advertised for "young, skinny, wiry fellows, not over 18. Must be expert riders, willing to risk death daily. Orphans preferred." Billy Cody, who later became famous as Buffalo Bill, became a Pony Express rider at age fourteen.

The service completed 308 runs in each direction during its brief operation from April 1860 until the completion of the ocean-to-ocean telegraph line in October 1861. Several of the young travellers among the twenty thousand people heading west in 1860 reported sighting the Pony Express riders.

The emigrant families travelling overland to California now also encountered stage stops or stations along the way, sometimes only twenty-five to thirty miles apart, where they could replenish provisions or spend the night. One thirteen year old wrote in her diary, "Last night as the stage came into the station, the driver played 'The Star Spangled Banner' on his horn to awaken the station keeper. It sounded beautiful to us." The quality of the sleeping arrangements at such a station was ably conveyed by one "world traveler" named Richard Burton, who observed, "Upon the bedded floor ... lay in a seemingly promiscuous heap, men, women, children, lambs and puppies, all fast asleep in the arms of Morpheus."

In April 1861 the Civil War began. It cast its long shadows on the overland trails. Travel was light, with a migration of fewer than ten thousand individuals that year. Among the youthful diarists was sixteen-year-old Edith A. Lockhart, who travelled from Clark County, Missouri, to Honey Lake, California. There was dissent and tension in her wagon train, reflecting the anxiety of the emigrants fleeing the border states. The young girl noted in her diary:

> *June 9th: Mr. Clark ... turned his brother and children out of his wagon this morning. Mr. Calloway took his oldest daughter—and Mrs. Murphy his youngest.*
>
> *June 13th: A man came to our camp this morning, before breakfast, accompanied by a Newfundland dog, and said he had nothing to eat for several days—he had been with an Irish train and they treated him so badly, he determined to leave them.*
>
> *July 19: A man who was engaged in horse-stealing was shot last evening. ... He had been under guard and was very cleverly trying to make his escape— They buried him today—and inscribed on his head-board, "all who do likewise, shall so perish."*

In spite of increased threats of violence by the Sioux and Cheyenne tribes along the Platte River, overland travel was stepped up in 1862. Thirteen-year-old Ada Millington went that year from Keosaque, Iowa, to Santa Rosa, California, in the company of her parents, her sister Grace, her brothers Ira, James, and Seth, and the baby, George.

The Civil War was very much on her mind. Ada observed at their campsite in eastern Nebraska:

> *There are part of a family camped in the woods here who have been living away down in Missouri. ... They are waiting for the rest of their family to reach them, then they will move on to some of the Pacific States. The [Civil] War is what is driving them from their home, but it is not safe for them to all leave at once, for they would be prevented from doing so. Uncle Michael moved from that place last fall.*

The War Between the States even led to controversies over the naming of a newly acquired ox in their wagon train. "Its former owner had called it Abe

[Lincoln] and its mate Jeff [Davis]," wrote Ada, "but the men have named it Duke [to give no offense]."

Ada's journey followed the newly laid telegraph line along the Platte River. She admired the settlements that were beginning to spring up along the road.

> *On the opposite side of the [Horseshoe] Creek, is a station or ranch kept by a family who seem so nicely fixed. They had a nice grassy yard around the house, enclosed with a plank fence. The house and fence were whitewashed. The walls of the house were papered; the floors carpeted and the rooms furnished to correspond. A genuine sweet baby, dressed daintily in white, was cooing on the floor. All these unusual signs of civilization make our eyes stare and mouths water.*

Her train, consisting of four wagons, had not formally joined a company, but after her family left Fort Kearney they were "anxious to join up ... for we are approaching Indian country." Much to their surprise, their encounters with the Sioux were friendly: "They want to shake hands with us and say How! How!" wrote the girl in her diary. "They were a great curiosity to we children."

After they left Sioux territory and moved westward toward the tribal lands of the Cheyenne, the Millingtons came in sight of wigwams where "some Indians" were walking around. Ada described the incident.

> *When they saw us, they went into their camp and began to fire guns. This excited our suspicions and we stopped. ... The men loaded up all the rifles and revolvers we had with us and watched every movement of the enemy. After a long while, the other wagons came up and then we all went on. We found the wigwams to be tents and the "Indians" to be U.S. soldiers! We had a good laugh over the scare.*

They went on to the South Pass without encountering any serious Indian threats and replenished their provisions in Salt Lake City. From there, they followed the new stagecoach road to Carson City, Nevada. On the way, Ada's baby brother, George, fell sick. He died within four days. They were able to send his remains to Carson City on the stagecoach "free of charge," as Ada wrote, "but it cost $35.00 for one person who must go with it."

One of their hired men, Isaac, took on the lonely task of accompanying the small coffin. Twelve days after his departure on the stagecoach, the Millington family reached Carson City with their wagons. Wrote young Ada:

Ma, Pa, and we children went to see George's grave. It is about a mile from town … a desolate looking place enough. … The graveyard is enclosed by a fence with two railings. … Pa cut twenty notches on each rail near the head of his grave, for he is aged twenty months. … Then we went away, hoping to be able in a year at most to have George's remains brought to California to be buried near where we can settle.

On September 6 Ada's family reached Sacramento, and in another ten days, they arrived in Santa Rosa. "What a pleasing sight," wrote Ada, "to behold the inside of a house once more." The entry in her diary on September 16, 1862, reads:

To night is the one hundred and forty-first day of our journey Twenty weeks ago we got into our wagons and left our Iowa home. We are in excellent health, our journey has been prosperous, with as little trouble as could have been expected. No Indian difficulties to speak of were encountered, and none of our stock was lost or stolen. We are indeed blessed.

The Millingtons had forty-two dollars in cash left after their trip across the plains. They bought a dozen chickens, a few dishes, a calico dress apiece, and shoes for the girls and had a little money left for seed. Ada's father soon found an opportunity to exchange some of his teams and wagons for a farm near Santa Rosa, and they moved into their new home four weeks after their arrival. Ada later remembered:

Our farm was all fenced; had a nice, young orchard, vineyard, a good well and a tolerable house and barn. … We were very proud and pleased to be settled so nicely, so soon, and felt that we were at home. Still we lacked for a good many articles and for about a year everything we used, we had to buy.

Her father exchanged a gun for a table and some chairs and did day work for a neighbor to obtain some homemade bedsteads. He and his hired man cut wood and hauled it to town. They had chicken and eggs for pin money and a "pretty good" garden, which yielded enough fruit and vegetables to feed them; the men killed wild boars for winter pork.

With two horses—all that was left of the team that had crossed the plains—Ada's father put in a crop of wheat and raised about two hundred bushels in an exceptionally mild winter. Within the course of a year, he paid off his mortgage, made improvements in their new home, and sent Ada and her sister Grace to school at the newly established Pacific Methodist College.

The Millingtons had found their gold: It was in the fertile wheat fields of Bennett's valley.

In 1863 travel on the overland route continued unabated, motivated in part by the anxiety of many families to escape a father, uncle, brother, or son being drafted into one of the two opposing armies—the North or the South.

In 1864 about forty thousand emigrants headed west, twice as many as had made the trek the year before; this reflected increasing pressure to avoid the bloody war between the states. Fifteen-year-old Mary Eliza Warner was among the youthful diarists that year, travelling from DeKalb, Illinois, to Sardine Valley, California, with her parents, her brothers John Elliott, age thirteen, and Elon Lafayette, age eleven, and her little sister, Cora Elfie, age three.

A vivacious girl, she balked at wearing "bloomers," which were then in fashion with the travelling ladies, but she was eager to ride a horse and was willing to drive a team of horses all day. She also composed poetry "that was read before the company" and played checkers and chess. An elderly matron in her wagon train thought that "this was the first step toward gambling." At forts and telegraph stations on the overland route, she caught up with the news of the Civil War.

The Warner family went by stage route from Salt Lake City to Virginia City, Nevada, and Sardine Valley, California. They settled on a cattle ranch in the Sierra Nevada, where Mary Eliza was as adept at rounding up the herd as she had been at driving a team across the plains.

In 1865 the Civil War finally ended. Overland travel to California slowed to a trickle. Among the last of the pioneer children to tell of his travels to the Golden State that year was ten-year-old Francis Marion Watkins, who set out from Alba, Iowa, on April 1 with his parents, his five older brothers, his sister, Emma, age eight, his four-year-old niece, and his two-year-old nephew. There were ten horse-drawn wagons in their train when they crossed the Missouri River at Council Bluffs.

It was a dangerous year on the trail. Indian hostilities along the North and South Platte had increased in response to a massacre of around 150 Cheyenne by Colorado Volunteers in November 1864. Francis remembered: "The year 1865 was the worst year of all for Indians on the plains. It was just at the close of the war and any number of bad men who had been driven out of the war zone had gotten out among the Indians and were stirring them up."

They followed the same road along the Platte River that the overland stagecoach travelled. The stage stations were now only twelve to fifteen miles apart, close enough so the horses could travel at a stiff gallop all the way. The

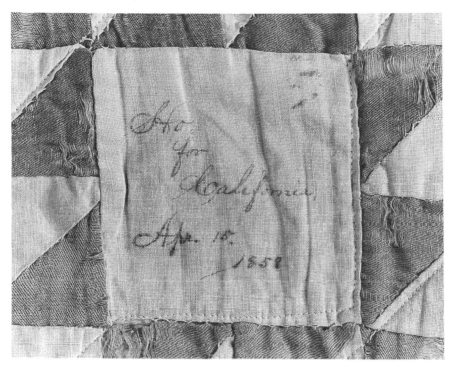

Quilt: "Ho for California" (collection of Ellen Reasoner Lopez; photograph courtesy Pat Ferraro, San Francisco)

attendants at each coach stop would hitch up fresh horses, and "away the stage would go again on the dead run." Every station was guarded by about twenty-five soldiers, and every coach was accompanied by eight cavalrymen to protect the driver and passengers from attack.

Along the way, young Francis counted fifteen freshly made graves with headboards reading "Slaughtered by the Indians," and at Julesburg he saw the burning stables of a settlement that had been set afire. But his own encounters with the Sioux were peaceful. He recalled only one incident that gave him a fright.

> *I got the scare of my life the morning we crossed the South Platte river. ...*
> *While we were still in camp waiting our turn to be ferried over ... I got ... a*
> *hundred yards away from the camp. I looked up in terror. There, coming*
> *right towards me at a jog trot on their little ponies were six or seven Indi-*
> *ans—all decked out in their feathers and war paint. ... I ran as fast as my*
> *... legs would go. I gained on the Indians and reached camp first. When they*

rode into camp they were … laughing their sides off. … The Indians had
come to sell us fresh [antelope] meat.

At Fort Laramie, his family joined the Crow train, composed of 240 wagons with 400 men, ages twenty-one to forty-five, "the largest and strongest train that ever crossed the plains." When they reached the desert, however, during the last third of their journey, the train broke up, and "it was every man for himself."

The Watkins family reached Petaluma, California, after four and a half months, without loss of life and property but with only twenty-five of the three thousand dollars in cash they had taken on their journey. Undaunted, they rented a ranch and started raising grain. Within three years they had cleared about fifteen thousand dollars and were ready to move again.

When they left Iowa in 1865, the construction of the Union Pacific Railroad had just begun. Four years later, in May 1869, a transcontinental railroad was completed that linked the Atlantic and Pacific Oceans. When Francis Marion Watkins returned "back East" that year to homestead in Kansas, it took his family only four days to reach Omaha by train from Salt Lake City. "Everything was changed," he remembered.

9

Vulnerable But Invincible

N EVER TAKE NO CUTOFS and hury along as fast as you can," wrote Virginia Reed to her cousin Mary in Springfield, Illinois, after she had survived her ordeal in the snow. A contemporary traveller, following her advice, will take a direct flight from St. Louis to San Francisco. Barring any unforeseen circumstances, she will traverse the two thousand miles from the banks of the Missouri to the shores of the Pacific in a little more than four hours. Virginia and her family took eleven months to complete that same journey. Everything has changed, indeed.

Yet there is a timelessness in the dimensions of the western landscape that passed in Virginia's view and in ours, in the vulnerability of the people who settled there, and in the invincibility of the children who travelled with them on the difficult roads west. What George Stewart wrote about the survivors of the Donner party could well be said about most pioneer children on their long and arduous journey on the overland trails: "Here if anywhere, we see ... children put to the final strain of body and spirit. ... Though despair is often close at hand, it never triumphs, and through all the stories runs a sustaining bond ... the sheer will to live."[11]

The terrors of our nature and of the world we live in remind us—forever—how vulnerable we are. Hence, biological and behavioral scientists, and historians as well, have spent a great deal of time and effort exploring the roots of our aggression, alienation, and unease. What is overlooked, but seems more awesome and miraculous, is our resilience as a species. Lately, we have begun to look for some of the roots of this resiliency. The answers are still tentative, but they invite other journeys to the world of children in more distant times and places. [12]

Psychologists have begun to study children and young people who overcame great adversities in their lives and grew into competent, confident, and caring adults. Among them are youngsters who were born and reared in chronic poverty; boys and girls who grew up in broken, disrupted, or troubled homes; the offspring of abusive, alcoholic, or psychotic parents; and children who experienced the horrors of the Holocaust and of contemporary wars.

Not surprisingly, these experiences left enduring scars on the lives of some individuals, but many more displayed a remarkable degree of resilience—a hardiness that resembles the grit and fortitude of the pioneer children in the mid-nineteenth century. Despite differences in the social and historical contexts in which these children lived, we can begin to discern a common core of individual characteristics and sources of support in the extended family and community that contributed to their capacity to overcome great odds. Perhaps, just perhaps, there is a certain timelessness in human resilience that transcends the here and now.

Like contemporary children who managed to cope successfully with chronic poverty, domestic conflict, and war, most pioneer children on the overland journey were active and outgoing youngsters—not passive onlookers. Their cheerful, easygoing personalities attracted the attention and affection of their fellow travellers—young and old alike.

Years after her fateful journey with the first band of emigrants to set out for California in 1841, Nancy Kelsey was still remembered by her fellow travellers for her cheerful nature. Without complaint, she had walked barefoot across the Sierra carrying her infant daughter, Ann. "She brought many a ray of sunshine [to] so many weary travellers," wrote one of her male companions in 1898.

Among the children of the ill-fated Donner party, the Reed sisters—thirteen-year-old Virginia and eight-year-old Patty—never lost their cheerfulness and their love of life. When the relief party finally arrived in Spring 1847 to rescue them from their ordeal in the snow, Patty Reed appeared in the cabin of the Donner children, "joyfully handing newly baked biscuits to each of us," remembered Eliza Donner. Patty later wrote how happy she had been in the company of her tiny wooden doll, which she managed to carry all the way to California.

Her vivacious half sister, Virginia Reed, could barely contain her joy when she was rescued. "I was ... feeling just as happy as a bird out of a cage," she wrote in a letter to C. F. McGlashan. "I laugh even to this day when I think of it." Although she had survived the same ordeal, thirteen-year-old Mary Murphy was far less sanguine. Her first message to her relatives back East in May 1847 reads, "William, Simon, Naomi and myself came through, but as for me, I have nothing to live for."

Seven-year-old Emma Griffis was more optimistic. Kidnapped twice in the spring and summer of 1849, she never lost her sunny disposition throughout her prolonged ordeal. Warren Saddler, the miner who rescued her and finally restored her to her parents, admired her "steadfast cheerfulness" and enjoyed her "happy company." So did a host of other caring strangers she met along the way—the miners who gave her a purse of gold, the woman who sewed her a new dress, the rancher who tracked down her parents.

Four-year-old Billy Lambkin, in contrast, was a far less appealing child. Kidnapped from his mother, abused, and finally abandoned by his father, he found a temporary home in J. Goldsborough Bruff's lodge in the wilderness on the Lassen Trail in winter 1849. During his two-month stay with his kind-hearted host, the boy was passive and withdrawn, appeared "indolent," and cried at the slightest provocation. When Billy died from food poisoning on New Year's Day, 1850, Bruff recorded sadly in his diary, "We've done all we could for the poor little sufferer." His efforts never restored in the little boy a feeling of security and trust that is the hallmark of resilient children—today as well as yesterday.

Such children—and we may surely count Emma Griffis and Virginia and Patty Reed among them—have the ability to attract love as well as physical and emotional support from members of their extended family and from friends and neighbors. This support could make the difference between life and death for youngsters who encountered serious adversities on their journey.

A case in point was the experience of the forty-one children of the Donner party. One-third—mostly infants and toddlers—died during that ordeal; two-thirds survived. The twenty-six survivors had the support of strong, competent mothers; of caring siblings; of cousins, aunts, and uncles; and of friends in their "travelling community." Those who perished were mostly young children below age five who lacked the support of an extended family and whose mothers were left to fend for themselves without a husband by their side.

"The mothers were the real heroes," wrote Patty Reed in 1879 in a letter to C. F. McGlashan, the historian of the Donner party. By then, Martha Reed Lewis had borne eight children of her own and could well appreciate the strength and fortitude of the women who had sheltered and protected her in the winter of 1846–1847. During that terrible ordeal two-thirds of the men perished, but only one-fourth of the women died. The children were their hope for the future.

A competent mother emerges as one of the major sources of emotional support in studies of contemporary children who have overcome great odds. That was true for the pioneer children on the overland trails as well. The only two families in the ill-fated Donner party to survive intact were the Breens and the Reeds, both of which were headed by strong, independent women. Margaret Breen, age forty, and Margaret Reed, age thirty-two, pooled their resources and never stopped thinking about how best to safeguard the lives of their children.

More isolated than the Reed and Breen families, Tamsen and Elizabeth Donner struggled at the Alder Creek camp to take care of twelve children the best they could—without the help of their husbands. Jacob Donner had died, and George Donner was seriously ill. The two determined women managed to send ten children who could walk or be carried out with the two relief parties that came in February and March 1847. Elizabeth Donner and her two youngest boys, Lewis, age three, and Samuel, age four, stayed behind and died from starvation.

In March 1847, Tamsen Donner—the last of the mothers in the Donner party to stay behind—died as well. She perished after her three young daughters had been rescued by the third relief party and her husband had died. With Tamsen's death vanished her dream of a "young ladies seminary" she had planned to open in California. A former schoolteacher, she left her daughters a legacy of a love of books and learning.

There were other indomitable mothers who followed Tamsen Donner on the difficult roads west. One was Sarah Royce, who had to abandon almost all of her possessions toward the end of her journey on the Carson Trail in 1849. Riding on a mule with her two-year-old daughter on her lap, she managed to bring to California her Bible, a tiny lap writing desk, and a children's book she had found among the objects strewn across the Nevada desert, left behind by other emigrants. "I thought it would please Mary, so I put it in my pocket," she wrote in her "Pilgrim's Diary."

And tiny Juliette Brier—all who knew her agreed—was by far "the best man" in the Jayhawker party that trekked across desolate Death Valley in the winter of 1849–1850. Carrying her four-year-old son on her back and leading his six-year-old and eight-year-old brothers by the hand, she drove her emaciated cattle across the barren mountains and the seemingly endless desert. "I couldn't give up," she said. When offered the chance to stay behind with her children at Travertine Springs and be sent for later, she emphatically declined. "I have never been a hindrance," she said. "I have never kept the company waiting, neither have my children. Every step I will take will be towards California."

Perhaps one of the most memorable mothers on the Gila Trail was the widow Brown who, in fall 1858, saved the lives of her children from an attack by Mojave Indians by barricading herself with her son and daughters in her covered wagon, behind quilts and featherbeds. When the attack was over, and after she had taken care of her wounded daughter Sally Fox and buried her husband, she rode on horseback into the searing heat of the Arizona desert, carrying her two-year-old son, Orrin, in her arms. When her horse gave out, she walked across the desert for hundreds of miles, carrying her little boy. He eventually died from dehydration. She buried him in New Mexico and then went on to California with his sisters.

Older siblings were often major sources of physical and emotional support for the children on the overland trail. They kept each other company, confided their hopes and fears to each other, and cheered each other up when the going got tough. They also shared food, drink, and shelter; nursed sick or injured siblings back to health; and, on occasion, saved their lives. If their parents were injured or died along the way, they took full responsibility for the welfare of their younger brothers and sisters.

Some of the most powerful descriptions of strong sibling bonds came from the narratives of the child survivors of the Donner party. Among the Jacob and George Donner families and the Reeds especially, there was a complex array of kinship ties. George Donner had been married three times and brought children from his second and third marriages on the journey. Betsy Donner, the wife of his brother Jacob, had been married twice, and two of her children from her first marriage had come along, together with the five children from her second marriage. Margaret Reed also had children from two marriages—the oldest, Virginia Backenstoe Reed, from her first marriage and the three younger ones by James Frazier Reed. But it did not seem to matter whether brothers and sisters were full or half siblings—the bond between them was strong and enduring, especially when disaster struck.

The Reed children were a close-knit group. Virginia was very fond of her half sister, Patty, and her two half brothers. During their ordeal in the snow, she entertained the younger children and read to them from her favorite books. She was especially solicitous of her five-year-old half brother, James Reed, on their long march to safety across the snow-covered Sierra. She wrote later in a letter to McGlashan, "We were, Mother and I, very much afraid that he would give out. So we encouraged him in every way, kept telling him that every step he took he was gitting nearer to Papa."

Elitha and Leanna Donner, George Donner's children from a previous marriage, were in that same relief party. Twelve-year-old Leanna was barely able to walk. Each day their food allowances were cut, and one evening Leanna, famished, ate her last ration of two small pieces of jerked beef at one time—saving nothing for breakfast. Her fourteen-year-old sister, seeing her distress, shared her own small portion with her. It was an incident Leanna would never forget.

Back at Alder Creek camp, their half sisters, the daughters of Tamsen Donner, shared the warmth of their bodies as well as food. Eliza, the youngest, remembered that during the coldest winter weather, she and her sisters were kept in bed. Her place was always in the middle, between Frances and Georgia. They snuggled up close, giving her of their warmth—and thus kept her from freezing to death.

The Brier brothers had to contend with the searing desert heat instead as they trekked through Death Valley in the winter of 1849–1850. They rarely complained, although they could barely talk, so swollen were their lips and tongues. Six-year-old John tried to cheer up his four-year-old brother, Kirk, by telling him of the wonderful water they would find to quench their thirst. But water was sometimes a menace to a young child, and an older sibling would risk her life to save a toddler from drowning. Ten-year-old Mary Ackley observed such an incident in 1852 at a river crossing when a wagon body with two children floated a mile downstream. The oldest child, a twelve-year-old girl, saved her two-year-old sister by catching hold of the wagon bows and holding her sister's head above the water.

Not every rescue attempt by a sibling had such a happy ending. Lorenzo Oatman was unable to save his brothers and sisters in the massacre on the Gila Trail. For five years, Lorenzo sought aid in the rescue in of his missing sisters. Finally, in 1856, he was reunited with his older sister, Olive, who had been released from captivity by the Mojave Indians. From then on, until Lorenzo's early death, the two were inseparable. Despite her brother's loyalty and caring, Olive continued for years to mourn the loss of their younger sister, Mary, who had died from starvation.

The emigrant children were often accompanied by other members of their extended families, who gave them affection as well as physical and emotional support along the way: grandparents, like Sarah Keyes; aunts and uncles, like Aunt Betsy and Uncle George Donner; and many cousins. Most wagon trains were made up of friends and neighbors from the same hometown.

Families that were part of this travelling community shared with one another as long as they had anything to share. When the Reeds lost most of their thirsty oxen west of the Great Salt Lake, their children crossed the desert on foot during the night. At daylight, they met the wagons of Jacob Donner. His wife invited them to ride with her. Patty Reed remembered gratefully that "we little ones were glad with the thought of riding with Aunt Betsy." Walking with her young daughters through that same salty wasteland, Tamsen Donner gave other suffering children small lumps of sugar moistened with a drop of peppermint and, when the situation grew more desperate, put a flattened bullet in each child's mouth to engage his or her attention.

Later, in their encampment at Donner Lake, the Breens took in Mrs. Reed and her four children when they were left without a home after they had eaten the hides that covered their makeshift shelter. Virginia Reed gratefully remembered that "Mrs. Breen prolonged my life by slipping me little bits of meat now and then, when she discovered I could not eat the hide."

Some of the members of the wagon train risked their lives by venturing off on their own to get provisions for the famished children. Among the most notable examples were McCutchen, the father of an infant daughter (who died from starvation), and the bachelor Stanton, who were the first volunteers to get supplies for the stranded Donner party. Later, two other fathers, William Eddy and William Foster, came back to rescue the remaining children, only to find that their own young sons, three-year-old James P. Eddy and four-year-old George Foster, had died during their absence from lack of proper food.

Three years later, risking death from thirst, John Rogers and William Lewis Manly (who had no children of their own) trekked more than five hundred miles through the desert to the Spanish settlements in the San Fernando valley and back again to Death Valley to get provisions for the Arcane and Bennett families and their four young children. "We said to each other," Manly wrote later, "if no women and children was out there, we wouldn't go back."

The pioneer children and their families also garnered physical and emotional support from other westbound travellers on the overland trails. Passing wagon trains would often take care of orphans who had lost their parents to deadly diseases. Luella Dickenson's husband reported the death of two "consumptives," a Mr. Hicklen and his wife, who died on the prairies in May 1846. The company dug a grave for the parents, in which they were placed side by side, wrapped in blankets. Their children, two-year-old Mary and baby Jimmy, were cared for by members of the company.

Three years later, in 1849, an ox train from Missouri "adopted" the Gilmore children whose parents had died of cholera near the Sandy River. And in 1852, Margaret Windsor, a young girl travelling "the plains across," during the last five hundred miles of her journey, cared for a baby whose mother had died en route. At each campground, Margaret would seek a woman to nurse the infant. She was, she later recalled, never once refused. [13]

Sometimes a passing wagon train would provide for stranded families that had suffered mishaps. In a magnificent gesture of kindness, the Smith train "adopted" the Brown family in summer 1858 after they had survived an attack by Mojave Indians in Arizona. Their captain, a Freemason, killed his own cattle so he could provide food for the lone widow and her young children. He later escorted her family safely to California, refusing any pay for his services.

One of the most memorable examples of a good neighbor was the captain of the Washington City and California Mining Association, J. Goldsborough Bruff, the father of two young children he had left with his wife back East. In his refuge in the wilderness on the Lassen Trail in winter 1849, he ministered to the needs of an unending stream of young children and their families who passed by his campground. He offered them shelter and warm meals, found warm clothing for them, and comforted them.

Many of the civilians and soldiers who participated in the relief expeditions in the Sierra Nevada in 1847 and 1849 took money out of their own purses and gave it to destitute emigrant families after they had reached the California settlements. But perhaps one of the most moving acts of kindness extended to an emigrant child was that of a freckle-faced, red-haired boy who offered a cup of "the finest milk you ever tasted" to orphaned Eliza Donner after her rescue and arrival at Sutter's Fort.

The diaries, letters, and reminiscences of the pioneer children also tell us of many acts of kindness by the indigenous people they met on their journey. The children, perhaps less anxious and less judgmental than their parents, reciprocated with genuine feelings of gratitude and affection for the help they received from Native Americans.

Sarah Winnemucca, a small child at the time, recalled the many ways in which her grandfather, the chief of the Piute Indians, assisted the emigrant families that crossed their native lands. In October 1846 two American Indian guides from Sutter's Fort, Luis and Salvador, were the first to bring provisions to the Donner party. Eight-year-old Patty and five-year-old Jimmy Reed, footsore and weary, rode behind them on a mule on their way up the Sierra. Later, fourteen-year-old John Breen met a friendly "Digger" Indian who gave him some soap roots he had in his pack and then went on his way. The hungry boy never forgot this simple act of kindness.

In the westward migrations of the late 1840s and early 1850s, the Crow Indians were especially helpful at dangerous river crossings, taking emigrant children and their mothers safely across on horseback. Elisha Brooks gratefully remembered how the Crow looked after his mother and her five young children when their teamster abandoned their wagon on the plains. Ironically, he had feared an Indian attack.

On the Gila Trail in the mid- and late 1850s, the Arapaho and Yuma Indians supplied the emigrants and their children with fresh vegetables and fruit and welcomed them into their homes. Wounded in the massacre that wiped out his family in 1851, Lorenzo Oatman could not have survived without the help of friendly Pima Indians. In 1853, nine-year-old Maggie Hall gratefully remembered the Moncapah Indians at the Gila River who supplied them with fresh melons and beans. "They were so friendly," she wrote, "they never tired of watching us and our ways." Even the warlike Apache were protective of white children. The Apache Chief Cochise, who visited Sally Fox in her camp in spring 1859, assured her that he was "bueno"—a good man. True to his word, he let her train pass undisturbed across his native land.

The narratives of some youngsters on the overland trail tell us of their budding friendships with Native American children. Ten-year-old Kate McDaniel was enamored by the fifteen-year-old daughter of a Sioux chief. Eliza McAuley grew fond of the American Indian Povo and his small son. Olive Oatman became attached to the daughter of the Mojave chief who had adopted her and her little sister, Mary. Years after Olive had been released from captivity, the Mojave princess still hoped she might tire of her "pale-faced friends" and return to her.

The Donner children maintained a lifelong friendship with their teamster John Baptiste Trudeau, son of a French trapper and a Mexican mother. During their stay at Alder Creek camp in the winter of 1846–1847, he was the only person who remained strong enough to gather firewood. He saw to it that the children of Jacob and George Donner were kept warm and entertained. After their rescue in spring 1847, he accompanied seven-year-old Mary Donner, whose foot was badly burned, to the Naval Hospital in San Francisco, still feeling an obligation to look after her. Throughout the 1850s, he continued to visit Eliza and Georgia Donner in Sonoma, where they were living with their adopted "grandpa" and "grandma" Brunner. On his first visit he brought them two beautiful bunches of raisins to soften their recollections of the hungry times they had endured together.

Equally thoughtful and solicitous of the welfare of the emigrant children on the southern routes were the Spaniards and Mexicans who lived in Arizona, New Mexico, and southern California. The del Valle family at Rancho San Francisquito waited carefully on the emaciated Arcane and Bennett children who had escaped the ordeal of Death Valley in 1850, plying them with oranges and tortillas. The Hispanic women of Albuquerque and Socorro, who took care of the needs of the Brown children and their widowed mother, did likewise.

Most pioneer children, then, could rely on the love and encouragement of members of their extended family, on the physical and emotional support of their "travelling community," and on the kindness of caring strangers. But the young emigrants also gave something in return: They had skills or special talents that were valued by their elders and peers on the long journey West.

Seventeen-year-old Moses Schallenberger, who spent a solitary winter in the Sierra Nevada in 1845, was an expert hunter and trapper. The two young Ferguson brothers, left alone to guard their family's wagon on the Lassen Trail in 1849, were handy with their rifles. Sarah Ide and Virginia Reed were accomplished horsewomen.

Seventeen-year-old Eliza McAuley, who went across the plains with her older brother and sister in 1852, was the chief cook for her company; like Sarah Ide, she could also drive a herd of cattle, and, like the Ferguson boys, she knew how to handle a pistol. Fifteen-year-old Mary Eliza Warner, who came westward in 1864, knew how to cook, sew, and nurse a sick child, and she also wrote poetry "that was read before the company" and sketched the beauty of the western landscape. Like any young man in her wagon train, she could ride, drive a team of horses, and play ball. She was an avid chess player as well and was no slouch at checkers.

Many young emigrants on the trail also had musical talents that helped them pass the time on the long journey west, especially when their wagon train was bogged down because of poor weather or they encountered unforeseen obstacles. Susan Thompson entertained her company with the violin; Jasper Hill and the young miners he befriended were, by his own account, "very good musicians who passed off the idle moments by playing on their instruments, while others were singing."

The pioneer children on the overland trail had plenty of opportunity to practice "acts of required helpfulness." Like contemporary children who have proven their resilience in the face of great odds, they were frequently asked to take on responsibilities on which the well-being of family members and of friends and neighbors depended. These experiences taught them self-reliance, gave them a sense of worth, and strengthened their conviction that hard times could be endured and overcome.

As long as they were healthy and could walk, even the youngest children were assigned duties on which the welfare of the wagon train depended. They took care of the chickens, cows, horses, mules, and oxen and fed the dogs. They also helped provide extra food and fuel for their company. They gathered berries, caught fish, and hunted for antelope and buffalo meat. The older girls assisted their mothers with the cooking—in good weather and bad. Standing guard at night was an important task for boys as young as age ten or eleven—even in rain, hail, or dust storms. If they fell asleep, as Elisha Brooks and his brother did only once, the company risked the loss of their cattle from a stampede or marauding Indians.

During the day, many youngsters who were good on horseback rode ahead of the train. Sometimes they would pick out a camping place or a good prospect for feed and water, as fifteen-year-old Henry Wade did in Death Valley. At other times, they would drive the cattle. Girls like Sarah Ide, Eliza McAuley, and Maria Eliza Warner were as expert as the teenage boys at that job. The girls also nursed the sick in the wagon train. Mary Ackley and Maria Elliott would minister to a fever-ridden baby or bind the wounds from an accidental gunshot or replace the splints on a broken leg. Teenage boys, like John and Edward Breen, would help bury the dead. Wrote John Breen, who was fourteen at the time, "Death had become so common an event that it was looked upon as a matter of course."

The emigrant trains that confronted an early and severe winter in the Sierra Nevada or lost their way exacted still greater demands from their young. Moses Schallenberger in 1845 and the Ferguson boys in 1849 spent weeks alone in the snow guarding the wagons that contained the earthly possessions of their company and their family.

In an emergency, young girls took unusual risks as well to safeguard the welfare of their parents. Under cover of dark, Virginia Reed followed her stepfather, who had been banished from their wagon train for killing a man. His company had denied him access to provisions and arms. Undaunted, his stepdaughter slipped out of camp at night to bring him his rifle, pistols, ammunition, and food. Her mother was left alone with four young children. "When I saw the distress of my mother," Virginia later wrote, "with the little ones clinging around her and no arm to lean upon, I realized that I must be strong and help mama bear her sorrows."

And they bore up with fortitude—the children of the Donner party in 1846 and those on the Lassen Trail in 1849—carrying their families' last possessions on their backs and their infant brothers and sisters in their arms. When they finally arrived in California, they often took over the responsibilities of a parent who had died or become seriously ill or disabled on the journey.

The Scharmann brothers, eleven-year-old Hermann and fifteen-year-old Jacob, worked all day with their father at placer mining on the Upper Feather River. Each night they returned, exhausted, to their "home," a sheet of canvas stretched on piles. Their mother was ill and eventually died from diarrhea and dehydration, so the boys would cook a makeshift meal before they fell asleep on the ground, wrapped in their ragged blankets.

Young girls became expert gold miners as well. At age eleven, the orphaned Martha Gentry worked in the California diggings and found enough nuggets to support herself and what was left of her family. And in the town of Ringgold, John Wood found two daintily dressed little girls who carried dirt in buckets to their father, who was rocking out the gold. Their mother and brother had died on the plains—"leaving none but father and us," said one. Said her sister, "I had to drive the ox-team many a day on the mountains."

In neighboring Nevada City, fourteen-year-old Rebecca Nutting and her father eked out a living by providing meals for miners. The young girl took care of the cooking and most other chores, for her father's health was very poor. When he recovered, Rebecca's father went to Bear River and opened up a boardinghouse for miners and loggers. Rebecca carried on without complaint, trusting that God would help those who helped themselves.

Contemporary studies of resilient children reveal that they usually have a strong religious faith that gives meaning to their lives, even when they experience great pain and suffering. That was true for most of the pioneer children. Even when confronted with seemingly insurmountable hardships, they believed life made sense and that they had some control over their fate. Their faith was not necessarily tied to a specific religious orientation but, rather, to confidence in some higher power, some center of value. It did not seem to matter whether they were nominally Catholic, like the Breens, or mainstream Protestant, like the Reeds and Donners, or Methodists, like the Briers, or Mormons, like the Oatman family. What mattered was their conviction, embodied in their faith, that "things will work out in the end."

Sometimes this conviction blinded them to real dangers that lay ahead and threatened their survival. A case in point was the Oatman family. Despite repeated warnings by the local people about the imminent danger of Indian raids along the Gila Road, "my father resolved to proceed under the protection of God," wrote Olive Oatman. He led his exhausted wagon train right into a bloody massacre that claimed the lives of six members of his family.

But more frequently, a strong faith mobilized the pioneer children and their families to perform acts of charity, compassion, and discipline that assured the survival of their travelling community. It also provided them with positive role models. Eliza Donner remembered that her mother "held us children spellbound with wondrous tales of Joseph in Egypt, or Daniel in the lion's den, of Elijah, healing the widow's son ... and of the Master who took young children in his arms and blessed them."

The Breens were the only Catholic family in the Donner party, and despite all hardships, they maintained a regular routine of prayers in their snowbound cabin—day and night. Little Patty Reed was very much impressed by the ritual of lighting candles from little sticks, split up like kindling wood, which were constantly kept on the hearth. "All of us," she wrote in a letter to McGlashan, "would kneel to hear and feel ... God have mercy!"

Virginia Reed, snowbound with her family in the Breen cabin, made a vow one night "that if God would send us relief and let me see my father again, I would be a Catholic." She lived up to that vow after her family was safely reunited. At age sixteen, at the time of her marriage, she converted to Catholicism. Since God had kept his side of the bargain, Virginia Reed kept hers.

Juliette Brier and her three young sons, trekking across Death Valley in 1849, never lost their abiding faith. "I couldn't give up," she later wrote. "We needed all our hope and faith." Ten years later, seven-year-old Julia Brown, another sojourner across the southwestern desert, kept walking for more than five hundred miles with the conviction "one thing assures me; the Lord will provide."

They never lost hope. The narratives of most pioneer children tell us of moments of sadness and fear, but there is little talk of despair or the thought of suicide when confronted with seemingly insurmountable odds or the loss of people they cherished. The orphaned Mary Murphy, who hoped she would not live long because she was "tired of this troublesome world," was an exception rather than the rule.

More typical was the response of Moses Schallenberger. Left alone to guard his company's wagons, he was saddened by the departure of his friends, but he quickly regained his optimism. "They had not been long out of sight," he later wrote, "before my spirits began to revive, and I began to think ... that something might turn up." And Patty Reed, separated from the rest of her family after they had departed with the first relief party, consoled herself with the thought that "mama, sister and brother had plenty to eat and drink ... and that they were well cared for."

Children on the trail often tried to impart hope to despairing parents or siblings. The two Jenkins boys, ages twelve and fourteen, did just that when they stopped, cold and wet, one evening at Bruff's camp. Bruff wrote, "The mother sat with her elbows on her knees, and her face in her hands, weeping. … The old man stood opposite, sighing and despondent, while the two brave little boys were endeavoring to cheer them up, and to encourage them." But the most memorable entry in Bruff's diary dates from an encounter he had experienced on the Lassen Trail a few day earlier: "A father with two children, a boy and a girl, were driving a lot of lame oxen along. The children were very small, and the little girl said to her brother, 'Never mind, Buddy, t'aint far to grass and water.'"

Some children never reached that promised land, which had plenty to eat and drink for them and their weary animals. One of five of the youngsters whose journeys I have traced here died on the way to California. Fifteen children in the Donner party perished in the snows of the Sierra Nevada; six children of the Oatman family died in or after the massacre near the Gila River. Other youngsters—like the Alford brothers, Billy Lambkin, George Millington, Orrin Brown, and the little Scharmann girl—died from accidents and illnesses.

Some youngsters were disappointed when they reached the "promised land." After the deaths of their little sister and their mother, the two surviving Scharmann boys and their father returned to New York. "California is a land of vice and gruesomeness," Hermann Scharmann wrote in a newspaper article in the *New York Staats Zeitung* in 1852. Others, forever restless, sought greener pastures in other states. Francis Marion Watkins went "back East" to homestead on free land in Kansas; Benjamin Bonney and his family settled in Oregon.

A few of the youngsters on the overland trails were scarred, physically or emotionally, by the ordeal. In the McGlashan collection of letters by the surviving children of the Donner party is a brief note, written by Nancy Graves in 1879, in which she declines an interview. The memory of having partaken of the flesh of her dead mother was still too painful for her—even as a middle-aged woman. Olive Oatman, after her release from captivity in 1856 until her death in 1903, was prone to frequent weeping spells, according to the testimony of her friend Susan Thompson Lewis. "We erased the tatoo marks from her face, but we could not erase the wild life from her heart," she wrote in her reminiscences.

Eighty of the one hundred survivors who settled in California left records of their adult lives—lives that were long and productive. Among the men were fishermen, ranchers, and vintners; freighters, stagecoach operators, and innkeepers; skilled craftsmen, machinists, and businessmen; teachers and school principals; lawyers, judges, and preachers. Among the women were writers, lecturers, and schoolteachers; the daughter of the first (and only) governor of the California Republic; the wife of a U.S. senator; and the sister of a Harvard professor of philosophy.

Most remained spry and active into old age and lived well into their eighties and nineties, especially the women. Bright and witty Virginia Reed never lost her enthusiasm and her love of life. Her spelling improved with time. She wrote to her cousin Mary in spring 1847: "We are all very pleased with Callifornia. ... It is a beautiful Country. ... It aut to be a beautiful Country to pay us for our trubel giting there."

In 1980, 133 years later, English writer Gwen Moffat retraced Virginia's steps on the California Trail driving a sturdy four-wheel-drive Scout, christened Old Crump, in memory of the faithful ox that had carried four small children out of Death Valley in 1850. In the epilogue of her book *Hard Road West,* she pays a proper tribute to the pioneers—men, women, and children—who first made the long journey from the banks of the Missouri to the shores of the Pacific.

> Their fortitude was almost incomprehensible; they learned to accept grief and they learned how to cope with fear. Cold and sad but without panic, they took the measure of fear and walked through it, realizing in the empty centre that there was nothing to be afraid of except death, and that was an old acquaintance and therefore could be disregarded. So they lived, and they survived, with dignity. (p. 191)

10

Postscript: Narratives of Mary Murphy, Sallie Hester, and Elizabeth Keegan

T HIRTEEN-YEAR-OLD Mary Murphy lost six members of her family—
her mother, three brothers, a niece, and a brother-in-law—during the entrapment of the Donner party. She wrote this letter at Johnson's ranch after her
rescue by the first relief party in spring 1847.

THE LETTER OF MARY MURPHY,
AGE THIRTEEN, MAY 25, 1847

California Territory, May the 25 1847

*Dear Uncles, Aunts and Cousins. I take my pen in hand to say a few
words to you all. I will give you a small sketch of our travels. After we left,
we went on to St. Louis and FOSTER and SARAH came with us and then
we cam on to Independence and there we wrote to you and then we left the
United States and in about six hundred miles from there to Sweetwater river
and there wrote again and then crost the rockey mountouns and took Has-
ting new rout by the big salt lake and had to make our road which kept us
behind about two or three weeks and we got out of provisions and had to kill
our oxens. There was about 85 persons in our company. MR FOSTER was
going to go ahead and come back with provisions but in loading the six
shooter it went of and shot MR PIKE in the back. He died in about one half*

hour and in that time he suffered more than tongue can tell. It was on the last day of October. We was then about 2 hundred miles from the settlements. That evening it commenced snowing. In three days we got to the dividing ridge of the Sierra Nevada or snowy range of the California mountains. It was snowing so that we could not find the road and we stoped by the mountain lake. It snowed 2 weeks. It was beyond hope almost for us to go father so we killed what few cattle we had left. We made several atempts to go on foot but the snow was soft and we would almost sink to our neck. After we had been there 2 or 3 months a company of ten men and five women went over on snow shoes. FOSTER, SARAH, HARRIETTE and LEMUEL was in this company. They ware thirty days coming 100 miles. They starved till they ware so weak that they could not stand up and they lived on thare friends that ware dying every day. LEMUEL died among the rest. There was but 2 men got through. FOSTER was one that got through. All the women got through and a company went out after the rest that were in the mountains. When they got there half the company had starved to death and LANDRUM, GEORGE and little CATHERINE, HARRIETTE's baby and my poor illfated and persecuted Mother was all dead. WILLIAM, SIMON, NAOMI and myself came through but as for me I have nothing to live for, a poor orphan, Motherless and almost Friendless. CHARLOTTE, you have been the companion of all my thoughts. Now just think of me in a strange country and to think on my poor mother and brother that are dead, their bodies to feed the hungry bears and wolves, for there was no burying them the snow was so deep. This is a very small sketch of what we have sufard but I hope I shall not live long for I am tired of this troublesome world and want to go to my mother. I know that she is in a better world. I must close these few lines. This is for all my friends and relations. I have not mind enough to write a letter. I will bid you all a long and perhaps a last farwell.

MARY A. M. MURPHY

DIARY OF SALLIE HESTER,

AGE FOURTEEN, MARCH 20, 1849–JUNE 3, 1850

Sallie Hester went overland in 1849 at age fourteen, with her parents, two brothers, and one sister. Her father was elected district attorney and later appointed judge of the Third Judicial District in San Jose, where her family settled in 1850.

Bloomington, Indiana, Tuesday, March 20, 1849.—*Our family, consisting of father, mother, two brothers and one sister, left this morning for that far and much talked of country, California. My father started our wagons one month in advance, to St. Joseph, Missouri, our starting point. We take the steamboat at New Albany, going by water to St. Joe. The train leaving Bloomington on that memorable occasion was called the Missionary Train, from the fact that the Rev. Isaac Owens of the Methodist Church and a number of ministers of the same denomination were sent as missionaries to California. Our train numbered fifty wagons. The last hours were spent in bidding good bye to old friends. My mother is heartbroken over this separation of relatives and friends. Giving up old associations for what? Good health, perhaps. My father is going in search of health, not gold. The last good bye has been said—the last glimpse of our old home on the hill, and a wave of hand at the old Academy, with a good bye to kind teachers and schoolmates, and we are off. We have been several days reaching New Albany [Indiana] on account of the terrible conditions of the roads. Our carriage upset at one place. All were thrown out, but no one was hurt. We were detained several hours on account of this accident. My mother thought it a bad omen and wanted to return and give up the trip.*

New Albany, March 24. This is my first experience of a big city and my first glimpse of a river and steamboats.

March 26. Took the steamboat Meteor *this evening for St. Joe. Now sailing on the broad Ohio, floating toward the far West.*

St. Louis, April 2. Spent the day here, enjoyed everything.

April 3. On the Missouri River, the worst in the world, sticking on sand bars most of the time.

Jefferson City, April 6. Stopped here for one hour, visited the State House, enjoyed everything.

April 14. Our boat struck another sand bar and was obliged to land passengers ten miles below St. Joe. Having our carriage with us, we were more fortunate than others. We reached the first day an old log hut, five miles from town, where we camped for the night. Next day an old friend of my father heard of our arrival, came to see us and insisted that we stay at his home until we hear from our wagons.

St. Joe, April 27. Here we are at last, safe and sound. We expect to remain here several days, laying in supplies for the trip and waiting our turn to be ferried across the river. As far as eye can reach, so great is the emigration, you see nothing but wagons. This town presents a striking appearance—a vast army on wheels—crowds of men, women and lots of children and last but not least the cattle and horses upon which our lives depend.

May 1. *Crossed the river. Camped six miles from town. Remained here several days, getting things shipshape for our long trip.*

May 13. *This is a small Indian village. There is a mission at this place, about thirty pupils, converts to the Christian faith. Left camp May 6, and have been travelling all week. We make it a point to rest over Sunday. Have a sermon in camp every Sunday morning and evening. I take advantage of this stopover to jot down our wandering during the week.*

May 21. *Camped on the beautiful Blue River, 215 miles from St. Joe, with plenty of wood and water and good grazing for our cattle. Our family all in good health. When we left St. Joe my mother had to be lifted in and out of our wagons; now she walks a mile or two without stopping, and gets in and out of the wagons as spry as a young girl. She is perfectly well. We had two deaths in our train within the past week of cholera—young men going West to seek their fortunes. We buried them on the banks of the Blue River, far from home and friends. This is a beautiful spot. The Plains are covered with flowers. We are now in the Pawnee Nation, a dangerous and hostile tribe. We are obliged to watch them closely and double our guards at night. They never make their appearance during the day, but skulk around at night, steal cattle and do all the mischief they can. When we camp at night, we form a corral with our wagons and pitch our tents on the outside, and inside of this corral we drive our cattle, with guards stationed on the outside of tents. We have a cooking stove made of sheet iron, a portable table, tin plates and cups, cheap knives and forks (best ones packed away), camp stools, etc. We sleep in our wagons on feather beds; the men who drive for us [sleep] in the tent. We live on bacon, ham, rice, dried fruits, molasses, packed butter, bread, coffee, tea and milk as we have our own cows. Occasionally some of the men kill an antelope and then we have a feat; and sometimes we have fish on Sunday.*

Fort Kearney, May 24. *This fort is built of adobe with walls of same.*

June 3. *Our tent is now pitched on the beautiful Platte River, 315 miles from St. Joe. The cholera is raging. A great many deaths; graves everywhere. We as* *a company are all in good health. Game is scarce; a few antelope in sight. Roads bad.*

Goose Creek, June 17. *This is our day of rest. There are several encampments in sight, making one feel not quite out of civilization. So many thousands all en route for the land of gold and Italian skies! Passed this week Court House Rock. Twelve miles from this point is Chimney Rock, 230 feet in height.*

Fort Laramie, June 19. *This fort is of adobe, enclosed with a high wall of the same. The entrance is a hole in the wall just large enough for a person to crawl through. The impression you have on entering is that you are in a small town. Men were engaged in all kinds of business from blacksmith up. We stayed here some time looking at everything that was to be seen and enjoying it to the fullest extent after our long tramp. We camped one mile from the fort, where we remained a few days to wash and lighten up.*

June 21. *Left camp and started over the Black Hills, sixty miles over the worst road in the world. Have again struck the Platte and followed it until we came to the ferry. Here we had a great deal of trouble swimming our cattle across, taking our wagons to pieces, unloading and replacing our traps. A number of accidents happened here. A lady and four children were drowned through the carelessness of those in charge of the ferry.*

Bear River, June 1. *Lots of Indians in sight, mostly naked, disgusting and dirty looking.*

July 2. *Passed Independence Rock. This rock is covered with names. With great difficulty I found a place to cut mine. Twelve miles from this is Devil's Gate. It's an opening in the mountain through which the Sweetwater River flows. Several of us climbed this mountain—somewhat perilous for youngsters not over fourteen. We made our way to the very edge of the cliff and looked down. We could hear the water dashing, splashing and roaring as if angry at the small space through which it was forced to pass. We were gone so long that the train was stopped and men sent out in search of us. We made all sorts of promises to remain in sight in the future. John Owens, a son of the minister, my brother John, sister Lottie and myself were the quartet. During the week we passed the South Pass and the summit of the Rocky Mountains. Four miles from here are the Pacific Springs.*

Lee Springs, July 4. *Had the pleasure of eating ice. At this point saw lots of dead cattle left by the emigrants to starve and die. Took a cutoff; had neither* *wood nor water for fifty-two miles. Traveled in the night. Arrived at Green River next day at two o'clock in the afternoon. Lay by two days to rest man and beast after our long and weary journey.*

July 29. *Passed Soda Springs. Two miles further on are the Steamboat Springs. They puff and blow and throw the water high in the air. The springs are in the midst of a grove of trees, a beautiful and romantic spot.*

August 3. *Took another cutoff this week called Sublets. Struck Raft River; from thence to Swamp Creek. Passed some beautiful scenery, high cliffs of rocks resembling old ruins or dilapidated buildings.*

Hot Springs, August 18. *Camped on a branch of Mary's River, a very disagreeable and unpleasant place on account of the water being so hot. This week some of our company left us, all young men. They were jolly, merry fellows and gave life to our lonely evenings. We all miss them very much. Some had violins, others guitars, and some had fine voices, and they always had a good audience. They were anxious to hurry on without the Sunday stops. Roads are rocky and trying to our wagons, and the dust is horrible. The men wear veils tied over their hats as a protection. When we reach camp at night they are covered with dust from head to heels.*

Humboldt River, August 20. *We are now 348 miles from the mines. We expect to travel that distance in three weeks and a half. Water and grass scarce.*

St. Mary's River, August 25. *Still traveling down the Humboldt. Grass has been scarce until today. Though the water is not fit to drink—slough water—we are obliged to use it, for it's all we have.*

St. Mary's, September 2. *After coming through a dreary region of country for two or three days, we arrived Saturday night. We had good grass but the water was bad. Remained over Sunday. Had preaching in camp.*

September 4. *Left the place where we camped last Sunday. Traveled six miles. Stopped and cut grass for cattle and supplied ourselves with water for the desert. Had a trying time crossing. Several of our cattle gave out and we left one. Our journey through the desert was from Monday, three o'clock in the afternoon, until Thursday morning at sunrise, September 6. The weary journey last night, the mooing of the cattle for water, their exhausted condition, with the cry of "Another ox down," the stopping of train to unyoke the poor dying brute, to let him follow at will or stop by the wayside and die, and the weary, weary tramp of men and beasts worn out with heat and fam-*

ished for water, will never be erased from my memory. Just at dawn, in the distance, we had a glimpse of Truckee River, and with it the feeling: Saved at last! Poor cattle; they kept on mooing, even when they stood knee deep in water. The long dreaded desert had been crossed and we are all safe and well. Here we rested Thursday and Friday—grass green and beautiful, and the cattle are up to their eyes in it.

September 8. *Traveled fourteen miles; crossed Truckee twelve times.*

September 9. *Sunday, our day of rest.*

Monday, September 10. *Traveled four miles down to the end of the valley.*

Tuesday, September 11. *Made eighteen miles. Crossed Truckee River ten times. Came near being drowned at one of the crossings. Got frightened and jumped out of the carriage into the water. The current was very swift and carried me some distance down the stream.*

September 14. *We arrived at the place where the Donner Party perished having lost their way and being snowed in. Most of them suffered and died from want of food. This was in 1846. Two log cabins, bones of human beings and animals, tops of the trees being cut off the depth of snow, was all that was left to tell the tale of that ill-fated party, their sufferings and sorrow. A few of their number made their way out, and after days of agony and hunger finally reached Sutter's Fort. We crossed the summit of the Sierra Nevada. It was night when we reached the top, and never shall I forget our descent to the place where we are now encamped—our tedious march with pine knots blazing in the darkness and the tall, majestic pines towering above our heads. The scene was grand and gloomy beyond description. We could not ride—roads too narrow and rocky—so we trudged along, keeping pace with the wagons as best we could. This is another picture engraven upon the tablets of memory. It was a footsore and weary crowd that reached that night our present camping place.*

Yuba Valley, September 16. *We are now 108 miles from Sutter's Fort.*

September 17. *Left camp this morning. Traveled down to the lower end of the valley. Lay by two days. Had preaching out under the pines at night. The men built a fire and we all gathered around it in camp-meeting style.*

September 19. *Started once more. Roads bad, almost impassable. After traveling for twenty-five miles we halted for one day. Good grass three miles from camp.*

September 21. *Reached Bear Valley by descending a tremendous hill. We let the wagons down with ropes. Stopped over Sunday. At Sleepy Hollow we again let our wagons down the mountain with ropes. Rested in the hollow, ate our dinner and then commenced our weary march over the mountain. Left one of our wagons and the springs of our carriage. Cut down trees for our cattle to browse on. Thanks to a kind Providence we are nearing the end of our long and perilous journey. Came on to Grass Valley and rested four or five days.*

October 1. *Arrived at Johnson's Fort. Thence we went to Nicholson's ranch.*

Vernon, California, October 6. Well, after a five month's trip from St. Joe, Missouri, our party of fifty wagons, now only thirteen, has at last reached this haven of rest. Strangers in a strange land—what will the future be? This town is situated at the junction of the Feather and Sacramento Rivers.

Fremont, October 10. This is a small town on the opposite side of the river from Vernon. My father has decided to remain here for the winter, as the rains have set in and we are worn out. We have had a small house put up of two rooms made of boards with puncheon floor. On this mother has a carpet which she brought with us and we feel quite fine, as our neighbors have the ground for a floor. The rooms are lined with heavy blue cloth. Our beds are put up in bunk style on one side of the room and curtained off. Back of these rooms we have pitched our tent, which answers as a store room, and the back of the lot is enclosed with a brush fence. My father has gone to Sacramento to lay in provisions for the winter.

Fremont, December 20. Have not written or confided in thee, dear journal, for some time. Now I must write up. My father returned from Sacramento with a supply of provisions. Everything is enormously high. Carpenter's wages sixteen dollars per day; vegetables scarce and high; potatoes the principal vegetable; onions, fifty cents each; eggs, one dollar apiece; melons, five dollars, and apples, one dollar each. The rain is pouring down. River very high.

Christmas, 1849. Still raining. This has been a sad Christmas for mother. She is homesick, longs for her old home and friends. It's hard for old folks to give up old ties and go so far away to live in a strange land among strange people. Young people can easily form new ties and make new friends and soon conform to circumstances, but it's hard for the old ones to forget. Was invited to a candy pull and had a nice time. Rather a number of young folks camped here. This is a funny looking town anyway. Most of the houses are built of brush. Now that the rains have set in, people are beginning to think of something more substantial. Some have log cabins, others have clapboards like ours.

New Years, January 1, 1850. *It's gloomy old New Year's for us all. What will this year bring forth?*

January 11. *Raining. The river is very high. Six inches will bring it over the whole town.*

January 12. *Water over the banks of the river, all over town except in a few places. Our house has escaped, though it's all around us. Mother has planted a garden in the rear of [the] lot and that has been swept away. Nearly everybody is up to their knees in mud and water. Some have boots. As far as the eye can reach you see nothing but water. It's horrible. Wish I was back in Indiana. Snakes are plenty. They come down the river, crawl under our bed and everywhere.*

January 20. *Water receding.*

Fremont, February 27. *It's raining very hard. A little snow by way of variety. Horrible weather. Received several letters from schoolmates at home.*

March 30. *Nothing of importance has transpired worth putting down. I am invited out so much that I am beginning to feel quite like a young lady. Girls are scarce; I presume that is the reason. Young men are plenty. There was a wedding here a few days ago. Had one of those old-fashioned serenades—tin pans, gongs, horns and everything else that could be drummed up to make a noise. It was dreadful. Weather windy and cold.*

April 1. *Quite a number of our old friends who crossed the Plains with us have stopped here for the winter, which makes it pleasant for mother. My father has gone to San Jose, the capital, to look for a permanent home.*

April 27. *My father has returned from San Jose. He gives glowing accounts of the place and lovely climate. We have not seen very much as yet of the mild and delightful climate of California so much talked about. We leave next month for San Jose. We are all glad that we are going to have a home somewhere at last.*

Pueblo de San Jose, June 3, 1850 *[Tuesday]. Left Fremont the first of May. We traveled by land in our wagons. The first night out was unpleas-*

ant. Mosquitoes nearly devoured us. The second days we arrived at Cash [Cache] Creek. Wednesday were at Wolfscales [Wolfskill's]. Friday we reached Benicia. We were detained here three days crossing the straits. Continued our journey and arrived here on Tuesday. Rev. Owens, who crossed the Plains with us, is living here, and we have pitched our tent near his house, with adobe ell, built only as a temporary home for the present. Started school. Have met Mrs. Reed's family. They crossed the Plains in 1846. They were of the Donner Party. Two of the Donner girls are living with Mrs. Reed, Mary and Frankie. Mattie Reed is a lovely girl with big brown eyes. She is near my own age. She has a piano, and Mrs. Reed has kindly asked me to come there and practice. I go every day. There was a race here a few days ago—a $15,000 bet.

THE LETTER OF ELIZABETH KEEGAN, AGE TWELVE, DECEMBER 12, 1852

Twelve-year-old Elizabeth Keegan arrived in Marysville, California, on September 17, 1852, in the company of her mother, a servant girl, and a hired man. The brother and sister back in St. Louis to whom this letter was addressed came to California two years later.

Sacramento   Dec. 12th 1852

My Dear Sister and Brother

Having written to you twice before and not receiving any answer I am beginning to feel impatient I do not attribute the non-receival of a letter to your not writing but to the errigularities of the mail. I will send this one by express and I sincerely hope it will reach its destination in safety and find you both in the enjoyment of that inestimable blessing good health as this leaves all at present.

Our journey across the plains was tedious in the extreme. We were over four months coming it is a long time to be without seeing any signs of civilization, we left the Baptist Mission on 3rd May and arrived in Marysville on 17th Sept. at which place we remained three weeks and then came on here. I like this place very well. But I must first tell you something of the route. The first part of it is beautiful and the scenery surpassing anything of the kind I have ever seen large rolling praries stretching as far as your eye can carry you covered with verdure. The grass so green and flowers of every discription from violets to geraniums of the richest hue. Then leaving this beautiful scenery behind, you descend into the woodland which is composed mostly of Oak and interspersed with creeks. some of them very large there was one we crossed called the Big Vermillion whose banks were so steep that our wagons had to be let down by means of ropes. I rode through on horseback and I had a fine opportunity to see and examine everything of note on the way. We did not meet any sickness nor see any fresh graves until we came in on the road from St. Joseph. I forgot to say in its proper place that Kansas was our starting point which was on the 17th of May from that out there was scarsely a day but we met six and not less than two fresh graves. We were camped one night next to a train and they were digging a grave for one of their companions. Another night a man was taken ill and his cries of agony drove sleep from many a pillow that night. All from Aseatic Cholera in its worst form from the beginning to the end of the journey. "Thanks be to God" we did not have one sick amongst us. After we passed the first desert our road was uniformly the same thing every day passing across wide dreary wastes covered only with sage and greenwood this last mentioned is a small shrub resembling evergreen. This is mostly the kind of road untill you arrive at the last desert. This desert is very heavy and difficult of travel, it is forty-five miles across and must be performed in one stretch as there is no good water or grass on it. There is some boiling springs about the middle part of it you can see the steam a good distance off it was in the night when we passed them and I did not see them. I heard a woman and a boy were badly scalded. They went to look in at it and went to near and the earth caved in. The woman was so badly scalded that her life was dispared of. Many teams go in on this desert but few come out of it. We had great difficulty to get across the desert. The mules we had in our carriage gave out when we were about ten miles in on it. We had to take a yoke of oxen out of [a] large wagon which weakened the other that when we were within about twelve miles of being across we were compeled to leave the carriage behind and put all our force to one. When we got across we laid up for a week and sent back for the carriage. We then started for to cross the mountains. The crossing of the plains is nothing to the crossing of the mountains. Some of them are so high and steep that you would scarsley think if you turned the cattle loose they could scarcely get up. We were one whole day getting up four miles having double teams putting nine yoke to a waggon. After you cross the last of the mountains you descend into the Sacramento Valley long looked for by the weary emigrant. the heat can scarcely be endured particularly so on the first coming down from the mountains. It is very cold on them. One night it froze so hard that water in the bucket had half an inch thick of ice. After we got down into the valley all our difficulties were at an end. We met houses at every turn of the road and flourishing farms, called here ranches. When we came within five miles of Marysville we stopped at one of the ranches and engaged ranching for our cattle. We turned all our cattle out but one yoke. We then went into Marysville like a flash.

We slept that night in our wagons and the next day doffed our plains habilments and went down town, how that word sent a thrill through my frame no one can picture the feelings of those who have come that wearisome journey the joy they feel at once more beholding and mingling with their fellow creatures. Church we had not to go to, but we thanked God from the bottom of our hearts for preserving [us] through our trials and temptations, on the following sunday mass was celebrated in the house of a private family at which we attended. Rev. Dr. Arcker officiated. We procured a house and the second night of arrival in Marysville we slept inside of a house for the first time since we left the states. We remained as I said before in Marysville three weeks but hearing we could do better here, we came on. We started in our wagons again came within four miles of the city we could not get a house to go into and had to remain camped out on a ranch for three weeks. When the rains set in on us, we started again and came in in the pouring rain. Altogether we are not two months inside of a house. You must know we do not have a drop of rain during nine months of the growing season. the raining season sets in about the first day of Nov. and terminates about the first of Feb. The rains are very heavy in the mountains, so that it raises the river very high. There is a slough on one side of the city which comes and goes with the tide. Since the rains have set in it swollen produgrously so much that they apprehend an overflow like in "49. There is nothing to keep the water out but a clay enbankment. Our city has been visited with destructive fire which destroyed the principal part of the city, leaving only a few houses in the suburbs but it is almost built up again. I will tell you a little how houses are built here. they are all mostly frame, lined with furniture calico or canvas There is no such thing as plastering except in very few cases. There is no pavements here but plank walks. We have public places of amusement of every kind and description.

Dear Sister and Brother here I have written and thought over and over about filling this little book the task looks easy but it is hard to perform. I thought what I had to say would fill it full but here I have almost exhausted my store and it is half full. If I were writing to a friend I would feel obliged to offer some apology but as it is to a loving sister and brother I know they can more readily excuse the tediousness and sameness of its contents. I have not made any acquaintances so I cannot give you any account of the usages or manner of the people. ... There is every class of people here in California the rich and poor of every nation of the world.

See what gold can do it brings men from all nations here to this distance shore to make their fortune many go home worse than when they came others have wealth countless wealth thus it is some must fall that others may rise. It is night now and I labored seslously at this writing I must lay by til morning for I have to be up at half past four. ...

Mother Mary and Kate join in sending their most affectionate love to you both accept my Dear Sister and Brother the sincere love of you affectionate sister.

E.J.C. Keegan.

Notes

1. John Faragher, *Women and Men on the Overland Trail* (New Haven: Yale University Press, 1979), pp. 195–196.

2. Ruth Barnes Moynihan, "Children and Young People on the Overland Trail," *Western Historical Quarterly* 6 (1975): 279–294; Elliott West, *Growing Up with the Country: Childhood on the Far Western Frontier* (Albuquerque: University of New Mexico Press, 1989), pp. 1–21; and Judy Allen, "Children on the Overland Trails," *Overland Journal* 12 (1) (Spring 1994): 2–11.

3. Sandra L. Myers, ed., *Ho for California! Women's Overland Diaries from the Huntington Library* (San Marino, Calif.: Huntington Library, 1980); Lillian Schlissel, *Women's Diaries of the Westward Journey* (New York: Schocken Books, 1982); and John Unruh Jr., *The Plains Across: The Overland Emigrants and the Trans Mississippi West, 1840–1860* (Urbana: University of Illinois Press, 1982), pp. 321–352.

4. Merrill J. Mattes, *Platte River Road Narratives* (Urbana: University of Illinois Press, 1988), p. 5.

5. Georgia Willis Read, "Women and Children on the Oregon-California Trail in the Gold Rush Years," *Missouri Historical Review* 39 (1944–1945): 6.

6. David Nasaw, *Schooled to Order: A Social History of Public Schooling in the United States* (New York: Oxford University Press, 1980).

7. Patrick Huyghe, "Voices, Glances, Flashbacks: Our First Memories," *Psychology Today* (September 1985): 48–52.

8. Joseph F. Kett, *Rites of Passage* (New York: Basic Books, 1977).

9. Katherine Nelson, "Remembering: A Functional Developmental Perspective," in P. R. Solomon, et al., eds., *Memory: Interdisciplinary Approaches* (New York: Springer Verlag, 1989), pp. 127–150; and Gail S. Goodman, B. L. Bottoms, B. M. Schwartz-Kenney, and L. Rudy, "Children's Testimony About a Stressful Event: Improving Children's Reports," *Journal of Narrative and Life History* 1 (1991): 69–99.

10. Emmy E. Werner, "Protective Factors and Individual Resilience," in Samuel J. Meisels and Jack P. Shonkoff, eds., *Handbook of Early Childhood Intervention* (Cambridge: Cambridge University Press, 1990), pp. 97–116; and Emmy E. Werner and Ruth S. Smith, *Overcoming the Odds: High Risk Children from Birth to Adulthood* (Ithaca: Cornell University Press, 1992), pp. 189–209.

11. George R. Stewart, *Ordeal by Hunger: The Story of The Donner Party* (New York: Washington Square Press, 1960), p. 236.

12. Glen H. Elder Jr., John Modell, and Ross D. Parke, eds., *Children in Time and Place: Developmental and Historical Insights* (Cambridge: Cambridge University Press, 1993), pp. 241–250; and Norman Garmezy, "Foreword," in Emmy E. Werner and Ruth S. Smith, *Vulnerable But Invincible: A Longitudinal Study of Resilient Children and Youth* (New York: McGraw Hill, 1982), p. xix.

13. Unruh, *The Plains Across,* p. 327.

Bibliography

Ackley, Mary E. 1928. *Crossing the Plains and Early Days in California.* San Francisco: Privately printed.

Allen, Judy. 1994. "Children on the Overland Trails." *Overland Journal.* 12 (1) Spring: 2–11.

Allen, Sally Fox. 1859. "Diary." MS 42. San Francisco, California Historical Society Library.

Applegate, Jesse A. 1914. *Recollections of My Boyhood.* Roseburg, Oreg.: Press of Review. Reprinted in Maude A. Rucker, ed. *The Oregon Trail and Some of Its Blazers.* New York: Walter Neale, 1930.

Baur, John E. 1978. *Growing Up with California: A History of California's Children.* Los Angeles: Will Kramer Western American Studies Series.

Bidwell, John. 1890. "The First Emigrant Train to California." *Country Magazine.* November: 106.

Bonney, Benjamin Franklin. 1923. "Recollections." *Oregon Historical Quarterly.* March: 36–56.

Boyles, J. C. 1940. "He Witnessed the Death Valley Tragedy of '49." *Desert Magazine.* February: 1–5.

Breen, Harry. 1947. "Letter to Dr. Walter M. Stookey, February 12." Hollister, Calif.: Mimeographed.

Breen, John. 1856. "Account of His Experiences with the Donner Party as Told to Mrs. Eliza W. Farnham." In Eliza W. Farnham. *California In-Doors and Out.* New York: Dix, Edwards.

——. 1877. "Pioneer Memories." Manuscript C-D 51. University of California, Berkeley, Bancroft Library.

——. 1879. "Letters to C. F. McGlashan." Manuscript C-B 570. Box I, Folder 11. University of California, Berkeley, Bancroft Library.

Breen, Patrick. 1846–1847. "Diary." Manuscript C-E 176. University of California, Berkeley, Bancroft Library.

Brier, John Wells. 1903. "The Death Valley Party of 1849." *Out West Magazine.* March–April: 326–335, 456–465.

——. 1911. "A Lonely Time." *Grizzly Bear.* October: 1–2.

———. 1911. "The Argonauts of Death Valley." *Grizzly Bear*. June: 1–4, 7.

Brier, Juliette. 1898. "Our Christmas and the Terrors of Death Valley 1849." *San Francisco Call*. December 25.

Bristow, Gwenn. 1980. *Golden Dreams*. New York: Lippincott and Crowell.

Brooks, Elisha. 1922. *A Pioneer Mother of California*. San Francisco: Harr Wagner.

Brown, Dee. 1971. *Bury My Heart at Wounded Knee: An Indian History of the American West*. New York: Holt, Rinehart and Winston.

Bruff, J. Goldsborough. 1949. *Gold Rush: The Journals, Drawings and Other Papers of J. Goldsborough Bruff*. Georgia Willis Reed and Ruth Gains, eds. New York: Columbia University Press. California Centennial Edition.

Bryant, Edwin. 1848. *What I Saw in California: Being a Journal of a Tour by the Emigrant Route and South Pass*. New York: D. Appleton. Reprint; Lincoln: University of Nebraska Press, 1985.

Canfield, Chauncey, ed. 1906. *The Diary of a Forty-Niner*. San Francisco: C. L. Canfield. Reprint; New York: Turtle Point Press, 1992.

Cheney, Rev. J. W. 1915. "The Story of an Emigrant Train." *The Republican*. April 22, April 29, pp. 1–12.

Chiles, John B. 1898. "A Visit to California in Early Times." Manuscript. University of California, Berkeley, Bancroft Library.

Clappe, Louise Amelia Knapp Smith. 1851–1852. *The Shirley Letters from the California Mines*. Marysville, Calif.: *Marysville Herald*. Reprint; New York: Alfred A. Knopf, 1949.

Dawson, Nicholas. 1841. "Notebook Kept on a Journey to California." Manuscript. University of California, Berkeley, Brancroft Library.

Dedera, Don. 1979. "The Gila Trail, Pathway in the Desert." In Robert L. Breeden, ed. *Trails West*. Washington, D.C.: National Geographic Society.

Dickenson, Luella. 1904. *Reminiscences of a Trip Across the Plains in 1846 and Early Days in California*. San Francisco: Whitaker and Ray. Reprint; Fairfield, Wash.: Ye Galleon Press, 1977.

Dillon, Richard. 1981. "Tragedy at Oatman Flat: Massacre, Captivity, Mystery." *American West* 18: 46–59.

Donner, Eliza. 1879. "Letters to C. F. McGlashan." Manuscript C-B 570. Box I, Folder 20. University of California, Berkeley, Bancroft Lbirary.

Donner, Eliza P. Houghton. 1911. *The Expedition of the Donner Party and Its Tragic Fate*. Chicago: A. C. McClung.

Donner, Frances. 1879. "Letters to C. F. McGlashan." Manuscript C-B 570. Box II, Folder 54. University of California, Berkeley, Bancroft Library.

Donner, Georgia. 1879. "Letters to C. F. McGlashan." Manuscript C-B 570. Box I, Folders 2–4. University of California, Berkeley, Bancroft Library.

Donner, Leanna. 1879. "Letters to C. F. McGlashan." Manuscript C-B 570. Box I, Folder 1. University of California, Berkeley, Bancroft Library.

Donner, Tamsen. 1846. "Letter of May 11, Written on the Trail to Her Sister in Independence, Missouri." Manuscript. San Marino, California, Huntington Library.

Reprinted in Kenneth L. Holmes, ed. *Covered Wagon Women,* vol. 1, Glendale, Calif.: Arthur H. Clark, 1983.

Elder, Glen H. Jr., John Modell, and Ross D. Parke, eds. 1993. *Children in Time and Place: Developmental and Historical Insights.* Cambridge: Cambridge University Press.

Elliott, Maria J. Norton. 1859. "Diary." Microfilm C-F 129. University of California, Berkeley, Bancroft Library.

Faragher, John. 1979. *Women and Men on the Overland Trail.* New Haven: Yale University Press.

Farnham, Eliza. 1856. *California, Indoors and Out.* New York: Dix, Edwards.

Faulk, Odie B. 1973. *Destiny Road: The Gila Trail and the Opening of the Southwest.* New York: Oxford University Press.

Ferguson, Henry. 1918. "Recollections of a 1849 Journey." Typed transcript C-2, 187. University of California, Berkeley, Bancroft Library.

Freedman, Russell. 1983. *Children of the Wild West.* New York: Clarion Books

Goldsmith, Oliver. 1896. "Overland in Forty-Nine: Recollections of a Wolverine Ranger." Reprinted in Georgia Willis Read. "Women and Children on the Oregon-California Trail." *Missouri Historical Review.* October 1944: 11.

Goodman, Gail S., B. L. Bottoms, B. M. Schwartz-Kenney, and L. Rudy. 1991. "Children's Testimony About a Stressful Event: Improving Children's Reports." *Journal of Narrative and Life History* 1: 69–99.

Graves, William. 1879. "Letters to C. F. McGlashan." Manuscript C-B 570. Box I, Folder 98. University of California, Berkeley, Bancroft Library.

———. 1877. "Graves' Crossing the Plains in '46." *Healdsburg Russian River Flag.* April 26–May 17.

Haight, Henry W. 1850. "We Walked to California in 1850." Manuscript. Iowa City, State Historical Society of Iowa.

Hall, Maggie. 1853. "Recollections." Manuscript C-F 152. University of California, Berkeley, Bancroft Library.

Haun, Catherine Margaret. 1849. "A Woman's Trip Across the Plains in 1849." Manuscript HM 538. San Marino, California, Huntington Library. Reprinted in Lillian Schlissel, ed. *Women's Diaries of the Westward Journey.* New York: Schocken Books, 1982.

Heath, Katherine. 1881. "A Child's Journey Through Arizona and New Mexico." *The Californian* 3, January:14–18.

Hester, Sallie. 1925. "The Diary of a Pioneer Girl." *Argonaut* 97, September 12–October 24: 231–246. Reprinted in Kenneth L. Holmes, ed. *Covered Wagon Women,* vol 1. Glendale, Calif.: Arthur H. Clark, 1983.

Hewitt, James. 1973. *Eye-Witnesses to Wagon Trains West.* New York: Charles Scribner's Sons.

Hill, Jasper S. 1964. *The Letters of a Young Gold Miner, Covering the Adventures of Jasper S. Hill During the California Gold Rush.* San Francisco: John Howell Books.

Hite, Mary Fetter Sanford. 1853. "A Biographical Sketch of Abraham Hite and Family. A Trip Across the Plains, March 28–October 27." Transcript 9CB H67S. Sacramento, California State Library.

Holliday, J. S. 1981. *The World Rushed In: The California Gold Rush Experience.* New York: Simon and Schuster.

Huyghe, Patrick. 1985. "Voices, Glances, Flashbacks: Our First Memories." *Psychology Today,* September: 48–52.

Ide, Sarah Healy. 1888. "Recollections." Manuscript CE-82. University of California, Berkeley. Reprinted in Simeon Ide. *The Conquest of California: The Biography of William B. Ide.* Glorieta, N.M.: Rio Grande Press, 1967.

Johnson, Leroy, and Jean Johnson. 1987. *Escape from Death Valley.* Reno: University of Nevada Press.

———. 1981. *Julia: Death Valley's Youngest Victim.* Roseville, Minn.: Privately printed.

Karshner, Gayle. 1991. "Nancy Kelsey." *Humboldt Historian.* November–December: 1–4.

Keegan, Elizabeth. 1852. "A Teenager's Letter from Sacramento." Manuscript. Sacramento, California State Library. Reprinted in Kenneth L. Holmes, ed. *Covered Wagon Women,* vol. 4. Glendale, Calif.: Arthur H. Clark, 1985.

Kelsey, Nancy. 1915. "A California Heroine." *Grizzly Bear.* February: 6–7.

Kett, Joseph F. 1977. *Rites of Passage.* New York: Basic Books.

King, Joseph A. 1992. *Winter of Entrapment: A New Look at the Donner Party.* Toronto: P. D. Meany.

Koenig, George. 1984. *Beyond This Place There May Be Dragons: The Route of the Death Valley 1849ers Through Nevada, Death Valley and on to Southern California.* Glendale, Calif.: Arthur H. Clark.

Laury, Jean R. 1990. *Ho for California: Pioneer Women and Their Quilts.* New York: E. P. Dutton.

Levy, Joann. 1990. *They Saw the Elephant: Women in the California Gold Rush.* Hamden, Colo.: Archon Books.

Lewis, Donovan. 1993. *Pioneers of California: True Stories of Early Settlers in the Golden State.* San Francisco: Scottwall Associates.

Lingenfelter, Richard E. 1986. *Death Valley and the Armagosa.* Berkeley: University of California Press.

Lockhart, Edith A. 1861. "Diary." Manuscript. Reno, Nevada State Historical Society.

Lothrop, Gloria. 1984. "True Grit and Triumph of Juliette Brier." *The Californians.* November–December: 11–35.

Maino, Jeannette Gould. 1987. *Left Hand Turn: A Story of the Donner Party Women.* Modesto, Calif.: Dry Creek Books.

Manly, William Lewis. 1894. *Death Valley in '49.* San Jose, Calif.: Pacific Tree and Vine.

———. 1888. "From Vermont to California." *Santa Clara Valley* 5 (5) July–5 (10) December.

Marsh, John. 1842. "Letter to His Parents." Reprinted in James Hewitt, ed. *Eye-Witnesses to Wagon Trains West.* New York: Charles Scribner's Sons, 1973.

Mattes, Merrill J. 1988. *Platte River Road Narratives.* Urbana: University of Illinois Press.

McAuley, Eliza Ann. 1852. "Diary." Manuscript. Sacramento, California State Library. Reprinted in Kenneth L. Holmes, ed. *Covered Wagon Women,* vol. 4 Glendale, Calif.: Arthur H. Clark, 1985.

McClosky, Joseph J., and Hermann J. Scharmann. 1959. *Christmas in the Goldfields 1849.* San Francisco: California Historical Society.

McDaniel, Kate Furniss. 1853. "From Prairie to Pacific. A Narrative of a Trip Across the Plains of a Family from Illinois with a Covered Wagon and Oxen." Edited by Mai Luman Hill. Typescript 9CB F98. Sacramento, California State Library.

McGlashan, C. F. 1880. *History of the Donner Party: A Tragedy of the Sierra.* Truckee, Calif.: *Truckee Republican.* Reprint. Stanford: Stanford University Press, 1940.

McWilliams, John. n.d. *Recollections of John McWilliams: His Youth Experiences in California and the Civil War.* Princeton: Princeton University Press.

Millington, Ada. 1862. "Journal Kept While Crossing the Plains." Manuscript C-F 11. Photocopy. University of California, Berkeley, Bancroft Library.

Moffat, Gwen. 1981. *Hard Road West: Alone on the California Trail.* New York: Viking Press.

Moynihan, Ruth Barnes. 1975. "Children and Young People on the Overland Trail." *Western Historical Quarterly* 6: 279–294.

Murphy, Mary. 1847. "Three Letters Written to Dear Uncles, Aunts and Cousins, May 25." Typescript. Covillaud Family Files. Marysville, California, Yuba County Library.

Murphy, William G. 1896. "Address at Shores of Donner Lake." Reprinted in Eliza P. Houghton Donner. *The Expedition of the Donner Party and Its Tragic Fate.* Chicago: A. C. McClung, 1911.

Myers, Sandra L., ed. 1980. *Ho for California! Women's Overland Diaries from the Huntington Library.* San Marino, Calif.: Huntington Library.

Nasaw, David. 1980. *Schooled to Order: A Social History of Public Schooling in the United States.* New York: Oxford University Press.

Nelson, Katherine. 1989. "Remembering: A Functional Developmental Perspective." In P. R. Solomon, G. R. Goethals, C. M. Kelly, and B. R. Stevens, eds. *Memory: Interdisciplinary Approaches.* New York: Springer Verlag.

Nutting, Rebecca Hildreth Woodson. 1850–1858. "Recollections." Manuscript. University of California, Berkeley, Bancroft Library.

Paden, Irene. 1949. *Prairie Schooner Detours.* New York: MacMillan.

Peoples, John H. 1849. "Report to Major D. H. Rucker, December 12." In *General Smith's Correspondence. Executive Documents. The Senate of the United States. First Session of the Thirty-First Congress.* Washington, D.C.: William Belt.

Pettid, Edward J. 1968. "Olive Ann Oatman's Original Lecture Notes." *San Bernardino County Museum Quarterly* 16: 1–39.

Read, Georgia Willis. 1944–1945. "Women and Children on the Oregon-California Trail in the Gold Rush Years." *Missouri Historical Review* 39: 1–23.

Reed, James. 1847. "Diary." Folder 85, Martha Reed Lewis Papers. Sacramento, California, Sutter's Fort Historical Museum.

Reed, Martha (Patty). 1879. "Letters to C. F. McGlashan." Manuscript C-B 570. Box II, Folder 38. University of California, Berkeley, Bancroft Library.

Reed, Virginia. 1846. "Letter Written to Her Cousin, Mary C. Keyes, July 12." Manuscript. Los Angeles, Southwest Museum.

———. 1847. "Letter Written to Her Cousin, Mary C. Keyes, May 16." Manuscript 89/127c. University of California, Berkeley, Bancroft Library. Reprinted in *The Illinois Journal* (Springfield), December 16, 1847.

———. 1879. "Letters to C. F. McGlashan." Manuscript C-B 57. Box II, Folder 48. University of California, Berkeley, Bancroft Library

Reed, Virginia Murphy. 1891. *Across the Plains in the Donner Party: A Personal Narrative of the Overland Trip to California, 1846–47.* Special (July) edition of *Century Magazine.* Reprint; Golden, Colo.: Outbooks, 1980.

Reid, Bernard J. 1983. *Overland to California with the Pioneer Line: The Gold Rush Diary of Bernard J. Reid.* Stanford: Stanford University Press. Reprint; Urbana: University of Illinois Press, 1987.

Rodgers, John H. 1884. "On the Plains, 1849." *Merced Star,* April 26.

Ross, Jennie E. 1914. "A Child's Experience in '49 as Related by Mrs. Martha A. Gentry." *Overland Monthly,* April: 402–403.

Royce, Sarah. 1932. *A Frontier Lady: Recollections of the Gold Rush and Early California.* New Haven, Conn.: Yale University Press. Reprint; Lincoln: University of Nebraska Press, 1977.

Rucker, D. H. 1849. "Report to Major General P. F. Smith: September 2–December 3." In *General Smith's Correspondence. Executive Documents. The Senate of the United States. First Session of the Thirty-First Congress.* Washington, D.C.: William Belt.

Saddler, Warren. 1849. "Journal of a Gold Prospector." Manuscript C-F 73, Vol. 1 University of California, Berkeley, Bancroft Library.

Schallenberger, Moses. 1885. "Overland in 1844." Reprinted in George R. Steward, ed. *The Opening of the California Trail.* Berkeley: University of California Press, 1953.

Scharmann, Hermann B. 1852. "Scharmann's Overland Journey to California." *New York Staats Zeitung.*

Schlissel, Lillian. 1982. *Women's Diaries of the Westward Journey.* New York: Schocken Books.

Steed, Jack, and Richard Steed. 1988. *The Donner Party Rescue Site: Johnson Ranch on the Bear River.* Sacramento, Calif.: Pioneer Publishing.

Stephens, L. Dow. 1916. *Life Sketches of a Jayhawker.* San Jose, Calif.: Nolta Brothers.

Stewart, George R. 1962. *The California Trail: An Epic with Many Heroes.* New York: McGraw Hill. Reprint; Lincoln: University of Nebraska Press, 1983.

——. 1936. *Ordeal by Hunger: The Story of the Donner Party.* New York: Henry Holt. Reprint; New York: Washington Square Press, 1960.

Stratton, R. B. 1957. *Captivity of the Oatman Girls.* New York: Carlton and Porter. Reprint; Lincoln: University of Nebraska Press, 1983.

Street, Franklin. 1851. *California in 1850.* Cincinnati, Ohio: R. R. Edwards. Reprint; New York: Promontory Press, 1974.

Strentzel, Louisiana. 1849. "Letter from San Diego." Reprinted in Kenneth L. Holmes, ed. *Covered Wagon Women,* vol. 1. Glendale, Calif.: Arthur H. Clark, 1983.

Thompson, Susan Lewis Parrish. 1860. "Reminiscences." Reprinted in Virginia Root, ed. *Following the Pot of Gold at the Rainbow's End.* Downey, Calif.: Elena Quinn, 1960.

True, Charles Frederick. 1966. *Covered Wagon Pioneers.* Madison, Wis.: Sally Ralston True. Reprinted as *The Overland Memoir of Charles Frederick True: A Teenager on the California Trail 1859.* Independence, Mo: Oregon-California Trail Association, 1993.

Unruh, John Jr. 1982. *The Plains Across: The Overland Emigrants and the Trans-Mississippi West: 1840–1860.* Urbana: University of Illinois Press.

Villegas, Ygnacio Pedro. 1927. "Villegas' Diary." *Salinas Daily Journal,* March. Reprinted as Albert Shumate, ed. *Boyhood Days: Ygnacio Villegas' Reminiscences of California in the 1850's.* San Francisco: California Historical Society, 1983.

Wade, Alma. 1894. "Recollections." *San Jose Pioneer,* December 15.

Ware, Joseph E. 1849. *The Emigrant's Guide to California.* St. Louis, Mo: J. Halshall. Reprint; Princeton, N.J.: Princeton University Press, 1932.

Warner, Mary Eliza, 1864. "Diary." Manuscript C-F 66 A. University of California, Berkeley, Bancroft Library.

Watkins, Francis Marion. 1935. *The Story of the Crow Emigrant Train of 1865.* Written by Ralph Leroy Milliken from conversations held with Mr. F. M. Watkins of Los Baros, California. *Livingston Chronicle,* January 14, pp. 1–14.

Weeks, Florence Blacow. 1859. "Notes to the Diary of Lorina Walker Weeks." Manuscript. University of the Pacific, Stockton, Holt-Atherton Center for Western Studies.

Werner, Emmy E. 1994. "Resilience in Development." In Sandra Scarr, ed. *Current Directions in Psychological Science.* Cambridge: Cambridge University Press.

——. 1990. "Protective Factors and Individual Resilience." In Samuel J. Meisels and Jack P. Shonkoff, eds. *Handbook of Early Childhood Intervention.* Cambridge: Cambridge University Press, pp. 97–116.

——. 1986–1987. "Hope Amid Times of Hardship." *California Historical Courier* 38 (5): 1, 12.

Werner, Emmy E. and Ruth S. Smith. 1992. *Overcoming the Odds: High Risk Children from Birth to Adulthood.* Ithaca, N.Y.: Cornell University Press.

——. 1982. *Vulnerable But Invincible: A Longitudinal Study of Resilient Children and Youth.* New York: McGraw Hill. Reprint; New York: Adams, Bannister, Cox, 1989.

West, Elliott. 1989. *Growing Up with the Country: Childhood on the Far Western Frontier.* Albuquerque: University of New Mexico Press.

Winnemucca, Sarah Hopkins. 1883. *Life Among the Piutes: Their Wrongs and Claims.* New York: G. P. Putnam Sons. Reprint; Reno: University of Nevada Press, 1994.

Wood, John. 1871. *Journal of John Wood as Kept by Him While Traveling from Cincinnati to the Gold Diggings of California in the Spring and Summer 1850.* Columbus, Ohio: Nevins and Myers.

About the Book and Author

BETWEEN 1841 AND 1865, some forty thousand children participated in the great overland journeys from the banks of the Missouri River to the shores of the Pacific Ocean. In this engaging book, Emmy Werner gives 120 of these young emigrants, ranging from ages four to seventeen, a chance to tell the stories of their journeys west.

Incorporating primary materials in the form of diaries, letters, journals, and reminiscences that are by turns humorous and heartrending, the author tells a timeless tale of human resilience. For six months or more, the young travelers traversed two thousand miles of uncharted prairies, deserts, and mountain ranges. Some became part of makeshift families; others adopted the task of keeping younger siblings alive. They encountered strangers who risked their own lives for the youngsters and guides whose erroneous advice led to detours and desolation. The children endured excessive heat and cold and often suffered from cholera, dysentery, fever, and scurvy. They also faced thirst and starvation, cannibalism among famished members of their own parties, kidnappings, and the deaths of family members and friends. From the teenaged Nancy Kelsey, who carried her infant daughter across the Sierra Nevada in 1841, to the survivors of the ill-fated Donner party in 1846–1847, the Gold Rush orphans of 1849, and the youngsters who crossed Death Valley and the southwestern deserts in the 1850s, the eyewitness accounts of these pioneer children speak of fortitude, faith, and invincibility in the face of great odds.

EMMY E. WERNER is a developmental psychologist and Research Professor at the University of California at Davis. Her research has focused on high-risk children who have been exposed to extraordinary odds—physical handicaps, chronic poverty, family discord, and psychopathology. She is especially interested in the roots of resiliency demonstrated by contemporary child survivors: their personal competencies and the sources of support that have enabled them to overcome adversity. She is the author of *The Children of Kauai* (1971);

Kauai's Children Come of Age (1977); *Cross-Cultural Child Development: A View from the Planet Earth* (1979); *Vulnerable But Invincible: A Longitudinal Study of Resilient Children and Youth* (1982, 1989); *Child Care: Kith, Kin and Hired Hands* (1984); and *Overcoming the Odds: High Risk Children from Birth to Adulthood* (1992).

Index